Tom Cruise

Tom Cruise

ROBERT SELLERS

ROBERT HALE · LONDON

ISBN 0 7090 5441 6

Robert Hale Limited
Clerkenwell House
Clerkenwell Green
London EC1R 0HT

4 6 8 10 9 7 5 3

Photoset in North Wales by
Derek Doyle & Associates, Mold, Clwyd.
Printed in Great Britain by
St Edmundsbury Press Ltd, Bury St Edmunds, Suffolk.
Bound by WBC Book Manufacturers Limited,
Bridgend, Mid-Glamorgan.

Contents

'I have a theory that the camera likes some people – and the people it likes can't do any wrong.'

– Howard Hawks

'Even if you're on the right track, you'll get run over if you just sit there.'

– Will Rogers

'He believes anything is possible. That's the key to Tom Cruise.'

– Don Simpson

Illustrations

1   Formula for Success

Ambitious to an almost absurd degree, unassailably confident, Hollywood's most competitive star, demanding, single-minded, programmed to succeed at all costs, with squeaky-clean good looks, Tom Cruise was self-evidently the 1980s All American Boy. The uncomplicated image of an intense young man with a mission, the total workhorse, the ultimate party animal, scored big with a teen generation raised to believe through Ronald Reagan the illusion of an America great again and that there was nothing wrong with the yuppie philosophy of going all out for number one. Some of Cruise's most successful characters personified the eighties culture and many of that decade's potent preoccupations – greed and winning at any cost: Maverick (*Top Gun*), Vincent (*The Color of Money*), Flanagan (*Cocktail*). He was the perfect actor for the decade.

Diversity has hardly been a topic for discussion in Cruise's career. Early on he found a series of winning formulae and has methodically lived by them in nearly every one of his movies. Why mess with something when it ain't broke? In four films he's in military uniform; in numerous films his characters are tormented by the restless spirits of deceased patriarchs (an intriguing case of art imitating life); five times he's been the cocky young brat taken under the wing of a father figure/mentor; in five films he sexually wrestles with older women, and in another two romances wealthy socialites; he's played a Harvard-educated lawyer twice; a demonstrably high number of times he's karaoke'd to golden oldie songs; and he always seems to be roaring around on some form of trendy transport – motorbike, jet aircraft, sports car – with a pair of Ray Ban Wayfarers perennially welded to his face.

Cruise movies are punctuated with scenes of self-glorification, scenes where crowds either cheer him on as if he's just scored the winning touchdown in the superbowl, or are mere fawning vessels of congratulation; where if he's not punching the air after having gained yet another blinding achievement, he's letting fly with that characteristic victory yell ('whooah'). No Cruise movie is complete without at least one of these carved-in-stone rituals being played out. Such juvenile idiocy reached an embarrassing climax in *The Firm* when Cruise defies gravity and does an impromptu somersault on a pavement. A majestically daft moment.

Cruise has made a habit of making films that feature some element of personal test or, mastery of a new skill – anything from flying and racing to shooting pool and mixing cocktails. The heroes of all Tom Cruise movies start out arrogant, selfish and callow braggarts, are put on the rack and emerge as mature, moral beings. In other words, they are voyages of personal endurance and self-discovery. Typically Cruise gets the girl or wins the scholarship or prize. Though he might mislay his innocence along the way, or be briefly tempted, he always regains his integrity by the last reel to embark upon some new golden phase as the credits roll. Something about Cruise roles exudes the spirit of human triumph. And all the time he's smiling with that immovable grin, filled with a natural self-confidence best summarized by the scene in *Top Gun* where he scans a crowded classroom of fellow pilots to zero in on the one guy who's the serious rival to his status as number one – Val Kilmer's Ice Man.

The fact remains that Tom Cruise has yet to fully challenge his audience's expectations, risk their alienation or significantly react against a certain stereotyping in his roles. It's a major part of the Hollywood syndrome, wanting always to be admired on and off camera; some actors never want to be disliked – even in character. And Cruise hogs the squeaky-clean hero roles. Admittedly, from the point of view of staying successful and having clout in the business, it's tough for stars to change their spots, to do diametrically different work to what their public expects. On the other hand, if he is to gain the legendary status of some of his famous co-stars – Newman, Hoffman, Nicholson – he will surely have to abandon the grinning hero and hit *Born on the Fourth of July* territory rather more often. But the blame isn't solely his: back in the eighties there wasn't much choice in the material offered to young actors, and critics complained when Cruise just played cocky teenagers. 'It always amazed me when I was 19 and they'd say, "Well, he's always playing teenagers." I'd think,

"Look at me, this is all I can play right now." ' As he matured so did the material, *Rain Man* being his first 'grown-up' role. But so long as he's attracted to characters with heroic haloes, cocky young males, usually haunted by ghosts of fathers, who've matured to manhood by a film's final reel, the longer producers will want him to play them.

Things may be changing following Cruise's recent performance as the androgynous bloodsucker Lestat in *Interview with the Vampire*, in the face of derisive howls of him being miscast (strange that he's criticized for always playing good guys but when he finally wears the cloak of a nasty the moaning minnies bellyache about his unsuitability). He has previously refused to play villains, complaining they often weren't the leading part and has inhabited films – of the violent/slasher genre – with which, morally, he really doesn't want to be associated. 'But if it was a good part though, I might consider a villain. Some villains are very compelling.'

2   *The Nomad*

Something bad's going to happen – he can see it coming as clearly as the hand in front of his face, like the lights of an onrushing train piercing through the veil of night. When you've roamed around as much as Tom Cruise you develop a sixth sense about these things. The small town on the outskirts of Ottawa, Canada, is just one of many places this eleven-year-old has lived in – always the new kid on the block, the outsider trying to find his niche, having to make new friends, uncover the stranger's mask. The story always ends the same, a boy rejected and alone. Through it all he's at least had the love and support of his family, a doting mother and a father who stood by him when things got rough. But he knows that today something is terribly wrong.

Bleak patches of grey cloud pregnant with rain drift ominously overhead; outside in the yard piles of stray garbage are tossed up by the wind. Tom watches them whirling in endless circles from the window, while around him sit his three sisters, Marian, Lee Anne and Cass. Their parents have summoned them to the lounge to tell them what Tom has suspected all along, their marriage is over. Around the room the flow of tears is uncontrollable; it's like there's been a death in the family. Tom feels a fatherly arm around his shoulder and is led outside to the lawn where together they hit a few baseballs for old time's sake. It's the last thing they'll do as father and son. But nothing can heal what's just taken place. Tom cries so hard he finds himself struggling for breath. Everything he'd ever trusted and felt secure about has fallen apart. Cruise's mother, Mary Lee, spent a week planning her divorce and told her only son to keep a suitcase under his bed. He packed his baseball glove and went to sleep every night with one great fear echoing through his mind: what's going to happen to us now? What next? The answer tapped him on the shoulder one morning at 4:30. With the coast clear – her husband was absent from the house, none had dared tell him for fear of a high-speed pursuit – Mary Lee was piling everybody into the car and making for the United States border. The young Tom, dazed and confused, sat in the front watching his mother's emotions doing cartwheels – tears one minute, laughter the next or a singalong to the tunes on the radio. The closer they edged to the border the more she turned on the gas, the more she looked in the rearview mirror. 'We felt like fugitives' Cruise says now. He was eleven years old. And his childhood had ended.

Penniless, unemployed, with four kids to support, Mary Lee was left with no choice but to return with her brood to Louisville, Kentucky, where the Cruises had their roots and where she and their father first met. It was a time of great poverty and hardship. 'A time of growing, a time of conflict' have been her only public words on the subject. Relocation, fashioning a new life for themselves, trailing after their mother as she began a pilgrimage for work was nothing new for Tom and his sisters. They'd done and seen it all before roving around North America with their father, Thomas Cruise Mapother III, enrolling in numerous schools before their teens.

The Cruise family record for staying in one town the longest stands at two years; on average they never resided in the same place for more than eighteen months. Tom's father, born in 1934, was a graduate of the University of Kentucky, a bit of a science boffin, and hard-working (a Mapother tradition). As an engineer for General Electric with dreams of developing his own inventions and making his fortune, he kept his family perpetually on the move, working on research projects up and down the country – Missouri one year, Arizona the next, then on to Wayne in New Jersey, then Canada. But every fresh start in every new town brought with it the same problems, money and security being at the root of most of them. Tom's father was always coming up with money-making schemes which usually failed, landing the family into financial straits. It created incredible tensions, not helped by Tom Snr's sometimes erratic temper. His burning obsession with becoming a self-made millionaire was starkly at odds with the unambitious Mary Lee, who sought only fulfilment in her children and a contented family life. This difference in expectations may have acted as the catalyst for their eventual separation. Ironically, Tom's father never lived to see his son become a millionaire several times over.

The survival instincts, self-confidence, drive and determination that have steered Tom Cruise's meteoric rise from peripheral Brat Pack member to the single most bankable actor of his generation were forged at an early age and honed over the years to a laser-like perfection. From the moment of his birth – 3 July 1962 in Syracuse, New York state (he was christened Thomas Cruise Mapother IV) – Cruise was a nomad, a wanderer whose traumatic upbringing is an emotional well from which he seems to draw even today. That time has shaped his personal mythology, and the bitter memories of a difficult, often lonely, adolescence have never truly been laid to rest. If a computer needed to come up with the perfect adolescence for an actor it wouldn't be too far from this one – the insecurity, the doing without, the yearning, the calculated performances, the determination and the anger to fuel it all. A wrecked marriage, a broken home, innocence scarred by an abusive father – with Cruise you get it all.

He lived out the nightmare of the self-conscious adolescent: always the new boy in class, always looking for acceptance from a new gang of kids, kids who were already ensconced in their rigid little cliques. Tom found the politics of always being the new boy in a system intensely painful. In one corner you had the Democrats, in the other Republicans; country-club kids always stuck together, while athletes and artists sorted themselves out into other camps. And then there was Tom, who didn't fit in anywhere and nobody was interested in seeing the new kid for who he was. They just wanted to size him up fast: was he a jock, a swot or a plain nerd (one of the possible reasons why Cruise has always detested being typecast as an actor)? Sometimes it was frustrating never to be able to smash through all those social barriers, cut through all the posturing. 'If someone was new or different, it was just brutal.' Life was like some grim theatrical tour where at each stop Tom learned to adapt and ingratiate himself with a new audience. Already he was a performer, playing different roles and learning new accents (if they moved south Tom would drop his Canadian accent and adopt a southern drawl). He was forced to cope with constantly shifting horizons and alien environments, to adapt to new situations as best he could – it was a matter of survival. In every town he became a wholly different person, assuming the role of what he thought the local kids were, what he thought was 'in'. As well as creating self-sufficiency and inner strength, this fitting-in, playing at roles, was the earliest form of

Cruise the actor. The nomadic lifestyle that film-making dictates, the constant changes involved in slipping in and out of characters, and the very unpredictability of acting – is it any wonder that Cruise chose it as a career? Part of being an actor is that you're always moving. Naturally Cruise liked to have roots, to have a home, but he used to feel (before settling down with second wife Nicole Kidman) the need to push on after only a few months. He craved change in his life: being in one place for a long time wasn't the way he was raised. Could this also be why he's so hooked on car racing, a sport constantly on the move, with meetings taking place at differing venues week to week?

Bullying was a problem too, for new kids made tempting targets. Playground bullies always made a point of coming over to knock seven bells out of the new boy and you quickly learned to either fight back or be routinely abused. 'It was sink or swim. I chose to swim.'

Even after the divorce the constant moving around from town to town didn't stop – three high schools in four years – breeding a kind of desperate frustration about having to always make adjustments. Tom never got those feelings of security a kid most probably needs; he was always feeling left out of things. This sense of rootlessness made him unable to form the usual lasting childhood friendships, for as soon as he'd got to make friends and begun making progress at his studies it was time to move on. The divorce left Tom wounded and vulnerable, a sensitive boy who took his father's desertion to heart. There were many nights when he cried himself to sleep. And travelling around as much as he did closed him off from people. He didn't feel he could talk to anyone, because no one could possibly understand: they hadn't had the childhood he'd had. As a consequence Tom kept the pain of his parents' separation bottled up inside. Sure he had a smattering of friends in each town, but no *real* friends, no one who really knew him; the closest people around him were always his family.

Tom always found it difficult making friends as a teenager, as he was a somewhat withdrawn, lonely figure, not given to expressing himself. That feeling stuck with Cruise well into adulthood and maybe had something to do with making him a solitary figure – explains, perhaps, why he likes driving fast, riding motorbikes and other dangerous, solitary pursuits like skydiving. Since he was always the new boy on the block Tom often played alone, developing, in the process, a very active imagination. He was a kid who craved adventure, playing out in the backyard, dreaming up monsters and dragons. Cruise was probably a constant daydreamer. His solitary nature was first glimpsed when he was barely out of diapers and knee-high to a milk bottle. A disappearing act one afternoon so panicked his mother that she called for the police who found him roaming nearby. Beaming from ear to ear Tom informed Mary Lee that he'd been having an adventure. There was no use being angry; she was simply relieved to have him back safely. But next time, she said, it would be wiser if she came along too. Later that week off he went again, this time with his mother and sisters in tow. They followed him down the street and deep into a neighbouring wood where Tom stopped beside a rancid pond that simply invited death by drowning. His mother was horrified that her son had been coming to such a dangerous and desolate spot alone. And what did he spend his time doing there? 'Oh, I just sit and think and throw rocks in the water.'

Tom went through a period after his parents' separation of desperately wanting to be accepted, craving love and attention. Never really able to fit in anywhere, Tom became self-destructive, reckless, something of a rebel, fighting his demons by cutting school and raising hell, brawling to survive. In Louisville he was even the leader of a gang, getting into fights with kids from other neighbourhoods, rewarding loyalty with cigarettes.

A young man in a hurry, bursting to get out – nothing in life moved fast enough for him during his high-school years. School was a horror show of narrow-minded teachers, a place to do time as painlessly as possible. Walking to class with his sisters he'd say to them: 'Let's just get through this. If we can just get through this somehow.' Cruise never once has returned to any of his old schools for a nostalgic wallow. 'I look back upon high school and grade school and I would never want to go back there,' declares Cruise today. 'Not in a million years.'

The sports field proved his salvation. Sport has always been seen as a great leveller, a time-honoured way for children to make friends, and Tom discovered he had natural ability, as well as a strong, stocky body that stood him in good stead with almost every activity he attempted. Thus he became an obsessive athlete, because athletes are automatically liked. It was a way of expressing himself, of proving his worth at the myriad schools he was forced to parade through, and also the perfect outlet for his natural aggressiveness. With typical gusto he tried his hand at everything – baseball, basketball, football, skiing, lacrosse – and though he was never Mr All-Star Athlete, what he did have, and in abundance, was hyperenergy. It's easy to imagine coaches falling over themselves to recruit a player like Tom: someone who's aggressive, who's driven to be number one. In basketball Tom was really only ever a B player, due to his size, but through sheer determination got on the varsity team. The sports hero has been a recurring role in the Cruise career – footballer in *All the Right Moves*, pool hustler in *The Color of Money*, stock-car driver in *Days of Thunder*, knuckle-duster in *Far and Away*. No opportunity is wasted to show off his sporting proficiency, even if it is just incidental – volleyball in *Top Gun*, baseball in *A Few Good Men*, basketball in *The Firm*.

When Tom got involved in ice hockey his mother became concerned because of the inherent violence associated with the game. Tom used to play hockey over the Kentucky border in Indiana with kids older and bigger than he, but his speed on the ice kept him out of trouble. In one match, however, an opposing player got so exasperated that he picked Tom up by the scruff of his neck and the seat of his trousers and physically threw him outside the boundary.

For Tom, sport was a way of channelling all that reckless unfocused energy, helped him to make friends quickly in a new town and lent him some self-esteem – esteem he didn't usually get in the classroom. Walking into a new school he'd find that the standards were different or that his classmates were studying different phases of a subject. Although he wasn't slow-witted, Tom invariably found himself among the lower ranks of achievers and always seemed to be running to catch up. After years of being branded a slow learner and being taunted mercilessly by other kids, it was discovered that Tom suffered from word blindness or dyslexia, a learning disorder that hampers the ability to read and spell. In kindergarten teachers had forced Tom to write with his right hand when he preferred using his left. Consequently he began to reverse letters, copying down from the blackboard backwards, and he was never sure whether letters like C or D curved to the right or left. Entire words and sentences could sometimes look back to front. Not surprisingly his spelling was atrocious and he found reading a terrible strain. All his school work suffered. Placed into remedial classes Tom found himself not just the new boy but the new boy singled out, labelled a dunce everywhere he went.

Cruise told *Today* in December 1994:

> It was tough because a lot of kids would make fun of me. That experience made me very tough on the inside because you learn to quietly accept abuse and constant ridicule ... I now look on it as a character building stage, although I hated every moment of my life in those days. I would come home crying so many times because of the misery of not being able to do as well in school as I knew I should be able to.

He'd travel to one school and they would have already learned what nouns and verbs were, the correct usage of punctuation, and moved on to the next thing. Meanwhile Tom would still be going, 'What's a verb?' Written tests drove him to despair. He'd get incredibly nervous and skip questions and lines. And he'd sit in dread of being called out to read aloud in front of the class. The simplest school acts, writing and reading, were already performances.

When he took up acting Tom's lack of verbal skills made reading for film parts a precarious business, carrying with it the fear of public humiliation. Even today he travels with a dictionary and looks up difficult words on demand: got to keep pushing himself, keep on learning: self-made movie star, self-taught man. 'He comes into my office,' *Top Gun* co-producer Don Simpson told *Time* magazine in December 1989, 'and goes over my stack of books, taking notes. Last night he used the word plethora. Two years ago, he didn't know the word.'

Only since achieving stardom has Tom started educating himself with writers and books (one of the film-making processes Cruise most enjoys is working through a script with its writer). While growing up, reading was never at the top of his list; it was such a chore and took up so much time and when he got tired he'd see things backwards and skip lines. Consumed by rage and grievance, Tom would always turn to his mother for help and guidance. Tom's teachers had successively failed to recognize his problem (had he not always been moving from school to school perhaps the condition would have been diagnosed earlier). Mary Lee, however, was a sufferer herself and had practical experience of working with hyperactive and dyslexic children, her own daughters included, and she identified what was wrong. A constant source of encouragement, she spent hours helping Tom with homework, instilling into him an unflinching confidence in his battle to overcome this debilitating handicap. While it may never be completely cured – 'You're always dyslexic,' he said in 1989. 'You just find different ways of dealing with it' – today it isn't really a major problem. Cruise has even claimed that Scientology eradicated dyslexia from his life. 'There was a study technology that L. Ron Hubbard had that I applied,' he told *Empire* in October 1993. 'In applying it, I had the ability to learn and read anything that I wanted to. Who knows whether I actually had dyslexia or not? Maybe I had the wrong approach to studying as a kid.' Cruise himself became a figurehead of sorts in the campaign to recognize and deal with the special requirements of dyslexics. By talking openly about his own difficulties he gave hope to countless others engaged in personal struggles of their own. In 1985 Tom was invited to the White House to receive an award: Outstanding Learning Disabled Achievement. I wonder whether Cruise would now accept an award with the word 'disabled' in its title.

Tom will never forget the debt of gratitude he owes his mother for the special help she gave him, nor the way she rallied the family when times got rough. After the divorce she was a rock to which Tom and his sisters clung. 'OK, things have changed,' she announced soon after the separation. 'This is the new game plan.' An intensely proud woman – 'incredibly noble' says Tom of her – Mary Lee did everything she could to avoid public assistance (social security), but as her husband didn't pay child support and her pride prevented her from going cap in hand to her in-laws, who had the financial means to help, the family were sometimes forced to go on welfare. Once she went to apply for food stamps and was horrified by the long queues of people. 'I don't care what it takes,' she said on arriving back home. 'I'm not going back there again.' So she juggled jobs, hosting trade conventions, selling electrical appliances, anything going, relying on her vitality and religious faith to keep the family's spirits up. Tom, the epitome of the devoted and dutiful son, is not embarrassed by his public admissions of love for his mother: she was always there for him and now he makes a point of being there for her. He must get an enormous amount of satisfaction from being able to treat her like a queen. Cruise must be one of the few 'big' stars ever to take their mum along to the Oscars – and how about skydiving! When his mother reached fifty Tom organized parachute lessons for her as an Easter gift.

Watching his mother struggle in a male-dominated world, fighting prejudice and harassment in the work place, gave Tom a rare perspective on life; he saw what his mother had to go through to keep him clothed and to send him to good schools. Growing up in an all-female household, and later with his aunt, Cruise learned to love and respect women. They're not a mystery or a threat to him the way they are to some men. 'I've always felt much closer to women than guys because they enjoy talking about what they feel and how they feel. With men, there's too much competition and ego involved. It takes a lot longer to get into an open friendship with another guy than it does with a woman. That's why I've always had girls as best friends.'

There was a time, though, when the world's biggest sex symbol was scared to death of the opposite sex, too shy to approach a girl he might fancy to ask her on a date for fear of rejection, unless the girl herself made it obvious she was interested. She would always have to make the first move. I suppose this is true of all kids going through puberty, but when Tom Cruise looked in the mirror he didn't like what he saw. But the advantage of having three sisters, and thus being in the close proximity of women day and night, cured him of his crippling sexual hang-ups. Now, as he says, he prefers the company of women to men – hardly surprising since the single most important man in Tom's life betrayed and deserted him. 'I love women,' Cruise once confessed. 'I love the way they smell.'

All through the late seventies the Cruise family struggled to make ends meet. There was always food on the table, they never starved, but it was tight. Tom had to wear his ill-fitting cousin's cast-offs (his is literally the classic rags to riches story), which was embarrassing for a fashion-minded youngster. There was also the time he went to the senior prom in a baggy suit he'd bought two sizes too large so he could wear it in the years to come. Money was so tight that on their first fatherless Christmas no one could afford to buy any presents. Instead they picked names out of a hat and carried out a special deed for that person – making their bed, leaving a flower on the pillow, writing poems which were read aloud. It soon became obvious that if the family was to have any chance of surviving, the children had to find part-time jobs after school.

Tom immediately went to work, giving every penny he earned to his grateful mother. While his sisters were waitresses in local restaurants Tom began a paper round, getting up at dawn in bitterly cold blizzards. That first winter was one of the worst on record, but it didn't deter him – he'd go out in the snow wrapped up like an Eskimo. Tom also did odd-jobs around the community, including raking leaves and mowing the lawn for neighbour Bill Lewis. No job was too dirty or difficult as long as it paid money to help his mother out. 'While most other kids were out raising hell, he had his nose to the grindstone and was working day and night,' Lewis recalls. 'I told Mary Lee she should be awfully proud of him.'

Given the choice, would Cruise have preferred a happier childhood and a loving father? Would he have liked things to have turned out differently? Maybe he wouldn't be where he is today if they had. There are no accidents, he believes. Cruise is apt to take negative situations and turn them into positive ones, and that's something he's done with his own childhood. He now looks upon the pain and suffering as having been an adventure, a challenge; the continual dislocation fertilizer for his future as an actor. 'Some people might think of my childhood as being difficult, but now I see it as extraordinary.' The hard times can never be truly buried, though, particularly one abiding memory of his, a mother weeping because she couldn't give her children the things other parents could. Tom was acutely aware of his family's poverty, surrounded as he was by infinitely better-off kids, and a piece of that poor boy from Louisville lives on in the superstar, refusing to allow him to be corrupted by the trappings of fame. Remarkably, his feet are still pretty much in touch with the ground. Cruise never had a superstar attitude to life. 'I find life is a very humbling experience and that keeps you honest.'

The Cruise homestead closely resembled a tight sorority in which Tom served as patriarch, brother and friend. As the sole remaining male Tom became head of the family, taking on a responsibility beyond his years (not for nothing did Don Simpson call him 'the youngest patriarch I've ever encountered'). It bred into him strong survival instincts and a loyalty to family that has never waned. Today he is as close as ever to Mary Lee and his sisters; they frequently visit him on location and turn up at the premieres of his latest movies. Tom even took Cass on holiday with him to Hawaii around the time of *Top Gun*'s release and later hired elder sister, Lee Anne, to work for him at his production company. Tom, keeping it in the family, also has close friend and cousin William Mapother on the payroll.

Struggling through those lean years brought Tom and his sisters closer together than most siblings who live out their adolescence squabbling and fighting (though they had their fair share of bust-ups). All this gave him a healthy insight into the opposite sex; he always got the inside juice on what they thought about boyfriends and what women liked and how they dealt with problems. He grew extremely protective of them, and they of him. 'I remember beating up some guy because he tried something with my sister on a date,' Cruise told *You* magazine in January 1989. 'I was always real careful on my dates – it was someone's sister for god's sake.' He'd pounce on anyone who dared even to stare at one of his sisters in a suggestive way. 'Whenever any of us girls started dating anybody we were serious about, having them meet Tom was a big deal,' Lee Anne told *Vanity Fair* in October 1994. 'His opinion has always weighed very heavily with all of us.' Once when this guy was going out with his little sister, Cruise told him that if he ever tried to feel her up, he'd kill him. 'My sister still wonders why that guy never kissed her!' They were always best of friends, looking out for each other. While Mary Lee was out working they'd cook the meals; everything was always a team effort.

That team was split up when, to ease the financial strain at home, Tom spent his freshman year of high school on scholarship in St Francis', a Catholic seminary near Cincinnati, an imposing mock-Gothic mansion. The building, which looked like the kind of place The Munsters might send their offspring to, only heightened the tension young Tom was feeling about being separated from his family. A sense of religious vocation festered inside the confused mind of thirteen-year-old Tom, which he confided to Bill Lewis, with whom he'd struck up a friendship. The fifty-year-old had become a father figure of sorts, someone to turn to for help and advice; though in his company Tom never once mentioned his real father. Bill scarcely doubted the seriousness of Tom's heavenly calling, and told the youngster that the church would provide a good life, but to follow the path most likely to make him happy. But more than anything the move to the seminary had to do with the fact that Mary Lee couldn't afford to give him a private education. Being subsidized, the Franciscan monastery school could put clothes on his back, feed him and provide what turned out to be the finest period of education in his academic life (the small class sizes meant each pupil received extra individual attention); even better, it was free. They also provided him with a set of rules to obey, a sense of order and structure, so desperately needed after the chaotic rollercoaster ride of the last few years.

But Tom found the priests weren't the only strict taskmasters. Pupils were obliged regimentally to walk up every stair leading to their classrooms. Late for a lesson once, Tom missed a step in his hurry and a tyrannical nun slammed him hard against a wall. She screamed into his petrified face: 'Don't you ever, ever, miss another stair again!' Misbehaviour was not tolerated, and Tom's holier-than-thou masters missed little opportunity to dish out their medieval punishments. The usual penance was writing lines, but once a lad caught with alcohol was severely beaten. Such behaviour today would be condemned as child abuse and the offending establishment shut down. In 1980, due to financial pressures, St Francis' closed its doors as a school: no one wanted to go there anymore. The building was almost used as one of the locations in *Rain Man*. Instead director Barry Levinson decided to film at another convent nearby where Cruise was reportedly standoffish with the nuns, the complete opposite to Hoffman.

The regime was tough, more like a bout of national service in the Algerian army than a school term. Cruise shared a dormitory with twenty other boys, sleeping in makeshift cubicles with a flimsy curtain for privacy. At 6.40 a.m. each morning pupils were stirred from slumber by a clattering bell. Breakfast was at 7.00 a.m. prompt, and woe betide anyone who was late. Classes began at 8.30 a.m., interrupted by an hour's mass and a spartan midday lunch. The afternoon consisted of more classes then recreation. The sports-enthusiast Cruise must have salivated when he laid his eyes on the seminary's sports facilities; they must have seemed like manna from heaven – playing fields galore, tennis courts, a swimming pool and a man-made lake. It was a huge campus, some 150 acres, for such a small school, consisting of only 100 pupils when Tom arrived in the autumn of 1976. The day ended at 4.30 p.m. with a study period, followed by supper. At 9.00 p.m. it was lights out. The regime was strict but it helped Tom enormously, it being the first time he'd spent such a long time away from home. Slowly too his self-confidence improved. His favourite teacher and confidant, Father Jack Schindler, remembers, 'Tom was very shy and was afraid girls wouldn't like him because he was so short. He

even asked, "when will girls be interested in me?" It took him a
while to get over it, but then he bloomed overnight. He turned
into a different person.'

As Tom's fancy turned to matters carnal, his interest in the
priesthood waned; he never gave becoming a priest another
serious thought. The idea of being celibate – no way! On weekends
he and a clutch of friends would sneak out of the seminary to visit a
girl's house in town, sit around, talk and play Spin the Bottle –
whomever the bottle ended up pointing at was subjected to an orgy
of kisses. Those evenings made Tom realize that he loved women
too much to give them up.

In the autumn of 1978 Tom met his first proper girlfriend, his
first taste of real romance, sixteen-year-old Laurie Hobbs who
lived close by and found Tom irresistibly cute. 'But not what you'd
call cool. And he had a chipped tooth that embarrassed him so
much that he decided to have it fixed.' Hobbs was also struck by
the boy's shyness; he was very uneasy when it came to chatting up
girls. So shy in fact that Laurie had to make the first move, finally,
in a state of exasperation, asking him: 'Are you going to take me
to the school dance or what?'

Tom was sixteen and approaching his senior year in high school
when Mary Lee announced she was remarrying. She'd met Jack
South, a plastics salesman, at an electronics convention and right
away Tom felt threatened. News of the impending union shocked
and upset him ('There's a part of you that's in love with your
mother'). Of course he wished his mother every happiness, but
had enjoyed being the man of the family, which was how his
adoring sisters treated him. He saw Jack, who was also determined
to be head of the household, as endangering this exalted role,
irrespective of the fact that he was offering them the only stability
they'd known in years, the best chance for future happiness. Not
surprisingly things got off to a bad start and there was much bad
blood between them. Their fragile relationship was further
strained when Jack decided to move his newly acquired family to
Glen Ridge, a leafy suburb nestled discreetly among the rougher
neighbourhoods of New Jersey. Tom was furious that he was going
to have to change schools in the final year before he graduated.
But Jack was now the boss. Tom's attitude towards Jack changed
over time as he came to realize just how much he loved Mary Lee;
it's a special kind of man who willingly takes on someone else's
kids. 'He is such a wise, smart man.' They'd bet on football games

and as Jack was a lousy gambler, Tom would make a packet.

The family's socioeconomic status scarcely matched the overtly snobbish area into which they'd moved and it was a while before they were fully accepted. Still relatively reserved, Tom did have a handful of acquaintances he'd hang out with at discos or the local cinema; his favourite film was *The Blues Brothers*, which he saw countless times. In the local high school Tom had followed his usual pattern of launching himself into different sports as a way of gaining instant acceptance with his peers (Tom's nomadic childhood was responsible for many later insecurities. His penchant for doing most of his own film stunts stems from these days of proving himself as an all-round athlete.) He certainly made a name for himself in the football team when he got kicked out for being caught drinking. The incident was enormously embarrassing to Tom who hadn't been at Glen Ridge High long; so drunk was he that he couldn't walk straight and had to be supported by his then girlfriend, Nancy Armel. Nancy became Tom's steady at Glen Ridge, but at first had to be persuaded to go out on a date with him. Her uncle was the school's assistant principal, one of whose jobs was to look after the new pupils, make sure they settled in; it was his suggestion that Nancy befriend Tom. 'I'm certain you'll get to like him,' he told her. While Nancy's nickname for him was 'Little Muppet' – 'Tom was real small, and he was no heartthrob, that's for sure' – his beguiling charm won her affection. 'He was a real nice guy and great fun,' Nancy told the *Sun* in October 1990. 'He developed a great personality, really sincere. And he had a great gift of the gab – he could bullshit anyone.' Tom wasn't above getting Nancy to help improve his grades. At Glen Ridge he was still trying to overcome his dyslexia and would sit next to Nancy in class and sweet-talk her until she let him copy down the answers.

Shortly before the all-important school prom, one of the most significant days in the calendar of any American teenage girl, Tom unceremoniously dumped Nancy. 'He told me just two days beforehand that we weren't going together, that we had finished as an item.' It was a bombshell. Both arrived on the night of the prom with different dates, but by the close of the evening were back together. 'It all eventually fizzled out when he made *Risky Business* with Rebecca DeMornay,' Nancy recalls. 'And she became his main squeeze.'

Following his inglorious exit from the football team, Tom took up wrestling; his strong, sinewy five-foot-nine frame made him a natural. So much so that he briefly considered making a career out of it, setting his heart on winning a college scholarship as a wrestler, though he was of only average ability. On occasion his varsity matches made the sports pages of the local paper. But then disaster struck in the shape of a bizarre accident which ended his stint on the Glen Ridge wrestling team. Every night before a bout Tom exercised at home in a bid to lose a few ounces so he might weigh in at the correct poundage. Running up and down the stairs to sweat off any unwanted fat, Tom slipped on some school papers his sister had inadvertently left on the stairwell and went tumbling down the entire flight, crashlanding at the bottom in an unglamorous heap. The resulting injury, pulled knee tendons, meant a brief spell on crutches, but worse, sidelined him for the remainder of the season. Tom was devastated.

It was a teacher at the glee-club, where Tom had been dabbling in singing lessons, who was to rescue him from the abyss of misery to which he had sunk after the accident by suggesting he audition for a part in the school's production of the musical *Guys and Dolls*. Tom had nothing else to do so thought he might as well give it a shot – a decision that would ultimately change his life. Originally Tom was marked down as being only part of the chorus, but the teacher in charge of the show was impressed with his strong voice and pushed him into the co-starring slot of Nathan Detroit (the role made famous by Frank Sinatra in the Hollywood film version).

Mary Lee was not entirely surprised by her son's sudden conversion to drama, since as a tiny tot he'd shown an early theatrical aptitude, creating his own skits and imitating the likes of Donald Duck, Woody Woodpecker, James Cagney, John Wayne and W.C. Fields. 'He had it in him then,' Mary Lee told *Rolling Stone* in June 1986. Like all boys he loved to play imaginary war games (Like the young Ron Kovic in the title sequence of *Born on the Fourth of July*) and Mary Lee encouraged such playacting and self-expression. Imagination was sometimes his only friend. 'But as he got older, he was more into sports and it stopped completely.' Rather more strangely, though another early indication that he was a natural exhibitionist (as most actors must be), the twelve-year-old Tom Cruise loved to dress up. One picture has the young Tom done up like some Victorian lady, with pearls and a feather hat, lipstick and eye shadow. In another he's arm in arm with two boys in fancy dress – one as a gangster, the

other a cowboy; again little Tom preferred to come as a girl,
wearing what is probably his mother's wig, a necklace and a
particularly dapper blue dress. As the picture was taken he
suggestively lifted the skirt, displaying ample portions of the
Cruise thigh, as though he's Claudette Colbert attracting the
amorous attention of drivers in *It Happened One Night*. All
perfectly innocent, but very interesting.

Mary Lee, bubbly, outgoing and religious, was once an aspiring
actress herself; theatre had been her passion as a youth but she
never seriously pursued it in later life. 'When I was growing up, if
you went to Hollywood that was really risque. I would have lost
my religion, my morals, all those things that young girls thought of
back then.' Instead amateur dramatics consumed most of her
spare time; practically every town the Cruise family moved to had
one theatre group or another Mary Lee could join and when it
didn't, as in Ottawa, she established her own.

Thoughts of what might have been had she followed her own
childhood dreams of a stage career must have entered Mary Lee's
mind as she watched, with tears of pride swelling up in her eyes,
her seventeen-year-old son barnstorming his way through the role
of Nathan Detroit on the opening night of *Guys and Dolls*. 'I can't
describe the feeling that was there. It was just an incredible
experience to see what we felt was a lot of talent coming forth all
of a sudden. It had been dormant for so many years – not thought
of or talked about or discussed in any way. Then to see him on that
stage.' But Mary Lee had no inkling of what was about to happen
next.

Tom returned home to the warm congratulations of his whole
family; taking Jack and his mother aside he told them he'd decided
to become an actor, just like that (backstage an agent who'd
watched the performance declared him a 'natural' and advised he
seriously consider turning professional). Disbelief, surprise, a
whole gamut of emotions raced through both mother and
stepfather; was their son serious? Had he properly and rationally
thought the whole thing through? Evidently so, Tom had it all
mapped out, he was going to take a crack at showbusiness, give
himself a deadline of ten years (if anything, to ease his parents'
anxieties) and see how far he got. The ten years expired in 1990,
with Tom firmly entrenched at the apogee of the Hollywood
pyramid and coming as close as anyone gets to winning an Oscar.
He'd already ruled out college; the thought of further education

was anathema to him, having attended so many different schools, each time struggling anew with dyslexia and being an outsider. Tom had saved up a bit of money which he'd planned to use hitch-hiking across Europe – that should see him comfortably started. 'Just let me see,' he pleaded with his parents. 'I really feel that this is what I want to do.'

Jack was by far the least convinced, after all he was the one who would largely have to finance Tom's voyage of discovery. 'What's this going to cost me? Ten years of what?' – remarks which are now a famous family joke. He thought maybe Tom should first learn a trade, something to fall back on if things didn't work out (ironically, considering the movie which would make him a star, Cruise briefly toyed with a career in the air force). But Mary Lee saw in her son a 'God-given talent' that he had every right to explore. Tom's enthusiasm was contagious and soon everyone was smitten with the idea; Mary and Jack didn't find it too difficult giving him their blessing, thrilled that he had at last found something he truly loved. For much of his youth Tom had been a dreamer, anything but hard-working and focused. His parents worried about him because of this boundless energy and the fact that he could never stick to one thing for very long. If he worked in an ice-cream parlour – 'and I've worked in a lot of them' – he'd be the best for the first two weeks or so, then boredom would inevitably set in and he'd either quit or get fired. There was also the painful truth that he'd never really achieved anything. Even in sport, he compensated for his lack of skill by boundless energy, and, like work, tended to flit from one activity to another. 'If I could just focus in and do something,' he'd tell himself, 'I know I've got the energy and creativity to be great.'

Then all of a sudden, after all those years of feeling like nothing, he had something to say. Tom found that he could express himself through acting and the applause (on that opening night Cruise received a standing ovation: it was obvious he stood out from the rest of the cast) was doubt-proof evidence that he was loved. The attention he'd craved for so long was suddenly there; people who never turned their heads or said anything before were now taking notice of him. He felt good; he was doing something he really enjoyed and grabbing all this attention. But even better than that, he felt at home on stage; he'd found himself. This was it. Tom knew from that moment if he didn't seize the opportunity he might regret it for the rest of his life.

3 'Hollywood: Welcome, Cruise'

A few weeks prior to leaving for the Big Apple, and fortuitously for Tom, a would-be actress schoolmate who'd appeared in a few commercials got him signed up with her New York-based management agency. Mary Lee drove Tom to the interview in a battered Ford Pinto for which he'd paid fifty dollars. Aged only seventeen, he wasn't allowed a manager unless his mother was present to cosign the contract for him. Apprehension about the impending meeting ate away at his self-confidence like acid; the strained atmosphere, the result of a massive bust-up that morning, didn't help much. It was rush hour and, already late, Tom left Mary to park the car somewhere while he ran into the office.

The meeting was straightforward enough, the woman making him read the script for a chocolate bar commercial. 'It was one of those, "Yeah, yeah, babe, you're beautiful, I'm going to make you a star sort of situations." ' But the aftermath proved disastrous; she treated Tom like a commodity, a piece of meat. She'd call him over for allegedly important meetings only to get him to run errands or go grocery shopping for her. After a month he could stand it no longer and wanted to sack her. 'Well you can't,' she declared. 'You've signed a five-year contract.' Happily, as Cruise signed the agreement under-age, it wasn't legally binding and he hired a lawyer to prise him out of the deal. Then he went about finding another manager, interested in exploiting him as an actor rather than as a slave. 'Soon after that, I didn't want a manager any more. I just had an agent. Managers can be a Hollywood trap.' His impoverished upbringing had taught Cruise the value of the American dollar; the cash he earned as an actor was going in his pocket, not someone else's.

On graduation day at Glen Ridge High, Cruise (having deleted the clumsy 'Mapother IV' from his name) was present in body but his spirit was elsewhere, already scheming his assault on showbusiness in the face of pressure to back out. Friends thought it was a pipe dream and that he was crazy even attempting to become an actor. Spurred on by his success in *Guys and Dolls* and the further mini-triumph of landing the role of Herb over 500 other aspirants in a theatre production of the rock opera *Godspell*, his first professional experience in front of an audience, Cruise moved to New York in the summer of 1980 and tore into the struggling performer's life – waiting tables, unloading trucks, hustling to auditions by day, catching workshops at the local playhouse when time permitted, honing his raw talent (other actors took classes, Cruise inhaled them). 'It was great. I was like an animal in the jungle.' Years of surviving hand to mouth seemed ideal preparation for life as a starving artist on the mean streets. He economized, always walking to classes and saving the $1.25 to buy hot dogs and rice and shared digs with a colleague to keep costs low. Then he wangled a job as a superintendent's assistant in an apartment block in exchange for free accommodation. 'People would call me in the middle of the night,' he related to *Premiere* in July 1988, 'and say, "My heating's not working." And I'd say, "Well, my fucking heating's not working, either." '

   In position to play leads just as Hollywood's wave of teen flicks were beginning, the soon-to-emerge Brat Pack, whose dramatic, hunky looks established them as instant idols with cinema's biggest audience – (the 17- to 25-year-olds), Cruise was initially told by a TV executive that he wasn't pretty enough for prime time TV, when people were eating their dinners (ironic for someone who would later be named the sexiest man in the world). The producers and casting directors who encountered Tom in those early days recall an urgency in his acting and an angry edge – an overpowering energy driven by a totally blinkered obsession to succeed. This approach was sometimes his undoing. Potential employers backed off when Cruise came on too intense, best exemplified at one audition for a TV commercial when he yelled, '*Eat* the *Fritos*!' Talk about the hard sell. Not surprisingly Cruise was never asked to sell washing powder. In life as in art Cruise was brash and bold. His saving grace was that he had the confidence of ignorance – not knowing anything about the dog-eat-dog business to which he'd willingly become slave, he was immune from fear. He seemed to sail through each audition failure with a breezy good humour, as if he were on some great learning curve. 'I felt that the people rejecting me were there to help me in the long run,' he told *Interview* in May 1986. 'Sometimes it hurts, but I truly believe that there are parts I'm supposed to get and parts I'm not supposed to get and something else is going to come along.' Tom Cruise is one of the 0.5 per cent who made it and his rise to prominence was so remarkably swift there was no time to become disillusioned or embittered. Once he was up for a situation comedy. The network were keen and paid his flight over to Los Angeles. After his read-through the director said, 'So, how long are you going to be out here?' Cruise, under the impression he'd just delivered a shit-hot reading and was about to be recalled for a second audition, said, 'Oh, just a few days.' 'Well, get a tan while you're here.' Today Cruise can't tell that story without cracking up. The director's delivery was so cold, the words froze as they left his lips. Cruise walked away, thinking to himself, 'This is Hollywood: Welcome, Cruise.'

4   Brats United

'The term Brat Pack is a bunch of crap, a lot of bullshit.'
— Tom Cruise, 1988

The term 'Brat Pack' was first coined in a June 1985 article for *New York* magazine by journalist David Blum. He portrayed them as Hollywood's new bad boys – promiscuous and immature, babe-chasing, club-hopping young studs interested only in money and staying in the limelight, an updated variation of Frank Sinatra's Rat Pack cronies of the sixties. Tabloids had a field day devoting copious column inches to their latest antics and misdemeanours – in particular, which grubby *paparazzo* Sean Penn had clouted that week. Brat Pack members, they reported, were easily recognizable in their 'uniform' of sunglasses, designer T-shirts, jeans and expensive trendy sports jackets. They patronized only the most fashionable watering holes, like the Hard Rock Café in Beverly Hills. There the Pack's unofficial president Emilio Estevez regularly held court, accompanied often by beautiful young actresses, downing Corona beers and Stolichnaya vodka served chilled over ice, their favourite tipple.

To the actors' chagrin Blum's article and the subsequent media coverage had the effect of trivializing their image and calling into question their 'serious artist' credentials. Cruise was in New York when he heard about what Blum had written. 'And that's when I realized I was a brat. "I'm a brat, Mom. Girls, I'm a brat." What are you going to say about something like that?' Thus he complained to *Rolling Stone* in August 1988. 'I mean, how did I get lumped in with that?' Indeed Cruise, like many of the other so-called Brats, disputed that such an exclusive club ever truly existed, even if they did have the unerring habit of appearing in each others' films with alarming monotony. 'There really isn't a

35

community of actors. I mean, that is false, absolutely false.' Cruise's fear was that being lumped together with a group of other actors could seriously damage him professionally by encouraging the sort of typecasting he was desperate to avoid. Cruise had Brat pals but didn't really roam with the gang. One of them was Emilio Estevez, and they hung out a lot in the early days; in 1986 Cruise described him as probably his best friend outside his family. He was pally too with Sean Penn, though during Penn's stormy marriage to Madonna the two met infrequently.

Whatever happened to …? The Brat Pack roll call

MATT DILLON: Branded by *Time* magazine as 'the punk Montgomery Clift', his bruised good looks reminded one of the early Brando.

C. THOMAS HOWELL: Made his film debut in *ET*. Career went down the toilet with *Soul Man* and has remained firmly stuck in the U-bend ever since.

RALPH MACCHIO: A native of New York, found fame in *The Karate Kid* series. If there's ever a Nuremberg trial for movies, they're going straight to the gallows.

ROB LOWE: The prettiest of the bunch. Famous more for the video he didn't want released than for those that were.

EMILIO ESTEVEZ: Born a Hollywood brat, son of Martin Sheen, brother of Charlie. Grew up in the same Malibu neighbourhood as Lowe and Penn. Scored in *Stake-out* and as Billy the Kid in *Young Guns*. The pack's most adventurous limb, trying his hand at writing and directing, with little success. Now simply known as Emilio Who?

PATRICK SWAYZE: The only other Brat Packer to come close to scaling the heights of Cruisedom, with *Dirty Dancing* and *Ghost* – then Crudsville.

JUDD NELSON: Seemingly destined for great things after his barnstorming tour de force as the school rebel in *The Breakfast Club*. Since then never made another tolerable film.

ANDREW MCCARTHY: The shy and sensitive one. Made a string of duff eighties movies that did little to enhance a reputation that never existed in the first place. Responsible for the appalling *Mannequin*.

SEAN PENN: Oh, he's that guy who married Madonna, right, and decks photographers. What, he acts too?

A litany of crushed dreams, gossip casualties, potential blighted by scandal and fluctuating fortune. Cruise left his contemporaries, mere also-rans, for dust. But why? What made Cruise so different? Why should he have streaked so far ahead of his brother Brat Packers? In a BBC interview with Barry Norman Cruise was asked to explain this and was totally stumped for an answer. Unlike many of his contemporaries Cruise did not come from a showbusiness background: C. Thomas Howell is the son of a stuntman, Timothy Hutton's father was the actor Jim Hutton, Nicolas Cage happens to be the nephew of Francis Ford Coppola (the mind boggles at how he managed to get into movies) and Patrick Swayze's mother was a dancer who choreographed the John Travolta movie *Urban Cowboy*. Merely another pretty-boy face at career outset, a hunk for hire in a series of exploitative teen flicks, Cruise rose phoenix-like from the ashes of the pack's fall from grace in the mid eighties. With apparent grace and ease, he matured into a bona fide world star, achieving success in a seemingly endless production line of mega-hits, and reached more filmgoers than the combined efforts of all his contemporaries. Even his flops made more money than Rob Lowe's hits.

What did he have that separated him from the Brat Pack? He was never going to be as pretty-looking as Rob Lowe, or as volatile and unpredictable on or off camera as Sean Penn, or as mean and moody as Matt Dillon; but almost from the beginning he was marked as the one with the biggest box-office potential. Paul Newman, having considered Cruise's rivals, once said, 'Tom may be the only survivor.' He didn't envy the young star having to make his way in today's industry. 'The streets are littered with kids who started at 18, and just died by the time they were 25,' he told the *Sunday Times* in April 1987. 'But Cruise is going to survive that because he's sensible. He's willing to study, and he's got a great sense of ethics.' So what was the secret of his success? In a word: simplicity. His peers tended to be more in the rebellious mode of Dean or Brando, whereas Cruise promotes the more accessible image of an intense young man with a mission, a workhorse whose energies are focused on one thing: an ambition to be 'the best of the best' in whatever field – jet flying, shooting pool, mixing drinks, biting necks. Director Barry Levinson is certain Cruise's talents are underestimated by critics because he's not pushing the rebel image which is associated with being a good actor. One imagines if Cruise had emerged in the early seventies, the era of *M.A.S.H.*, *Easy Rider* and *Five Easy Pieces*, films that typified a rebellious youth at odds with authority and complacent middle-class attitudes, audiences would have laughed him off the screen as the worst kind of youthful conformist egomaniac. He had to wait until Ronald Reagan became president to become a star. If anything, Cruise is a throwback to fifties teen idols like Tony Curtis and Tab Hunter, who also made it in the magazine cover and bedroom wall stakes, but neither achieved anything close to Cruise's popularity. Cruise is the cleanest young man to become a popular actor since the juveniles of the fifties. Perhaps his politeness was integral to his appeal – he was an antidote to the snarling, self-involved Matt Dillon and Sean Penn.

That toothpaste-commercial grin, cartoon-handsome face and acting-class earnestness radiated American boyishness; there's always been an eager-to-please charisma about Cruise. Unlike many of his hard-drinking, hard-living Brat Pack colleagues, Cruise was never the promiscuous 'party animal' type, never led a rock 'n' roll, *paparazzi*-punching lifestyle. The recklessness and aggressiveness of youth is channelled into his work. Once on a night out with Sean Penn at a New York club, just after the release of *Risky Business*, he was mixing with a group of other actors – De Niro, Mickey Rourke – all attracting a fair quota of desirable female company. One long-legged specimen sauntered over to Tom and started chatting him up, and it soon became obvious she was only interested in his body. Cruise lost his cool and yelled, 'I have a girlfriend [then Rebecca DeMornay] I'm in love with!' No doubt unaccustomed to being rebuffed the girl angrily retorted, 'You should have told me that five minutes ago.' No other example is needed of Tom's determined intention not to become embroiled in the seedier side of fame. He may drive his Porsche, race his Harley and fly aerobatics in his plane when he's not jumping out of them, but he does it in the disciplined and determined way he approaches his career. 'Acting is not that glamorous. It's hard work. If you can make movie after movie and still find the energy to party and have a highly visible social life, my hat's off to you.' Seriously down-to-earth, Cruise is just not interested in the kind of self-destructive behaviour typified by his Brat colleagues.

Although Cruise only ever appeared in two 'official' Brat Pack projects (*Taps*, arguably the first Brat Pack movie, and *The Outsiders*), every one of his pre-stardom movies were 'brattish' in nature – *Legend* being the only real departure and significantly his biggest financial flop. They were aimed brazenly at America's cola-guzzling, Nike-wearing, MTV-mesmerized youth. Amazingly, within only five months of arriving in New York Cruise bagged a small role in Franco Zeffirelli's contemptible *Endless Love*. Apparently the renowned Italian director uttered but one word after Tom's reading – 'Bellissimo' – before signing him for his Hollywood debut. Nervous at the prospect of auditioning for, theoretically, one of the year's hottest releases? Not one jot: Cruise was unaware of Zeffirelli's impressive name and pedigree, and this undoubtedly worked in his favour.

Briefly appearing as teen arsonist Billy (so brief, in fact, that it only took a day to shoot), Cruise exhibits breathless non-star potential. Billed eighteenth in the cast credits he was only paid $300 a day. 'I didn't even know where the camera was when I did that movie,' Cruise enjoyably related to *Empire* in August 1996. 'They kept saying, "Hit your marks", and I was like, "What's a mark? You want me to hit Mark? Who's he?" ' In just two years his looks alone would guarantee him romantic leads, bestowed here upon Martin Hewitt (who vanished afterwards into the black abyss from which he was plucked) as a lovesick pup whose idea of winning the hand of his betrothed is to reduce her parents' home to blackened ruins.

James Spader was another rising actor making his feature debut in *Endless Love*, but with by far the larger role. For Cruise it was merely a learning exercise, an exhilarating experience to be on the set of a major Hollywood picture. For the first time he was inhaling the intoxicating atmosphere generated by a unit of some sixty professionals, with catering vans, actors' caravans, make-up and wardrobe wagons. The film belonged to its star Brooke Shields, who, following the smash success of *The Blue Lagoon* in 1980, looked set to become the decade's most celebrated teenage idol. But Zeffirelli, reduced to squeezing Shields' big toe off-camera during the sex scenes to provoke the desired orgasmic facial contortions, callously described directing her as, 'cracking the whip at a limping horse'. And when the film flopped spectacularly with public and critics alike, it was she who caught most of the fall-out, leaving her movie career in tatters. Today she floats among that curious clique of people who are famous for simply being famous. Reactions to the film were indeed uniformly hostile. Preview audiences booed at the screen, and reviewers booed in their columns: 'Zeffirelli directs with all the perception and delicate insight of a mentally handicapped walrus' – *Daily Express*; 'the sort of movie one yearns to put over one's knee and spank' – *New Statesman*; 'morally indefensible twaddle' – *Daily Mirror*.

Interestingly, the failure of *Endless Love* and the subsequent dimming of Miss Shields's star coincided with the rise of a new breed of teenage actor, embryonically evident in Cruise's very next film, *Taps*. It was the end of an era; Shields and her fellow 70s children, Tatum O'Neal and Jodie Foster (whose fortunes reversed only years later) were no longer considered box office. The torch was being passed from one generation of juvenile narcissists to another – the Brat Pack, to whom acting seemed almost incidental to their existence as pin-ups and products of publicity machines, now represented the new wave of Hollywood – 'a fresh group of young actors whose dramatic skills transcend their age and who will inherit the mantle of Newman-Eastwood-McQueen, Pacino-De Niro-Hoffman' – Lee Grant, *Los Angeles Times*. And, ironically, where Shields and her ilk had been conspicuously female (only the irksome child actors had been male, notably Ricky Schroder in *The Champ* and Justin Henry in *Kramer Vs Kramer*), the Brat Pack was predominantly male – indicative of just how much the male movie star would totally dominate the industry in the 1980s. This held true into the 90s, too, with the emergence of a new breed of Hollywood brats – Keanu Reeves, Christian Slater, Brad Pitt, Johnny Depp – who were certainly more talented and likely to stay the course than the Lowe/Estevez crowd.

Taps, about the doomed take-over of a military academy threatened with closure by its misguided cadets, was vastly superior to *Endless Love* and was the film where things really started happening for Tom Cruise. After that inauspicious debut he'd returned to New York and suffered the classic grinding poverty and rejection of the down-at-heel actor. Just when things seemed as low as they could get, when Cruise, in his own words, 'literally didn't have a dollar to my name,' his agent wangled him an interview first with director Harold Becker, then producer Stanley R. Jaffe. Ominously this meeting lasted all of two minutes, after which he was shown the door. Still convinced he'd done enough to get the part, despite the fact he was competing against 2,000 other hopefuls, Cruise visited his family in Glen Ridge, but because of his dire financial plight hitchhiked his way down. Walking up the driveway he saw his mother on the telephone through the window. Upon opening the front door she was scarcely able to suppress her excitement. 'It's your agent,' she said. 'You've got the part.'

Prior to filming the cast were assembled for a month's rehearsal, time enough for everyone to psych each other out and compare egos. Cruise and the other young actors like Sean Penn (making his debut) and Timothy Hutton (who'd just won an Oscar for *Ordinary People*), were being closely scrutinized by brokers in Hollywood, who wondered which of them might step into the spotlight. Competition between these rising young guns could well have spilled over into petty jealous rivalries; instead firm friendships were forged that still endure to this day. From the moment cameras rolled there was an overwhelming sense that everyone was on the ground floor of something special, proving for Cruise and his contemporaries a time of great trepidation and expectation. 'I felt like it was a chance for me,' Cruise revealed to *Interview* in May 1986, 'and a beginning. We were really scared and nervous and excited. We didn't know what was going to happen. It was a special time in my life.' Tom and Sean grew particularly close, prone to staying up half the night ruminating over the script and drama theory and would hang out with Hutton at weekends in his four-wheeler, sometimes driving for hours through the Pennsylvania countryside with music blasting out of the sound system.

There was also a master plan, brewed no doubt in the intoxicating haze of a late-night drinking session, with liberal borrowings from *Apocalypse Now*.

Near the Valley Forge Military Academy, the Merion Golf Club was hosting the U.S. Open that year, [Hutton related to *Rolling Stone* in May 1983] and we had access to helicopters and smoke bombs. So we went to the sound department and asked them if they could rig up some speakers on the helicopter. We realized that on Sunday all the heavies in the

golf world were gonna make their final putt for the big bucks.
So, we were gonna have a radio up in the helicopter and be
kind of flying around the area, listening to the golf broadcast,
and then at the key moment, swoop down and land on the
18th green. We were going to drop out of the sky just as the
announcer was saying, "And now, here's Tom Watson,
thirteen under par, birdy-triple-doo-dah-dang. The crowd
has gone deadly silent." ' At this point Hutton bursts into an
impromptu rendition of Ride of the Valkyries, interspersed
with machine-gun fire. 'We were gonna jump out, carrying
machine guns with blanks, and say something like, "just
kidding." But we were so charged up about the idea that we
didn't keep it to ourselves, and it got to the police. They sort
of came down and said that it wouldn't be such a great idea.'

Friendships were further strengthened during a month-long stay
roughing it at the Valley Forge Military Academy in Pennsylvania,
where much of the film was shot. There they ate, slept and trained
with real recruits until the kind of discipline that turns bed wetters
into crack commandos, spit 'n' polish terrorists willing to take a
bullet in the head for flag and country, became almost second
nature. His body blown up with a junk-food diet (cheeseburgers,
fries and milk-shakes), solidified by pumping iron and topped with
a crew-cut that would have made Yul Brynner wince, Cruise
already looked every inch a Red Beret wannabe. Even his
strutting parade ground walk had, according to Sean Penn, the
crisp exactness 'a kid at a military academy might work 3 or 4 years
for'. With scenes at a premium and needing to make a visual
impact Cruise had gained the extra 15 pounds necessary to lend his
first major role on-screen 'weight'.

His zealous dedication drew affectionate sniggers from Penn
and Hutton. 'Very intense, 200 per cent there,' Penn recalled in
Rolling Stone in June 1986. 'It was overpowering – and we'd all
kind of laugh because it was so sincere. Good acting, but so far in
the intense direction that it was funny.' Cruise had originally been
cast as a sidekick of David Shawn, the fanatic cadet whose brains
go AWOL, but the actor cast wasn't firing on all cylinders. 'Cruise
was so strong that the other guy didn't have a chance,' says Penn.
Just days into production Harold Becker offered Cruise the
substantially greater part of Shawn. 'While we were in rehearsal I
began to notice Tom,' recalled the director. 'He became the

character and he just blew me away with his intensity. So I replaced one of the leading actors with him. It's what I call a battlefield promotion.' It was on *Taps* that Cruise first displayed his now famous gung-ho working methods and provided his earliest opportunity to employ his inner resources to create a character. To the bafflement of his colleagues Cruise rejected Becker's offer – 'O fuck' was his immediate reaction, on the grounds that being so inexperienced he was content simply to observe proceedings on set and watch more seasoned performers like George C. Scott go through their paces. He also didn't want to upset the other actor. Besides, they'd already greatly increased his role thanks to a veritable fountain of ideas – he'd wanted scenes that showed his character in his dorm room determinedly courting pain – and he got them. Cruise relented only when it was pointed out to him that he either accept or pack his bags. The producers cornered him, threatening. 'Look, buddy, if you don't want to do it, leave. We want you for this part, but we're not going to beg you.' Penn recalls, 'It was incredible how innocent and naive he was when he came in to do *Taps*.'

Maniacal and obsessed, a wildly energetic misfit, the role of David Shawn seemed tailor-made for a young determined Cruise. Echoes of his own troubled childhood existed in the tortured furrows of Shawn's fictional psyche. 'A lot of that character was my childhood,' he admitted. 'I wasn't intense like that but the character is just fear. That's what he does when he's afraid – he fights.' Murderously gung-ho, Shawn is the definitive macho-warrior steeped in marine tradition. His face beams every time the chances of an armed exchange escalate, and he becomes a symbol of man driven by an appetite for killing rather than by ideals. Yet absurdly he's also the film's ultimate idealist, though his idealism takes the form of trying to massacre everyone in sight. The aggressive side of Cruise's nature was given free rein as he fell easily into the character, marching around the set, snapping to attention and barking out orders in drill sergeant fashion. He displayed a steely look in the early parade ground scenes – the look of a Top Gun and apparently Becker promoted Cruise from background player to featured role after witnessing first hand his physical expertise marching alongside a cadre of bona fide military muscleheads. As intense off-camera as on, the actor had his red-beret group in the movie and beyond the movie, none of whose members were averse to wild drunken binges that lasted all night. 'We would get a keg of beer and go crazy.'

But the aftershocks of all this were devastating. Playing Shawn had a serious residual effect on Cruise, and the psychological fall-out hung in the air for months after filming. His behaviour distressed his mother and sisters, for the aggressiveness he'd channelled into the character was spilling over into real life. At home he was prone to dark mood swings, and his company became most unpleasant – 'I became an asshole.' Told to lighten up Cruise escaped to the wilderness of southern Kentucky and the sanctuary of his grandfather's log cabin, where he did little except unwind and return to normality. Cruise had yet to learn that he needn't live a character 100 per cent of the time. This wouldn't be the last time Cruise was unable to shake off a character, and curiously it would be another marine – Ron Kovic.

Considering how many military types he's played since, it's significant that Tom Cruise first came to the attention of audiences in a uniformed role, and in his first major film of the eighties, as in his last (*Born on the Fourth of July*), Cruise plays the gung-ho soldier boy blown away in the fantasy of combat. 'It's beautiful, man! Beautiful,' is Shawn's exultant death cry of suicidal idealism as he manically sprays the campus grounds with machine-gun fire before being mown down by itchy-fingered National Guards, precipitating the inevitably tragic and shocking finale. For the first and only time in his career, Tom Cruise dies. (I don't include *Interview with the Vampire* here; he's already dead in that one.)

Of all his pre-stardom movies *Taps* was possibly the most well received. The critics were lukewarm but teenagers lapped up the fantasy spectacle of youngsters playing at war with real bullets. One reviewer referred to *Taps* as 'a *Straw Dogs* for thinking tots'; another saw it as '*Straw Dogs* goes *Animal House*.' I see it as more Lindsay Anderson than Peckinpah, a well-crafted film, flawed but worthy, with enough weighty virtues to command attention and earn respect. In this school for little killers, brainwashing teenagers with archaic notions of death before dishonour, it's little wonder they're driven to crazy measures to uphold their distorted principles and patriotism. Cruise himself cites the film as a major breakthrough, a milestone in his career. After *Taps* he informed his agency that he wasn't interested in doing commercials or television – that following his experience on *Taps* he wanted to make movies.

Calamitously, Tom's very next film was a stone's throw from wrecking his fledgling career. *Losin' It*, his least-known picture and for sound reason – it's pretty dire stuff – was amongst a batch of teen movies riding on the back of the absurd success of *Porky's* and *Lemon Popsicle* (all little more than sixties beach party movies updated to include easy sex and drugs). He'd done it as a knee-jerk reaction to being typecast as a bit of a psycho – his first two films had cast him as loony tunes (Shawn is *Endless Love*'s Billy in uniform). Today Cruise ruefully refers to *Losin' It* as 'my cable classic. You know you're in trouble when it's a comedy and everybody making the movie is miserable.' Warning bells sounded the moment he read the script, and they got louder when he met the two shysters in California who were producing the film. 'Don't worry about the script, Tom,' they said, like dentists informing their patient that it won't hurt, then producing a nine-inch syringe. 'We'll work on it, it'll be fine.' When you hear those words in Hollywood – run. Cruise's agent was vehemently in favour of him taking the role of Woody, a caricature of shy and innocent nerddom on a sex joyride to Mexico with brattish high-school chums. Unable to perform the dirty deed with local whores, he loses his burdensome virginity to a young runaway bride played by Shelley Long. Prior to *Top Gun* Cruise specialized in virginal-types; indeed Woody now appears as a forerunner to his equally sexually naive but more corruptible persona in *Risky Business*. *Losin' It* courted a good deal of hostile critical reaction – 'a film made for morons by morons' – *Daily Express*; 'a film that gives garbage a bad name' – *Daily Mirror*; 'a repellent, witless farce' – *Observer*. That Cruise survived such an unbridled barrage is perhaps his greatest achievement and despite being a creatively stifling experience, it was none the less a benchmark in Cruise's career. Taking the film's failure to heart, calling it 'a terrible time in my life', he learnt an important lesson, namely never to make any more movies like that one and never to rush into anything but examine all the elements of a project carefully, choosing one's collaborators wisely. Even this early on Cruise was already thinking about control. 'That's an important film for me. I can look at it and say, "Thank god I've grown." I thought anyone could make a great movie, all you had to do was just knock yourself out. I didn't know anything about anything.' I suppose Cruise thought he could take cold comfort in the fact that whatever crap he appeared in in the future would pale into insignificance compared to *Losin' It*. Wrong: *Cocktail* was a mere five years away.

It was during this low period that Cruise put himself in the hands of agent Paula Wagner of CAA (beginning an important relationship) to whom he outlined his credo: work only with the best people, that was the key, classy film-makers who'd help him grow as an artist. He must not delude himself by saying, 'Well, I'm gonna do this pretty crappy film, but I'm going to be the star of it.' And not to care, too much, about money. 'Money was never a factor with me – I wanted to learn on a film. Money goes, but what you learn can't be taken away from you.' He has followed this dictum through his entire career, working with a catalogue of directors that would make even the most seasoned actor green with envy: Francis Ford Coppola, Stanley Kubrick, Martin Scorsese, Oliver Stone, Ridley Scott, Barry Levinson, Sydney Pollack, Neil Jordan, Brian De Palma. 'The times Tom has been brilliant are the times when he's worked with great directors,' Nicole Kidman (his wife) told *Movieline* in March 1994. 'It makes you salivate to look at the list of directors he's worked with.'

As if out to prove a point Cruise turned down $70,000 and a first-class plane ticket to star in a horror movie; he didn't want to be associated with that kind of juvenile exploitation any more. Remember that in the early eighties the horror genre consisted solely of teen slasher flicks – high school kids on summer vacation wiped out by nutter with axe. Horror had returned to the respectable mainstream by the time Cruise made *Interview with the Vampire*, with heavyweight contributions in the order of Coppola's *Dracula*, De Niro's *Frankenstein*, Nicholson in *Wolf* and Julia Roberts's *Mary Reilly*. So chillingly effective as the demented David Shawn, Cruise was offered a slew of teen psycho roles, deluged with offers for 'every horror movie and killer movie and young-teen movie going, really bad, bad stuff'. He told Paula Wagner to bin the lot; too many of his contemporaries were hostage to such adolescent pap, hot one month, out of favour the next. Cruise was convinced many of his peers were prostituting themselves by agreeing to star in teen exploitation flicks. Cruise was determined to stay the course, and he knew the greats whom he admired (Newman, Hoffman, De Niro) took their time in nurturing their careers. 'I'm working toward the long range of what I can be as an artist,' he said in 1986. 'And I work my ass off trying. Because I know what I want to be.' And that was not getting typecast or rotting away playing one teen hero after another. There was little future in being that week's pin-up on the bedroom wall of American girls.

Learning that one of his favourite childhood books, S.E. Hinton's *The Outsiders*, was to be filmed by Francis Ford Coppola, Cruise moved to Los Angeles to participate in workshops the director had set up preparatory to casting. There he stayed at the home of Emilio Estevez over Christmas then moved in with the brothers Penn, Sean and Christopher. At the audition Cruise displayed the fearless tenacity for which he would soon become noted, striding over to Coppola and saying, 'Look, I don't care what role you give me. I really want to work with you. I want to be there on the set and watch. I'll do anything it takes; I'll play any role in this.' His courage was rewarded with the part of petrol-pump attendant Steve Randle, who, as in *Taps*, is another Cruise character so intense you think he'll self-detonate any second. In terms of size the part was negligible, but that didn't concern Cruise. He was nineteen and making a movie with Francis Ford Coppola, spurning other offers of lucrative work to do so. One agent thought it was madness: 'Francis! He's not going to pay you anything!' But that was beside the point.

Hinton's book, like so much teenage Americana, depicted a rite of passage from adolescence to adulthood and in whose pages Cruise saw mirrored the painful truth of his own displaced youth. It was written, remarkably, while the author herself was still at school, starting life as a short story that ballooned into a novel as she shared her 'work-in-progress' with classmates. Based on her own experiences growing up in Tulsa, Oklahoma, the plot details how an oil-affluent city typical of the Midwest is corrupted by a class structure dictated by economic status, giving rise to warring gangs of teenagers – the 'socs', affluent middle-class kids and 'greasers', poor white trash. It was published in 1967 under the genderless signature of S.E. Hinton (Susan Eloise), and quickly proved cult reading for kids across America who saw their own private rebellions and anxieties made flesh in characters like Ponyboy, Dallas and Sodapop. If it weren't for such a vivid group of schoolchildren, *The Outsiders* might never have reached the screen.

In March 1980 Coppola received a letter from Jo Ellen Misakian, a librarian at the Lone Star Junior High School in Fresno, California, stating that her students had nominated him to turn their favourite book *The Outsiders* into a movie. A hand-signed petition from the children was attached. 'We have a student body of 324,' wrote Misakian. 'I feel our students are representative of the youth of America. Everyone who has read the book has enthusiastically endorsed this project.' Intrigued, but not wholly convinced, Coppola passed the flimsy paperback over to his producer Fred Roos. 'I bet kids have a good idea of what should be a movie,' he said. 'Check it out, Fred, if you want to.' He didn't really, until, weeks later, when finding himself bored on a plane trip and fed up with carrying the blasted thing around, he decided to give it ten pages. 'I ended up reading it from cover to cover, and I agreed with the kids. I thought it was a movie.'

In negotiating the film rights of the book, Hinton asked for $5,000, not unreasonable in an age of million dollar movie/book deals, but Coppola, crippled by his mega-flop *One from the Heart*, was staring down the barrel of financial ruin and persuaded her to accept a down payment of just $500. Once this deal was successfully negotiated, the Coppola crew flew out to Tulsa, almost two years to the day after receiving Misakian's letter. The next and most important priority was finding a young cast with the natural unselfconsciousness that characterizes the best in American acting. In retrospect, this was accomplished with breathtaking astuteness as the majority of the fresh-faced leads subsequently carved out lucrative careers, some achieving major or cult stardom: Matt Dillon, Patrick Swayze, Emilio Estevez, Rob Lowe, C. Thomas Howell, Ralph Macchio and Diane Lane – the brat pack in its first flowering and arguably the greatest cast of gonnabes ever assembled. Or should that now read 'not any mores'.

Cruise is a master of research; it's the currency of his acting, and once in Tulsa he met with Susie Hinton, 'which was really wonderful' (the author appears fleetingly in the film as a nurse). He also spent a week with locals who were greasers themselves back in the sixties (he prepared similarly for *Risky Business*, hanging out with local rich kids in the Highland Park area of Chicago). Extremely disciplined, too, he reshapes his body to suit each character. Cruise's obsessiveness about getting his body right for each part is remarkable and had critics talking about a new De Niro. For his role as drop-out Steve Randle the hair was untidily slicked back, and the cap from a front tooth, chipped by a flying puck in a hockey game, was temporarily removed at his own insistence. A tattoo (unpermanent) adorned one of his considerable biceps, thus toughening up his macho image as a greaser, a realism heightened no doubt by a refusal to shower during much of the shoot to the dismay of those downwind of him. And there was a stringent fitness programme, instigated by Coppola. Cruise and other cast members started each day with Chinese Tai Chi Chuan exercises, spent two hours every afternoon at a local gym working out on weights and even engaged in gymnastics lessons. Cruise put on six pounds of beefcake muscle, which he shows off as often as possible in a series of open-shirted tableaux. Most of the cast's sleek muscles are on show, and indeed the film succeeds most as a preening contest – best demonstrated by the infamous location photoshoot where the first batch of stills were scrapped for being too sexually provocative – giving rise to comments that Coppola teasingly treated the 'greasers' as objects of sublime homoerotic desire.

Off-set there was little discipline, much horseplay, prodigious downing of beers and, according to insiders, sex bouts between the visiting thesps and local girls. Horny females were everywhere, following the cast around, ever present at location sites and camped outside the hotel each night screaming for their fave teen magazine heartthrob. Apart from a couple of discos, there was little else in Tulsa to cool off the hot libidos – certainly the Atari games Coppola had installed in his production offices were inadequate. One thoughtful soul did organize a cultural excursion to a women's mud-wrestling match. Conversation usually revolved around which of the actors would emerge the biggest movie star. A scheming Coppola, seemingly intent on creating an atmosphere of antagonism, housed those actors playing Greasers in the crummiest rooms of the Excelsior Hotel, allocating them a paltry daily allowance and scripts in bargain binders. The Socs, on the other hand, reclined in top-floor suites with first-class room service, enough expenses to rent cars and dine out in style, and leather-bound scripts. Inevitably friction arose between the two camps, and an organized weekend football match resembled something approaching a war zone. Greasers and socs stuck with their own kind – on and off camera.

Pranks were played a-plenty. One night Cruise returned to his hotel room to discover Estevez had left a present of human faeces on his doorknob. 'There was this bellman in Chicago I ran into recently,' Cruise related to *Premiere* in July 1988, 'and he said,

"Mr Cruise, I was in the Excelsior when you were there." And I said, "Oh, my god!" ' No doubt he was recalling the time he chased C. Thomas Howell, trousers around his ankles, out of the elevator and into the lobby brandishing a belt and yelling, 'I'm going to spank you.' Lord knows what fellow guests made of this exhibition. The pair were reprimanded by the hotel manager. Having already distinguished himself by mooning in front of the cameras on *Losin' It*, ripping up spruce lawns in an army jeep in *Taps* and later in *All the Right Moves* having a water fight with co-star and buddy Chris Penn in a hotel at two a.m., it was on *The Outsiders* that Cruise earned a real name for himself as a prankster. He scrawled 'Helter Skelter', the notorious blood inscription written on a wall near the slain corpse of Sharon Tate, on to Diane Lane's hotel mirror and smeared honey on her toilet seat, among other jokes of an equally crude nature, dispelling the cast's previous perception of Tom as being a bit of a square. All this was childish behaviour perhaps, but it worked for the character. Coppola encouraged his actors to behave like brats, to the point of allowing them deliberately to behave like hooligans in a restaurant, flinging their food around and insulting the waitresses. Tom saw such crude manipulation for what it was, method acting at its worst.

Tom certainly enjoyed every minute, later describing filming as 'a hell of a good time'. Working with Coppola couldn't have been anything other than a valuable learning experience. So what if the role was near-irrelevant and his fee negligible ($30,000); at this early stage in his career such factors didn't matter to him. Watching a master like Coppola at work, simultaneously building up his own confidence as a performer, had no equal in monetary terms. It had been a growing experience, and after the shambolic direness of *Losin' It*, a breath of much needed fresh air.

The Outsiders found a responsive audience, but critics didn't buy this romantic melancholia. Coppola's idealized view of teenage angst was trashed with vitriolic glee. 'A frightening failure,' David Denby in *New York* called it. 'Directed by Coppola, who must have been temporarily deranged at the time,' wrote the *Daily Express*. *The Outsiders* really is excruciatingly awful, with a feeble script – *Tom Sawyer* meets *American Graffiti* – and very badly acted.

Coppola delayed his departure from Tulsa in order to make *Rumble Fish*, Hinton's third novel which he'd read while on location, using many of the cast and crew from *The Outsiders*. (Two other Hinton books got the Brat Pack screen treatment around the same period: *Tex* starred Dillon and Estevez, who also headlined *That Was Then, This is Now*, a project that for a time had Cruise's name attached.) Cruise would surely have taken up the director's request for him to stay on had he not been offered another film that same week. It was called *Risky Business*, another hymn to teenagedom, but this one was going to change his life forever.

Along had come this script from first-time director Paul Brickman that hooked Tom from the first brisk read-through; he scented a hit. 'I thought, finally, this is an intelligent, stylish piece of material.' The timing couldn't have been more apt. Prior to *The Outsiders* the enormous responsibility of carrying a film single-handed daunted him, still a little green round the edges. His intensity and energy compensated for a lack of real acting talent in those days, and he would have been hung out to dry by the critics. Now, the time had come, he felt, to make his 'starring' debut. Unfortunate, then, that the last thing Brickman wanted was Tom Cruise as the aptly named Joel Goodsen, a horny high-school senior cramming for his college exams who comes of age with a wallop when his affluent parents leave him home alone. He was against him even auditioning. Having seen *Taps*, Brickman couldn't visualize Cruise as a clean-cut suburban preppy, the model American son. 'This guy for Joel?' he ranted. 'This guy is a killer! Let him do *Amityville 3*.' Cruise's agent pushed hard; four months of auditioning had yielded no likely candidate, and they were desperate. Brickman finally relented.

Cruise flew into Los Angeles on one of his days off from *The Outsiders*, still very much in the guise of Steve Randle – torn sweatshirt, old Levis, chipped tooth, tattoo and speaking in an Oklahoma drawl: 'Hey, how y'all doing.' Brickman just sat there. Shawn the shaven-headed lunatic now didn't seem quite so bad. 'Let's just read a little bit,' he finally said. Cruise isn't at his best reading scripts cold. Because of his dyslexia he tended to start with a line then veer off in tangents and ad-lib, scrabbling his way through the pages. The assembled company shuffled impatiently, gearing up for the immortal, 'OK, thank you, next please,' when Cruise interrupted himself mid-sentence. 'Wait, let me try it this way,' and he began from the top again. 'That was a courageous thing for a 19-year-old to do,' recalled Brickman. 'But Tom is a courageous guy. He's got a will for excellence.'

The mood lightened and they ended up reading through half the script. Tom had won over the disapproving Brickman and was later recalled for a screen test, which, to work around his cramped schedule, took place at five a.m. in order for him to fly back to Tulsa where he was required on set that evening. Unable to tamper with his *Outsiders* image, unshowered, his hair looking as if it had been dipped in axle grease, Cruise's entrance had him coming face to face with, in his words, 'this stunningly gorgeous woman. And I'm thinking, "Oh my god." ' It was Rebecca DeMornay; Brickman wanted to see if the pair gelled. DeMornay, as the tart with the kind of business acumen that belongs in the boardrooms of ICI, gives Joel a lesson in American free enterprise that's twice as effective as anything he's learnt at school. Moreover, she gave *Risky Business* its risque sex appeal. Cruise may have brought in the teenage girls but DeMornay stole their dates. Cruise apologized for his appearance. 'Listen,' he told Brickman, 'you have to have a little imagination when you see me now. For your movie I'll lose weight and cut my hair, and I'll look younger and kind of Chicago prep.' Cruise ultimately shed 14 pounds in five weeks, achieved by jogging obsessively under the furnace-like Florida sun and adhering to a strict diet of fish, chicken and vegetables. Then he forewent exercise in order to put on a little layer of baby fat, since Cruise saw Joel as the kind of kid who'd be out of shape physically as well as mentally.

The test passed smoothly. 'His feel for the part of Joel was right,' noted John Avnet, the film's producer. 'And the chemistry between Tom and Rebecca was special.' Oddly Cruise didn't see it that way. 'We didn't test that well,' he recalled to *Interview* in May 1986. 'Paul just believed in me. I told him exactly what I was going to do. We talked about it for a long time and he trusted me.' The part was Cruise's. His fee is thought to have been in the region of $200,000. 'He had the right combination of heat and innocence,' remembered the director, who was after a young Dustin Hoffman type. 'I didn't want just a cute kid – I wanted physical intensity.'

When Tom Cruise thrashed an air guitar to Bob Segar's 'Old Time Rock and Roll' clad only in a white shirt, white socks and Y-fronts, audiences rocked in their seats and cinema managers reported teenage girls jumping to their feet, clapping with delight and shouting for more. It was the most sensational piece of beefcake posturing since Travolta's street strut in *Saturday Night Fever*.

There was no turning back now, no way this guy was going to be anything but a movie star. Bouncing about in his jockeys with frenetic energy Cruise seemed in his enthusiasm and freshness a real discovery. Joel was a perfect showcase for Cruise's style – equal parts comic vulnerability and dramatic strength. This combination of boyish charm and sexuality was an instant hit with girls, and Cruise's cool, macho style also gave him a sizable male audience. This is the very essence of Cruise appeal. He's like a boy scout, caring, brave, loyal, but there's a volatile edge; his honest-to-good-guyness is mixed with steely determination. That's what audiences find so compelling. Cruise made Joel's transformation from innocent to unlikely entrepreneur, who turns his parents' house into a brothel servicing his undersexed, rich pals utterly credible. His attractive and self-mocking performance diffused some of the morally outrageous aspects of Brickman's intended satire on contemporary materialism and yuppie values, which legitimized pimping as an occupation for middle-class teenagers as the ideal preparation for Princeton Business School. One ends up unsure whether it celebrates or condemns the irresponsible lifestyle it glossily depicts.

It started as one line in the script. 'Joel dances in underwear through the house.' Brickman took Tom aside. 'I want you to use the whole living room. Just do whatever would cause your parents to have a heart attack if they were sitting in the living room.' Brickman wanted Segar's classic or maybe some Elvis to play over the scene. 'But if you can come up with something else, Tom, great.' Cruise rummaged through his record collection, but in the end 'nothing beat Bob Segar'.

Brickman had the opening shot – this was the moment Joel bursts out of his dull workaday shell. Left with strict instructions from his parents to behave responsibly, Joel moves from mild rebellion – jumping on the furniture and drinking his pop's best whisky – to acute insurrection – getting suspended from school and driving the family Porsche into a lake. He wanted Tom to somehow jump out into the frame and that would start the ball rolling. But the scene wasn't happening, no matter how many ways they tried it. Then Cruise thought if he wore socks (Brickman had intended him to be barefoot throughout) added a little dirt to the polished hardwood floor he'd get a perfect slide right out to the centre of the frame. Grabbing a candlestick, he decided it would be perfect as a microphone, and it was a case of just ad-libbing, improvising his dance moves on the spot. (Growing up the dominant music was disco, made popular by the release of *Saturday Night Fever*. Cruise watched shows like *American Bandstand* and *Soul Train* and mimicked the dance moves, rehearsed all week for those Saturday trips to the local nightclub. He'd sussed that the only way to win over the interest of girls was if you were a really good dancer). It was a memorable one-minute sequence that took only half a day to shoot, yet it endeared Cruise to film audiences worldwide. 'It's the most hysterical scene in the movie,' Brickman told his young star after seeing the rushes.

Brickman bestowed upon Cruise a creative freedom he'd not previously enjoyed on a film set, and a healthy spirit of co-operation sprang up between director and star. 'It seemed like he and Paul were kind of a unit,' DeMornay recalled to *Premiere* in July 1988. 'They would show up on the set wearing exactly the same clothes: the jeans, the sweater, the loafers. It was Tom's outfit for the movie, but it just happened to coincide with Paul's real-life wardrobe. They were both Joel, as far as I could see.'

Top-heavy with star-making scenes, not least an erotic clinch in an express train between the young lovers and the dumping of the family Porsche in Lake Michigan, *Risky Business* proved the making of Tom Cruise. He was a hot property at just twenty-one. His critically acclaimed performance helped make *Risky Business* the sleeper hit of 1983, grossing $63 million domestically on an outlay of just $5.5 million. The film catapulted him into the public gaze (sales of Ray-Ban Wayfarers increased twenty-fold after Cruise wore them in the film), and in the process he won over a whole generation of moviegoers. *Rolling Stone* dubbed it, 'The *Easy Rider* of the MTV generation'. *NME* described it as 'the shape of teen movies to come'. David Denby in *New York* was one of the scant dissenting voices: 'A standard-issue baby-faced actor, Cruise has a slight, undeveloped voice and a nervous smile, which he relies on whenever the script reveals one of its innumerable holes.' That said, it was seen by many as the outstanding adolescent sex comedy of the early eighties, a then flourishing genre characterized by its portrayal of the shameless pursuit of immediate material gratification and sexual experience. *Risky Business* is a wish-fulfilment movie – Joel fulfils his daydreams about doing it with girls and making money – an updated coming-of-age fable set in the highly competitive realm of kids doing their all to get into the 'right' college. Brickman steers clear of the worst excesses of mindless juvenile lechery *à la Porky's* and Cruise's previous *Losin' It*, but like the reprehensible *Pretty Woman* prostitution is here depicted as a glossy occupation, not the sad, rotten business it really is: here 'working women' are vivacious, glamorous women who look like they've just stepped out of *Vogue* or *Playboy*.

Next on the Cruise production line was *All the Right Moves* (prophetic title indeed), a working-class version of *Risky Business* that brought Tom full-circle as Stefan Djordjevic, a high-school athlete and football star struggling for a college scholarship to avoid following his father and brother into the steel mills. Under the stewardship of Michael Chapman, a renowned cinematographer (*Taxi Driver*, *Raging Bull*) who never quite hacked it as a director, (*Moves* was his debut; the second virgin director in a row for Cruise, they hit it off immediately, working on the script together, altering dialogue to suit Tom's interpretation of the character and organizing weekly workshops for the cast) this modest and unpretentious movie comes over as merely another coming-of-age fable, brimful with cliches and crude stereotypes, albeit with a more serious tone than other frivolous teen movies of the period. Here at least our hero, the son of a struggling blue-collar family, is intent on bettering himself. Football is his only avenue of escape out of a dying home town, a place so depressing newlyweds travel to Pittsburgh on honeymoon for a bit of glamour. Chapman, who must have hoped his naive little film might prove itself football's answer to *Flashdance*, chose as his location Johnstown, Pennsylvania, a community in decline that perfectly mirrored the gunmetal drabness of the storyline. Local residents, many out of work, gladly hired themselves out as extras. The abject hopelessness of the town moved Tom deeply – he'd got to know some of the people quite well working out with high-school football squads. Prior to leaving he took out an ad in a local newspaper thanking everyone for their kindness, and saying that the place had struck an emotional chord. Stef's plight was akin to his own at that age, struggling to get ahead in life without the luxury of a head start.

Cruise approached the role with his accustomed zeal, working out viciously on weights to tone up his body, dyeing his hair jet-black to reflect the grim environment and getting stuck into the bruising gridiron sequences, in which he refused the use of a stunt double. He took such a pounding that Chapman, worried his leading man looked 'out of it', sent him to hospital where tests revealed a minor concussion.

Moves' decent showing at the American box office solidified Cruise's now pre-eminent position among Hollywood's young actors. He could pretty much write his own ticket, his fee having shot up to an estimated $1 million. Instead he became virtually invisible throughout 1984 and 1985. Where did he disappear to? One word: *Legend*. Ridley Scott's sumptuously vacuous fantasy kept Cruise in London for what turned out to be a year longer than he would've wanted. His part was Jack O' The Green, a woodland sprite adorned in sylvan shreds, a role he astutely described as 'another colour in a Ridley Scott painting. There was no character.' As a kid Cruise loved the fairy tales his mother used to read to him, and when Scott outlined his story with a passionate enthusiasm Tom desperately wanted to be part of it. Having just done the two extremes of high-school life, *Risky* and *Moves*, which wound up his youth movie period as he himself turned twenty-one, it was time for something different. *Legend* was different all right, turning out to be a physical challenge, a dire toll on his patience (a scene that might last thirty seconds on screen sometimes took a week to shoot) – and a mistake.

In common with Alan Parker, Adrian Lyne and other successful British directors-in-exile who've abandoned their roots, seduced by the all-powerful Hollywood magnet of money, Ridley Scott started out in commercials. With his own company, he established an enviable reputation, churning out around 3,000 ads in ten years, including those legendary sepia-tinted Hovis vignettes. Born in 1939 in South Shields, Northumberland, Scott discovered a 16mm Bolex camera in a cupboard whilst a student at the Royal College of Art, and this led inexorably to movies. An early amateur short made for under £100 and called *Boy on a Bicycle* starred his father and younger brother Tony, who would go on to direct not one, but two Cruise movies.

Given his background in commercials Scott has faced constant accusations that his films habitually overdose on ravishing imagery at the expense of story and structure, that they're all surface. He once misguidedly said, 'The design of a film is the script.' *Alien* and *Blade Runner* were proof conclusive of the director's style-over-content ethic. And *Legend* was no different: dazzling visuals, duff plot. Pictorially, it is one of the most breathtaking films of the eighties, with its gales of thistledown and fairydust, a satan who resides in a Wagnerian underworld lit by the glow of flaming souls, grotesque goblins reciting pantomime verse in camp

American accents, leprechauns chirping in stage Irish and Christmas grotto sets. It is as though Disney raped Tolkien and this is the bastard offspring. However, the script, by American novelist William Hjortsberg, even after fifteen revisions, still failed to emerge with anything faintly resembling a storyline, just some useless whimsy about satan killing the last unicorn and plunging the world into a perpetual wintry void – the eternal struggle between the conflicting powers of good and evil, etc., etc. Essentially this material was too skeletal to counter Scott's astonishing vitality and stylistic flair. *Legend*'s plot is as simple as a bedtime story and has the same effect, putting the kids to sleep. Visually this rococo fable has such an overpoweringly majestic beauty that it swamps everything else in sight – Cruise, in particular, who wanders through leafy sunlit dells and secret glades looking never less than befuddled. It's a one-dimensional role and that's how he plays it. Trusted with little in the way of actual dialogue Cruise expressed Jack by means of physical movement, after studying jazz dance and ballet. He did only the sketchiest research, filling his head with stories of unicorns and magic and explored the child inside himself, exposed as never before after the devastating loss of his father, who died prior to filming.

Filming began in March 1984 – eighteen months later, with industry gossip rife that his film was foundering, Scott was still working on the final cut. After hostile audience previews, Universal scrapped plans to open *Legend* in the summer of 1985; there was even talk of shutting the negative in a vault and pretending it never happened. Thereafter the studio set about reworking the film into a more commercial form, one which would appeal to a mass audience. Jettisoning his film-making principles, Scott witlessly eliminated twenty minutes from the European print, and, pandering to the MTV brat brigade, ditched Jerry Goldsmith's lush symphonic score in favour of an electronic soundtrack by Tangerine Dream (who'd scored *Risky Business*) and out-of-place rock songs. *Legend* belatedly opened in the spring of 1986 as the week's top-grossing film in the USA before plummeting down the charts quicker than a dozen Pavarottis on an ice floe. Nevertheless, it was an early indication that Cruise was a name that would bring opening-weekend audiences into cinemas whatever the dross he was in – even if they did disappear again just as quickly. Critics lavished praise on the film's beauty but found

everything else about it severely wanting, including the miscast
Cruise. 'Mr Cruise goes through all this nonsense gamely, as if it
were an initiation into a fraternity he wants very much to join' –
New York Times; 'Tom Cruise, the nominal hero, has only one
expression which is generally hidden by his hair' – *The Times*;
'One of the most thoroughly realised and visually seductive fairy
tales this side of Cocteau's *Beauty and the Beast*' – *Starburst*.

   Legend might be seen as one of those misjudgements actors
make from time to time, but Cruise never regretted doing it: 'You
look at some of those scenes in that movie and they just take your
breath away.' He treasured the memory of seeing the eyes of a
four-year-old visitor to the set fill with tears at the sight of a
unicorn and his own sense of awe working amidst such colossal
sets. 'It was like walking on a real old-time movie set, when they
built entire cities on studio lots.' It was a supreme test of his
endurance though (Scott's perfectionism meant insufferably long
gaps between camera set-ups), one of the most difficult periods of
his career. It taught him the value of being able to relax and be
patient – even the worst disasters Cruise is able to turn into
learning experiences. Marooned in London, cut off from his family
and new love Rebecca, who flew over several times to be near him,
Cruise would often take long lonely walks in Hyde Park.
However, he must have liked Pinewood enough to return not once
but twice, making *Interview with the Vampire* and *Mission:
Impossible* there back to back.

   Numerous technical problems compounded his misery, such as
having to deal with complex special effects for the first time, or
acting to a piece of black tape that was supposed to be some
monstrous hobgoblin. And yet he was never less than
co-operative, his enthusiasm and commitment never waned – even
when he injured his back or when, with just a few days of filming
left, the forest set burned to the ground. Manager Paula Wagner
and her husband were in England on their honeymoon and had
dropped in to say hi and have lunch with Tom at the studio. It was
the first time she'd visited her client on a movie set. While they
were eating a crew hand burst in: the stage is ablaze, he tells them;
everything is destroyed; months of work have gone up the spout.
Tom turns to Paula. 'I hope you'll understand,' he says, 'when I
ask that you never visit a set of mine again.' It was meant as a joke,
an immediate reaction to one of the most serious situations he'd
ever faced in his career. The source of the fire was uncertain, but

the miracle was that it happened when almost everybody was at lunch. The whole place went up like an incendiary bomb, and a hundred firemen fought intense heat and exploding gas canisters. The enchanted forest set, housed within the famously monolithic 007 stage, was utterly destroyed, and damages ran into the millions. Scott was heard to mutter 'shit' as he ran to his office to set about rejuggling the schedule.

What in God's name does he do now? It inevitably meant more delays. Does he wallow in self-pity, bang his head against a wall in frustration, or say, 'OK, that happened, now what do we do? Let's go ahead.' He'd placed a frantic call to Scott about the fire. 'Oh well,' the director coolly replied. 'I'm just going to play some tennis. Would you like to get some dinner later? How does that sound?' If he wasn't upset, Cruise figured, why the hell should I be? As with every problem, Cruise hurdled it brimming with determination and resolve: he'd learned how to cope the hard way. 'I always had that ability to just deal with things. My whole life has been like that: "Okay, what do I do now?" '

The answer was awaiting him on his return to the States.

5 Tom Cruise and the Work Ethic

'My mother taught us that if you work hard you get paid for it. And you do it better than anybody else has done.'

— Tom Cruise

The Cruiser's dedication to the work ethic, his expenditure of what Americans call sweat-equity, is legendary; a self-described 'shooter', for whom making movies ranks just below breathing, his passion and commitment to his craft borders on obsession. Its source? A character-building childhood of struggling and fighting against the odds. Anything but hard-working as a kid – he spent most of the time daydreaming – the young actor learned how to channel his imagination and energy into intense discipline. His workaholism was an inheritance from a mother who slogged her guts out to keep her young family afloat. 'I grew up as a very competitive individual, and when you're at a constant disadvantage, you learn to do whatever it takes to succeed in life. There's no substitute for hard work.' Known for his discipline, methodical determination and high expectations of others, Cruise is 100 per cent committed when he sets his mind on something. Talking once to racing pal Rick Hendrick about the dedication of drivers, Cruise asked, 'What is it about these guys?' Hendrick said, 'It's like bacon and eggs. The chicken may be involved, but the pig's committed.'

Directors fall over each other to work with him because of this reputation as an artist obsessed with doing the best job he can. Ask any director who's worked with Cruise and beyond the PR-friendly 'great to work with' stuff there seems to be a genuine affection for the man. 'Talking about working with Tom Cruise is boring,' Sydney Pollack told *Time Out* in September 1993.

It'd be much more interesting to say that Tom Cruise is really unpredictable but to say that he comes to work every morning with a smile on his face, full of energy, that he is well-prepared and can't wait to get started, that he takes direction, waits to be directed, that he will work until he drops – that's boring but that's the truth.

And this from Rob Reiner: 'You can't find a harder worker. He runs to the set. He's there five minutes early. If I could do every single picture with Cruise I would do it.' On the set of *Far and Away* Cruise famously sprinted to the toilet between takes, much to everyone's amusement. Perhaps those crew members who scoffed behind his back, in disbelief that someone could take their work so seriously, preferred those temperamental stars who turn up either late or not at all, fluffing their lines or drunk. Take your choice. Crews are usually responsive to the kind of rigorous working atmosphere on a Cruise movie. The work of the set hands and technicians doubles as soon as he arrives. He's the ultimate professional. Making *Interview with the Vampire* Cruise was never once late. He'd walk on to the set in make-up and say, 'Let's go.' Wasting time is anathema to him. 'It's respectful to the director and everybody else on the set to show up on time and do the best job you possibly can.' And on *Mission: Impossible* co-workers were invited to movie premières or to his London home for dinner. 'If he likes your energy and it gels with his, no question he's thrilled with you,' remarked one of the film's co-stars, Henry Czerny. 'Which is wise. Why surround yourself with people who make you feel like shit?'

He takes responsibility for all aspects of his career, from choosing his movies to signing his own cheques. Cruise has surrounded himself with the cream of Hollywood talent, people who are the best at what they do, and an army of advisers who cosset his every move. That doesn't mean platoons of yes-men who say, 'Oh, Tom, you're wonderful, you're doing great' when really he's falling on his backside. People like that just leave him cold. 'That's no good. I want people who are like me, who, when they get involved in something, get consumed by it' – figures like super-agent Mike Ovitz (who's probably helped guide Tom's career more than any other player in Hollywood) and billionaire mogul David Geffen (whose counsel Tom acknowledges because it is blunt and direct). When he struck big, Cruise might easily have just handed his professional life over to others and let them run with it; instead, he's chosen to be self-sufficient in the truest sense. He thinks it's dangerous to be otherwise. The man is one of the savviest money-manager stars in Hollywood. At an early age he was making decisions about millions of dollars, and where other actors don't want to know about the business side of the industry, leaving others to worry about their finances, Cruise gets stuck in. Showbusiness is a business first; the talent is almost secondary. 'It doesn't happen by accident that someone at such a young age becomes such a world-renowned movie star,' Sherry Lansing, one of Hollywood's top executives, told *Vanity Fair* in October 1994. 'Tom not only knows about all aspects of this business, he, more importantly, wants that knowledge.' Cruise learned to play the Hollywood game early, a far cry from when he first came to New York oblivious of agents, scripts and 'the business'. Cruise gets involved at the very early stages of all his films. He's never relied on readers to go over the hundreds of scripts which have come his way, he did it all himself. If this is still the case, one wonders how he spares the time, for practically every major script in Hollywood winds up on his desk first.

The energy that drives Cruise to push himself is prodigious. It is a seemingly endless fight against cold feet, waged on racing tracks, in the air and on movie locations. The game plan is to keep on taking chances; accepting challenges is the only way to learn and get better. Actors who stop taking risks and gambling with new roles, he believes, grow stale. It's easy to believe the story that he got the part in *Taps* by ramrodding his personality down the director's throat. Not everything has gone smoothly, yet there have been remarkably few mistakes in such a high-profile career. He's not in this business for the money alone or the soft option, since, if he were, he could have made *Top Gun 2, Son of Top Gun, Top Gun with a Vengeance* and retired for life. That's a testament to his total lack of greed – and to be applauded. Cruise has never made a movie purely for the money, a case in point being *Born on the Fourth of July* when he deferred his then customary $5 million fee in favour of a cut of the profits. It was a gamble, but where there's a Cruise, there's a profit. 'The competition is with myself,' he once said. 'I want to be able to say I've pushed it as far as I could.' The intent was there early in his career but Cruise never really pushed it until he played Ron Kovic. *Rain Man* was a gamble – the film, that is; the role Cruise played was, well, Tom

Cruise. It would have been more of a lottery had he played the autistic savant. But certainly in recent years he's shown a determination to play more challenging roles, even if his big-earning status suffers. 'I've lived with nothing my whole life. If the big offers vanish, they can't erase what I've learned and what I've done.'

Underneath the real domestic contentment he's found with second wife Nicole Kidman and his two children, Cruise is still as focused, driven and ambitious as ever. He's always been happiest when he's working. Pride in his work is something that characterizes Cruise, one of the healthy side-effects of his induction into Scientology? He is dedicated, relentlessly enthusiastic and indefatigably positive. A man who gives perfectionism a good name.

6   I Feel the Need, the Need for Speed

'It's strange that he's into speeding so much because he was
always the safest of drivers and never had a lead foot.'
                    — Nancy Armel, high school sweetheart

The evening before every race meeting Tom Cruise drives the
circuit in his mind's eye so that when he gets out there his natural
instincts take over. He wants to feel the rear wheels with his back,
the front tyres in his fingertips, and sense the speed of the car
without even looking at the speedometer.

Before the race proper the cars drive a warm-up lap to hot up
their tyres. The capacity crowd roars in anticipation, and the
countdown starts. Gas fumes are spreading, oil is burning, the
pounding of Cruise's heart is drowned out only by the furious
clamour of the engines, and the noise is deafening, as the pressure,
intense beautiful pressure, builds. It's like going into battle. But
he's got to be relaxed, stay calm, know the limitations of his
vehicle. The last thing you want is your emotions to run riot, to
lose control. He's thinking, always thinking: just enjoy yourself
out there. And then suddenly the flag hits the dirt. Knocking the
leather gear stick forward, blipping the throttle, he's off, hitting
the first bend with the force of a cannonball, his gaze like that of a
man possessed, firmly fixed on the track ahead. His frame
strapped tightly against the seat, only his arms and legs move,
turning the small steering wheel and stamping at the pedals.

The first two corners are the most important. You've got to
watch you don't get hit or that some driver doesn't break in front
of you, while at the same time trying to manoeuvre yourself on the
inside. Too many other drivers are gunning for that first corner,

trying to win the race in the first lap, no matter how many seasons of experience they've notched up. Cruise learned that what makes a good racer isn't a devil-may-care attitude but judgement, timing. At 150 m.p.h. a cool head outstrips machismo. It's all about nerves of steel and grace under pressure. The beauty is that mental discipline, the will to hold back at the right time, only makes racing more exhilarating. Exercising the lead foot could be great, but crossing that finishing line – perhaps in first place – that could be amazing. 'Everyone wants to win – it doesn't feel good losing.'

Sometimes on those crucial corners it's as if the car is easing down, almost crawling. Everything seems to be in slow motion, and in the mirror the other machines are catching up, bearing down on him. Then freedom. Out of the corner and Cruise punishes the accelerator, the G-forces make his head feel like it weighs a ton; as he roars down the straight, every time he blinks another 100 yards flashes by. Speed is all-important coming out of the corners. But the real excitement lies in the combative nature of the sport, being bumper to bumper, 'trading paint' with a challenger, like knights jousting in their Chevrolet steeds. It's not just about putting your foot to the ground or who has the fastest car, it's a chess game on four wheels everybody wants to win – losing's a downer – with the added attraction of flirting with your own mortality; mistakes or just plain bad luck can land you a stint in hospital or the morgue. Cruise is philosophical about the dangers involved, but he's confident he won't be in a race car when he goes. The dangers are probably over-rated. When he's motoring Cruise doesn't think about the death sentence that could be waiting for him around the next corner; he doesn't worry about hitting a wall or another car, it's them hitting him.

The race is seemingly over before it's begun. Drenched in sweat, the Cruise climbs out of his vehicle and is greeted by the crew chief. Together they go over the whole race and later, alone, Cruise will return to it, because every race presents new lessons, new opportunities to get better, and each race Tom Cruise has got better. 'It's a different world at that speed. When you're squeezing on that throttle and the car's just riding perfect – when that happens, you just feel like you can't do without that race car.'

Tom Cruise dreamed about racing long before he ever thought of acting. Go-carting was an early love, a hobby pursued with fervent passion until he developed a craving for the real thing – motorbikes and cars. The love affair began when he first sat behind a wheel at the age of three. His mother had left Tom and his sister alone in the car while she grabbed some groceries. Returning from the store Mary Lee was horrified to see her youngest clutching the steering wheel and backing the car down the street. Dropping everything she raced after them, yanked open the door, shoved Tom out of the driving seat and slammed on the brakes. Years later, and the young Cruise still hadn't learnt his lesson. As a teenager in Kentucky, well shy of the legal driving age, he'd coax his sisters to help him push the family saloon out of the drive at 4 a.m. so he might start it up out of range and use it for his paper round. His mother was totally oblivious of this until informed by a neighbour. And once he and a friend were stopped by police for driving the wrong way up a one-way street. Tom was still too young to drive, but, even worse, was at the time training to be a priest! Tom would liberally 'borrow' his mother's car as a teenager so he and a friend could go out cruising for girls in the early hours. A quaint American custom.

What feeds this craving for speed, this urge to race? Is it akin to his four-wheel mentor, Paul Newman, who no matter what his celebrity and acclaim has never experienced a thrill to compare with victory on the race track? 'I like to win,' Newman has said. 'I despise that in myself, but it's all there is.' Is it the intense competition, driver against driver? Or the solitude, a man alone with his thoughts and a steering wheel, the world and its problems flashing by, blurred, irrelevant? 'It's calming, you know? I'm in a world of my own. I just feel really relaxed.' Frankly, the thought of doing 100 m.p.h. round a track in a tin can doesn't automatically bring 'relaxing' to my mind.

Speed had always fascinated Cruise, not so much for the actual driving as the need to go fast, to rev it up, to be one with the engine, revelling in holding dominion over a piece of machinery bombing down a track at suicidal speeds. Trying to ingratiate himself with new friends he once boasted of his motorcycling proficiency, when in fact he'd never ridden one before in his life. Then a classmate called his bluff. He had one at home and challenged Cruise to come over after school to show him what he could do. Before hopping on the saddle Cruise looked the machine up and down desperately trying to figure out how the damn thing worked. Once on, this hell-for-leather urge, merging with an incessant impulse to prove himself, prevailed over caution. Turning the hand grip thinking it to be the brake, Cruise crashed the bike through a hedge, launching himself – wham! – against the side of a house. 'I nearly killed myself trying to be one of the guys.' Another time, years later, he and Sean Penn were out racing in the desert, jumping their bikes. 'Tommy hit the dust about fifteen times,' Penn recalled to *Premiere* in July 1988. 'It would have made a great montage. Tom knows how to go up, but when he comes down, you're talking about two separate falling items.'

Even after he became an actor this yen for speed never abated; indeed it took on new and elephantine proportions, from mum's car and motorbikes (Cruise owns a Harley Davidson, of course, and a Porsche) to hitching a ride in an F-14 jet fighter. And it also began to permeate into his work. That scene in *Top Gun* where Cruise guns the bike to drown out Kelly McGillis – his idea.

> 'Landing on an aircraft carrier at night – sex in a car wreck'
> —Top Gun pilot

In May 1983 *California* magazine published an article about the US Navy's elite combat-training school, Top Gun. Producer Jerry Bruckheimer happened to be flipping through a copy when a full-page photo of an F-14 streaking across an electric blue sky stopped him in mid-flip. If ever there was a subject for a mainstream movie this was it: these pilots were rock 'n' roll stars of the skies and it was all happening a scant two hours' drive from his Hollywood office. He consulted with partner Don Simpson, with whom he'd got formula movies down to a science (*Flashdance, Beverly Hills Cop*). It goes like this: take a star, mix liberally with fast planes, cars, motorbikes – anything really that'll puncture an audience's eardrum – add sexy subservient women, throw in some fights, a few gags, a jukebox soundtrack and, hey presto, you've got a critic-proof blockbuster. Bruckheimer sold the idea to Paramount then set about securing co-operation from the US Navy, vital if the project was to achieve any kind of authenticity. But he was fully aware that the Department of Defense didn't loan out their war toys to just anyone, and that prospective projects were carefully vetted by the public-relations arm of the Pentagon. Any movie purporting to show the military in an unfavourable or distorted light was given the shove. Flying into Washington for a meeting with Naval top brass, the producers launched into an impassioned hustle. Immediately recognizing the propaganda potential of the concept, the Navy proved 100 per cent receptive, offering near *carte blanche* access to facilities, aircraft and personnel. The catch was that Paramount had to agree to pay for costs, which didn't come cheap – the studio was charged $7,600 an hour for jet fuel, and the final bill came to $1.2 million, a tenth of the entire budget. Moreover, the Navy demanded script approval. Ultimately the Pentagon asked for relatively few fundamental changes and the biggest disputes arose over four-letter words. For an industry in the business of death, it seems hypocritical to be coy about profanity.

When it came to casting hotshot flier Pete 'Maverick' Mitchell, the youthful Reaganite role model, Simpson and Bruckheimer insisted there was only ever one candidate. 'From the first time we went down to Miramar,' said Bruckheimer, 'even before the script was written, we said, "These guys are Tom Cruise" ' (or should that read Sean Penn, the producer's hot pre-Cruise favourite for the role?). The producers had admired Cruise ever since first catching sight of him in *Taps*. 'We liked his work,' said Simpson, 'his look, his intensity.' A script was duly sent to London where Cruise had plenty of spare time to study it in between set-ups on *Legend*. On offer was, it seemed, the perfect antidote to the laborious, special-effects-laden production presently gnawing at his sanity. It was fast and immediate but, in his view, in need of drastic reworking. A meeting with the producers served as a confidence booster. 'They seemed like they had that fighter-pilot spirit – the Top Gun, the best of the best.' But Cruise brought with him an ultimatum. Either he be allowed to share in the development of the project or no deal – remarkable nerve for an actor who then had about as much pulling power in Tinsel Town as Rin Tin Tin. Simpson and Bruckheimer were certainly taken aback. Actors to them were hired hands, not creative partners, but Cruise, still smarting from his close encounter of the Ridley kind, merely wished for everything to be AOK before a frame of celluloid was shot. Never again did he want to squander a year making a picture.

As a shape of things to come, Cruise got his way: the birth of Cruise control. For a 23-year-old he was wielding Thor-like power, even down to the approval of his co-stars. Cruise already had a reputation for doctoring scripts; after all he's the one who'll look a fool spouting turnip dialogue. That said, there have been enough ripe lines in his movies to beg the question of whether he should have tampered more. Not being a glutton for punishment, naturally he'd prefer it if scripts were set before shooting, but then dollar bills don't grow on trees. *Top Gun* is significant in that it heralded the start of Cruise's passion for involving himself in all aspects of the post-production process, perhaps more actively than any other actor in Hollywood. Tony Scott equated Tom with a terrier: 'He locks on and hangs on.' Cruise attends dailies (rough footage of the previous day's filming), for example, despite his aversion to watching himself on screen, and checks over the rough cut. However, there's only so much Tom can influence or monitor. Perhaps that's why he wants to be a director, to wield ultimate control. Two months were set aside for the *Top Gun* rewrites and far from alienating his paymasters the Cruise perfectionism brought forth a fountain of praise. 'He was terrific,' Simpson told *Rolling Stone* in June 1986. 'Tom would show up at my house, grab a beer, and we'd work five or six hours on the script. Sometimes we'd act scenes out. The guy doesn't see things from just a couple of perspectives – he can really wrap his arms around something and see it from all angles. We had a lot of fun.'

The role of Pete 'Maverick' Mitchell, one of an elite core of nationalistic fighter pilots, all gleaming white teeth and bulging biceps, was the perfect showcase for Cruise's sizewell energy and tanned good looks. Curious though why the filmmakers seemed obsessed with obscuring his face, flying helmet in the air, sunglasses on *terra firma*. It's tough relating to a character clamped anonymously into his cockpit – indicative of how impersonal this film is. *Top Gun* was another rites-of-passage morality tale and the script reworks the scenario of the young hero's troubled passage into manhood from *An Officer and a Gentleman*. In the dreary tradition of these movies the death of our hero's best buddy improves his character, and he becomes a team player, proving he has the right stuff in battle. Like so many Cruise vehicles *Top Gun* is about the pursuit of excellence, undertaken with nobility of purpose. Maverick became the archetypal Cruise role. It defined his screen persona for the remainder of the decade – the cocky, wildcard flyboy of instinctive genius. He's arrogance personified, the embodiment of competitive zeal, but dangerously unorthodox and vulnerable beneath the bravado. Mourning his father, a top-flight navy pilot who died under suspicious circumstances in Vietnam, he flies by the seat of his pants in a deep need to prove himself. It is fun to speculate, considering his deep involvement in the rewrites, how much Cruise initiated this subtext for Maverick's reckless antics. A guy haunted by the spectre of a lost father sounds pretty close to home, after all.

Problems developed, however, when they cast Kelly McGillis as an impossibly glamorous astrophysics instructor. Inevitably rumours abounded about an off-screen romance. In fact the pair scarcely socialized at all, a deliberate ploy on Cruise's part in order to build up some sexual tension for the obligatory love scene. Both actually had great trouble 'relating', and at times things got so frosty between them that fears were raised about how it might affect their screen partnership. McGillis has apparently refused to answer questions about her Cruise encounter, turning off the tape recorder and rolling her eyes whenever such a question comes up. Her height also bred arguments that dragged on for weeks. There were daily discussions about whether to go with high heels or not. 'I have no problem if you wear high heels,' Tom told her. 'What's the big deal?' But Paramount were dead against the idea: it was blasphemy for the female to be taller than the male star, and they sent her a sticker of high heels with a red line through them, like those No Smoking signs. McGillis ended the picture suffering from terrible posture because of trying not to look taller than Cruise.

For this movie, image was everything (flight suits and helmets were designed to maximize visual appeal), the 'look' would be key to its success and appeal. Everything is really secondary to the film's pivotal purpose of worshipping the Cruiser's good looks against a gleaming backdrop of America's defence hardware. A poster of Cruise in his flyboy gear with McGillis fawning over his shoulder was the biggest seller in the United States that year. The flyer look went on sale in stores and sales of Ray-Bans increased by 40 per cent. (After *Risky Business* you'd have thought Cruise would have bought shares in the company.) Having discounted first choice David Cronenberg (that equates with Merchant and Ivory taking on *Full Metal Jacket*), Simpson and Bruckheimer took a white-water rafting trip in Colorado with other industry bigshots, among them Tony Scott, Ridley's directing brother, then in-between assignments (Hollywood-speak for unemployed). Like his more famous sibling, Tony had a fine arts background, was a graduate of the Royal College of Art and a director of commercials famous for their explosive visual style, notably one for SAAB motors that featured jet aircraft and cars in stunt harmony. That ad clinched the *Top Gun* deal for Scott, and around the camp fire producers and director chatted excitedly about the project. 'It was a marvellous idea,' cooed Scott, counting the noughts on his pay cheque. 'I read the first 3½ pages and I loved it.' Scott's visual flair proved perfectly suited to the shameless superficiality of *Top Gun*. With its admittedly breathtaking aerial sequences – the best ever captured on camera – join-the-dots plot and simplistic cartoon-strip characterizations, *Top Gun* embodied all that was both loved and loathed about eighties moviemaking. Scott and Cruise had already met in London during the *Legend* shoot and the director thought the young actor fitted the role of Maverick like a glove. 'I felt he had just the right arrogance in the best sense of the word.'

There's a large sign on the side of one of the hangars: 'Fightertown U.S.A.' Rather more menacing is a sticker on the back of a car in the parking lot: 'I'd rather be fighting commies in Central America.' Cruise attacked the Maverick role with even more of his customary vigour, sensing perhaps that this was the film that would send him into orbit. He commuted between Los Angeles and the Miramar Naval Air base for three months in advance of shooting, attending declassified Top Gun briefings and generally soaking up the heady atmosphere with the pilots. What he discovered was a breed of men who risk their lives just for the passion of flying, and he could relate to their love of speed. So immersed did he become in the gung-ho lifestyle the flyboys lead at Miramar – getting up at four o'clock every morning to exercise – that by the time filming began it was difficult to set him apart from the real thing (Cruise and the F-14 jets seemed made in heaven for each other). 'If you saw him around the base, you'd assume that he was a pilot,' said Simpson. 'They're cocky, brave, and full of strong character, and Tom embodies all those elements.' The Cruiser's first meeting with Top Gun pilots, a gang in their late twenties with the unlikely handles of Jaws, Flex and Jambo, was genial, if a little strained. 'Initially, we were very sceptical,' Jaws told *American Film* in June 1986. 'The first time any of us saw him, he showed up with a ponytail and we thought: Oh, no. But he's very responsive and a really professional actor. We went out drinking. He wanted to know about flying, and we wanted to know about parties and all the Hollywood stuff. I think at this moment he'd do anything to do what we do.' Cruise was in awe of these men, admiring their competitiveness and courage, their drive to be the best of the best. One of the pilots gave him his gold wings to wear in the film. Cruise undertook an intensive two-day training course – psychological tests, withstanding G-forces – to qualify for a backseat ride in an F-14. It was the ultimate speed trip, the ultimate high. 'It's one of those experiences that is bigger than life itself,' he described to *Interview* in May 1986. 'It blows your shit away. Flying is so intense and emotional.' On landing he couldn't wipe the grin off his face.

So when Cruise voiced a determination to become a pilot himself, an ambition treasured since childhood, the only surprise was that it had taken so long. *The Firm*'s director Sydney Pollack, an accomplished pilot, lent the enthusiastic Cruise books on the subject that prompted him to take lessons. With the encouragement of another friend, actor Kurt Russell, Cruise took to the skies soon after wrapping *Interview with the Vampire*. He decided to train in a Pitt Special S-2B, an aerobatic plane considered the most difficult to fly – 'Which is why I chose it, because I want to be a good pilot.' He named the plane Sweet Nic, after guess who, for good luck. Cruise loves to fly, even taking up journalists close to heaven as he had earlier given them white-knuckle rides in his sports car. 'I found it very freeing, like acting in many ways.' It's an escape route from the pressures of film-making. As proof, if any were needed, of how hot Cruise is, at a Los Angeles AIDS benefit auction in late 1994 a half-hour ride with the actor in his two-seater plane went for $25,000. Rob Reiner, on hearing Cruise was whizzing about like a real-life *Top Gun*, explained to *Vanity Fair* in October 1994. 'Tom likes to jump out of planes. He likes to race cars. He likes to ride motorcycles. He likes to climb rocks. He likes white-water rafting. And now he likes this aerobatic stuff. Let's just say there's not a drop of Jewish blood in him.'

Top Gun, akin to *The Outsiders*, though on a lesser scale, had a supporting cast of actors 'on the up'. There's Val Kilmer, for example, who, as the Cruiser's rival vying for the *Top Gun* crown, spends the entire film smiling daggers at Maverick. On reaching stardom Kilmer was dismissive, almost apologetic, about his involvement. 'I didn't want to do it, but it was a contract Paramount invoked. It was a horrible celebration of redneckness.' The three days' work put in by Meg Ryan, as the breezy, sexy wife of Maverick's co-pilot Goose, started to get her noticed in Hollywood; and, if you look closely, you can just make out a young Tim Robbins.

Filming began in late June 1985, mostly in Miramar for the scenes involving an impressive line-up of F-14 Tomcats (worth a

cool $46 million each), F-5 Tigers and A-4 Skyhawks. These
fighters were the real stars of *Top Gun*; they out-act the cast in just
the same way as the cars do in *Days of Thunder*, *Top Gun*'s
bastard twin. By mid July shooting relocated aboard the aircraft
carrier USS *Enterprise*, stationed 110 choppy miles off the San
Diego coast. Ferried in by helicopter the cast and crew were
assigned to junior officer quarters. On board, the ear-shattering
racket of planes taking off and the heartbeat thud-thud of engines
defied anyone to get a decent night's sleep. Most, however,
declined dreaming in favour of standing up on deck and watching
in awe as 50,000-pound jets doing 180 m.p.h. slammed every ten
seconds on to a parking grid the size of a football field. Cruise had
brought along his own camera to record the events of his four-day
stay, including the moment he found himself being taught how to
taxi on-coming jets on to the flight line. The thundering jet noise
frequently delayed filming. 'That noise could really scramble your
brains,' Scott related to *American Cinematographer* in May 1986.
'It was sometimes hard for an actor to remember his lines with the
roar of an F-14's after-burners behind him.' What with the thunder
of those engines and the continuous bombardment of a pounding
MTV soundtrack, *Top Gun* ranks as one of the loudest films in
history. Along with *Star Wars* this is a movie Dolby Stereo was
invented for: soft in the head but hard on the ears.

In one of the most hair-raising scenes, Maverick's jet goes into a
spin over the ocean and he is forced to eject. Cruise and Anthony
Edwards spent hours on end in the freezing Pacific Ocean waiting
to be saved by air-sea rescue helicopters. In the end it was two
Navy frogmen who came to Cruise's aid when he became tangled
up in his parachute and was being buffeted by waves and
repeatedly dragged under the water. The diver's lightning reaction
probably saved the actor from drowning; hauling him into a
lifeboat, one of them performed life-saving mouth-to-mouth
resuscitation. After an hour recuperating, Cruise was back in front
of the cameras.

At cinemas around the United States *Top Gun*'s bellicose
climax drew explosive cheers from teenage audiences too young to
know anything about Vietnam, but stirred by its Ramboesque
triumph over Communist forces. Even theatre owners themselves
were so intoxicated by the film's patriotic fervour that they
volunteered their lobbies as makeshift recruiting stations for the
Navy. Not very subtle. All this inevitably led to allegations that the

movie-makers were peddling jingoism and cashing in on the new patriotism that had audiences (mostly male) chanting 'U.S.A.' during the massacre scenes in *Rambo*. Cruise may have turned on the girls but it was the machines, not McGillis, that excited the boys. The film invokes flying and combat as sexual substitutes – war is the ultimate orgasm. The sexy glamorizing of death and destruction may have been offensive, but it worked. Enough people plugged in to make *Top Gun* the highest-grossing film of 1986 ($177 million in America alone; add to that 2.8 million domestic video cassettes sold, a record at the time). Simpson and Bruckheimer reacted angrily to accusations that *Top Gun* represented a return to America's hawkish values after the shame of Vietnam, that it upheld the jingoistic attitude of the Reagan administration. 'It has nothing to do with jingoism,' they countered, 'nothing to do with war,' – momentarily forgetting perhaps that *Top Gun* concerned fighter pilots who flew machines designed and equipped to kill people. Critics thought otherwise. Alexander Walker in the *Evening Standard* called it, 'a dangerous film. Irresponsible and conscienceless;' Kim Newman commented in *City Limits*: '*Top Gun* is the most politically and morally objectionable film I've seen since *The Triumph of the Will*. I'd rather see *My Little Pony* again than *Top Gun*, which is probably the most damning statement I'll make about a film this decade.'

And *Premiere*: 'As for Tom Cruise, well, the truth is that he could be charming in a movie about the Hitler youth. Which, when you come right down to it, this practically is.'

The militaristic pro-war nature of the story had worried Cruise from the off, and he knew full well the dangers of a backlash. But when controversy struck he was as vehement as his producers in defending his decision to make *Top Gun*. Hollow words? Not so, for Cruise courageously risked being dropped from the lead role in a movie he knew was a dead cert launchpad to stardom. Standing firmly by his principles, he had refused to commit to the project unless the more jingoistic, gung-ho elements of the script were watered down. He wanted a more human story, with the emphasis placed on the camaraderie and rivalry among pilots, rather than the mayhem and death they reap. A compromise must have been reached for the climax, where anonymous enemy pilots are clinically blown out of the sky like so many electronic blips on a Nintendo game screen – a triumph of American male over Russian machine. Cruise found that what drove men like Maverick to want to risk their lives was the flying, the need for speed. 'You're not a fighter pilot just because you want combat,' he said. 'It's the flying, the F-14.' Cruise refused to define them as warmongers, flying Rambos, and for the most part they're not. On the other hand these pilots are as if on a football team that's always practising but never gets to play. That breeds frustration, because eventually you're going to want to test yourself. Itchy fingers. What had excited Cruise first and foremost were the planes; essentially he saw the movie purely as a fantasy – '*Star Wars* with real aircraft.' War as a rock video? But isn't it far more dangerous, in this context, to blur the borders between fantasy and reality?

What Cruise couldn't excuse, and had no say in or control over, was the Navy's blatant hijacking of the film, the setting-up of recruiting stands outside theatres where it was shown. Thanks to *Top Gun* the military achieved its goal of increased personnel. During the film's release recruitment queries hit an all-time high – not surprising really as the whole thing's shot like a military training promo. 'When *Top Gun* came out we discovered that many of our new recruits had either heard of or seen the film,' William Hart, a public affairs official for the military told *Premiere* in September 1989. 'They did not necessarily want to become *Top Gun* pilots, but the film showed that the military was a good career and life.' Inadvertently or not Cruise and Co had beaten the war drum, and young men were signing up in droves to live out Tom Cruise's film fantasy. Let's face it, the thrill of flying is infectiously conveyed; these all-American heroes and their way of life must have been irresistible to teenage audiences, just as old John Wayne movies were to kids in the fifties, kids like Ron Kovic, the Vietnam vet Cruise played in *Born on the Fourth of July*. Even the pilots back at Miramar were under no illusion about what the film was trying to say. 'The intent of the movie is maybe a little bit to take advantage of the newfound patriotism and that's great,' one of them told *American Film* in June 1986. 'It's good for the Navy. We can't complain about the glamorizing.' One actress, Linda Fiorentino, even took herself out of the running for the McGillis role because of the pro-combat theme of the film, despite being personally courted by Cruise, whom she described as 'the sweetest guy in the world'. Strolling through Central Park with Cruise, Fiorentino voiced her objections. 'This is a bad movie for kids, and that's the target audience and I don't think it's right. Airplanes are one thing, but they have this scene where there's a war!' A puzzled and perplexed Cruise replied, 'Linda, it's just a movie.'

Oliver Stone, who released *Platoon* that same year, was the most vehemently outspoken public voice. 'You see a film like *Top Gun* if you're a kid, you join the Navy. It looks great,' he ranted in *New York* magazine in December 1986. 'I join the Navy, I get to wear that spiffy uniform, I get to ride at the speed of light, I get the machine under my legs so I get that sexual energy, plus I get Kelly McGillis if I blow up the MIG! Nobody mentions the fact that he possibly started World War III by doing that! So the message of the movie is "I get a girlfriend if I start World War III"' Apparently David Puttnam's *Memphis Belle*, about the crew of an American WWII bomber stationed in England, was written in reaction to the rabid pro-war posturing of *Top Gun*. Would that Puttnam's decent liberalism could guarantee the same mass audience.

Just another wholesome-looking teenager at the time of *Risky Business*, Cruise saw the phenomenal success of *Top Gun* turn him, practically overnight, into a multi-million-dollar property. The name Cruise now meant box-office appeal. He was 'hot' – *People* magazine labelled him the 'media morsel of the moment'. In Pete Maverick Cruise was already beginning to outgrow his teen-idol roles. With the death of his father the innocent, shy Cruise of *Risky Business* was left behind by the exciting young leading male of *Top Gun*, *The Color of Money* and *Rain Man*. Despite this, he continued to play in coming-of-age stories, usually as a young man in search of success who's taken in hand by a father figure.

'This isn't filmmaking. It's war'

—Tom Cruise

Midway through *The Color of Money* Cruise asked a favour of Newman. 'If we're still friends at the end of this, maybe you could get me into racing.' Paul Newman's astonishing second career as a championship racing driver, taken up at an age when most drivers are contemplating retirement, began after starring in the 1968 movie *Winning*. A frequent visitor to Newman's home in Connecticut and keen attendant of some of his races (Cruise was among the spectators at a Californian circuit who watched in horror as Newman's Nissan thudded into a wall at 100 m.p.h., the actor emerging without a scratch), Cruise was taken by the veteran

for a spin in a Porsche round his local race-track. After a few
red-hot laps Newman asked his guest if he wanted to take the
wheel. 'You bet!' Dumb question, right. 'OK,' Newman said,
shifting to the passenger side. 'Just don't show me how brave you
are, kid.' 'Aw,' replied Cruise. 'Stop givin' me shit.' Cruise
discovered he was a natural, taking at once to that adrenalin rush,
the thrill of crossing the finishing line first. 'I think one of the great
things in life is the feeling of accomplishment, choosing a goal and
achieving it,' Cruise said. 'I get that sensation with racing. I love
the intensity of it and the demands, physically and emotionally.'
He was hooked. The sport became an addiction more powerful
than any drug, as evidenced by his dashing the day after *Rain Man*
wrapped to attend a race meeting in Pennsylvania, during which
he lost control and spun into a wall, luckily escaping serious injury.
Headlines such as 'Tom Cruise wrecks sports car' really irritated
him. They were written by people who knew nothing about racing,
who couldn't appreciate that he was having to master a new skill in
the glare of media attention.

Cruise trained with Newman's Nissan team-mate Jim Fitzgerald,
and so intent was he to master the sport attended the Bob
Bondurant School of High Performance Driving, located north of
San Francisco, along with *Top Gun* co-producer Don Simpson,
whose fee of $25,000 Cruise paid. The evening before the final
exam, after one of the most gruelling days on the course, Cruise
took Simpson out for a meal but brought along his books and
made the producer grill him for an hour. It was Simpson, though
who came first in the class (the producer appears briefly in *Days of
Thunder* as a hot shot driver), Cruise an honourable third. Often
Cruise drove like a man possessed, in the process smashing up
three cars, one of which he split right down the middle. Each time
he'd just pull out his chequebook and write off the wreckage; by
the time he left the course he'd chalked up a bill approaching
$100,000. Newman admired Cruise's courage as an actor but was
startled at the risks he took on the track. 'His head,' the veteran
observed, 'has got to catch up to his balls.' Simpson has seen in
close-up the star's obsession with speed on a number of
goose-pimple-inducing occasions. 'I have been in a car with Tom
in Rome, in San Francisco, in Los Angeles, and each time he was
in the driver's seat and I was truly scared,' the producer disclosed
to *Rolling Stone* in January 1990. 'This is a man who is comfortable
taking major risks. He likes to be out there on the edge, whether

it's in a car or on the screen.'

Cruise started racing Nissans for Newman's team, making his professional racing debut at the Road Atlanta circuit in Georgia. But it was not without incident – a near miss during a practice lap, knocking one opponent off the track and spinning himself. Mimi Rogers attended, as she was often prone to do, cheering from the pits (although her nerves started fraying after a number of close-calls involving Tom; it's claimed she implored Newman to tell the kid to ease up). Cruise finished his debut race a commendable fourteenth in a field of forty-two cars. Cruise has raced but without the success achieved by Newman, whose own passion for the sport has finally dwindled with old age. One afternoon Cruise and Newman were out burning some serious rubber around the Daytona International Speedway. Cruise had been invited to drive there by his friend and one of NASCAR's (National Association for Stock Car Auto Racing) premier owners Rick Hendrick. The notion of a racing movie, almost a prerequisite genre for macho stars – Steve McQueen's *Le Mans*, Al Pacino's *Bobby Deerfield* and Newman's own *Winning* – fermented inside the Cruise brain while he chatted easily to the drivers and pit mechanics at the Florida track. Once behind the wheel and pushing hard on the accelerator Cruise felt as if he'd entered a different dimension. Sure he'd driven Porsches and Nissans with Newman, but stock-car racing, this was something else. Bombing around the tri-oval track with its steep curves and suicidal bends, Cruise was struck by the Panavision possibilities with the force of a hammer on the forehead. Screeching to a halt in the pit lane Cruise leapt from the car giving one of those trademark high-five yells we assumed he only does in movies like *Top Gun*. 'I'm going to make a movie about that!' he whoops in the direction of a grinning Newman.

That evening both men dined out with a group of stock-car veterans whose colourful anecdotes about maverick drivers and their hair-raising exploits convinced Cruise even more that he'd found a great angle for an action movie. As with *Top Gun* Cruise viewed his project as being not so much about the machinery but the dedication and artistry of the men who operated them. He started work immediately on a rough outline, pitching the idea to Ned Tanen, an executive at Paramount and fellow auto freak (he'd given George Lucas his big break by financing the car orientated *American Graffiti*). Tanen greenlighted the project without even seeing a script – which was just as well, because there wasn't one. The studio immediately recruited screenwriter Donald Stewart to embellish Cruise's sketched treatment. When a less-than-inspiring script came back Cruise enlisted his old *Top Gun* buddies Simpson and Bruckheimer, plus writer Warren Skaaren, and left them to it. Meanwhile, he went off to make the two best films of his career, *Rain Man* and *Born on the Fourth of July*. Seven drafts later everyone was scratching their heads, at a loss at how to make the beast work, not least the returning Cruise: 'There was frustration that the script wasn't getting there.' He desperately needed to connect with a young, mainstream audience again after those two pretty heavyweight offerings; his image needed lightening up. All the time Cruise knew the risk he was running: Hollywood had never made a decent motor racing movie, let alone one which made money. No amount of exciting racing footage – and in *Thunder* they are superb, in their way as exhilarating as the dogfights of *Top Gun* – ever compensates for a paper-thin premise. Cruise wasn't prepared to fall into that trap, making it plain in interviews that *Thunder* was a character-motivated piece rather than lots of cars just expensively banging into each other. While away Cruise had kept in constant touch with developments, inviting Rick Hendrick, enlisted as technical consultant, to his movie sets or flying down to Hendrick's home base of Charlotte, North Carolina. Despite such passionate determination Hendrick began to doubt the film would ever get off the ground. 'Tom had been talking about this movie for years,' he told *Rolling Stone* in July 1990. 'You know, it's been like a dog with a bone – he has never let it alone.' Was the script destined to linger in development hell?

Even if a script had emerged of *Citizen Kane* standard it would still have been binned if NASCAR turned round and said no to them using their racetracks and facilities. It must have entered Cruise's reckoning that without official co-operation he didn't have a movie. There was no back-up plan. However, despite the lack of a decent script, the feeling among NASCAR officialdom was that having attracted millions of fans and hundreds of millions of dollars in sponsorship money during the eighties the sport needed to maintain that growth in the nineties. And a Cruise movie opening in 2,000 cinemas across the United States is not bad advertising. Just ask the Navy. 'We're going to take the image of stock-car racing as most of the public perceives it and turn it around,' pitched Simpson to NASCAR president Bill France Jr. 'We're going to show them just how high-tech and professional it really is.' It was Simpson at his classic best and France could only sit back and admire the sheer nerve of it. 'Son,' rasped France, 'I've had the best salesmen come through here. I had Howard Hawks come in here and tell me about *Red Line 7000* [racing-car drama from the mid sixties with James Caan] and what a terrific movie that was. And you know what, son? It was a piece of crap. But you're a helluva kid. I like your style. I'm gonna do it.'

NASCAR in, but scriptwriter Skaaren out, from sheer exhaustion. Enter Robert Towne, who'd salvaged troubled stories in the past. He bailed out Warren Beatty by polishing the final draft of *Bonnie and Clyde*, without taking screen credit, and won an Oscar for *Chinatown*. Now just what one of the most respected screenwriters in the business was doing getting himself into this quagmire is anyone's guess. Or maybe it was all terribly simple – Simpson and Bruckheimer weren't known for being the most frugal employers. The uninitiated Towne, with Cruise as guide, flew to a race meeting at Watkins Glen, New York. 'He was hesitant,' remembers Cruise. 'He said he'd check it out and I was trying not to put on too much pressure. After a few hours he came up to me smiling and said, "I get it, Cruise, this is fantastic." '

Junking Skaaren's work, Towne started from scratch and continued writing almost nonstop throughout filming. New script pages would be thrust into the hands of actors, sometimes just minutes before the cameras rolled. Cruise's brainwave, which almost cost him his life, was to tape pieces of his script on to the car's dashboard so he could recite dialogue whilst bombing around the track. Not such a great idea – the first time he tried it his car slammed into a wall. Next Towne read Cruise the dialogue through his headphones; he'd get a feel for it and then speak it back. 'So in the movie, when it looks like my crew chief is talking to me and I'm listening intently, I was actually waiting for my next line.'

Everyone's goal was to capture on film, as never before, the gritty intensity of motor racing, to bring a fresh look to a sport America watches every day on cable TV. 'I wanted to take an audience for a ride at 200 miles an hour and have them live to tell about it.' – Cruise. Director Tony Scott vividly evokes the greasy heat of summer racetracks in middle America. To achieve a heightened sense of realism, *Thunder* includes authentic race-day footage. High-test, professionally built cars driven by stock-car pros were given permission to race in NASCAR events alongside real competing teams, providing they dropped out early on to ensure they didn't influence the outcome of any race. In order to capture the action remote-controlled cameras were housed in special crash boxes front and back – even so $500,000-worth of equipment was junked; every time a car hit the wall an $85,000 camera went up the spout. Most irritating was that during the race, as the other teams changed tyres, *Thunder*'s own pit crew were changing rolls of film. Scott shot at a number of race circuits, most notably Daytona International Speedway, Florida, where the season culminates in that explosion of male hormones known as the Daytona 500. Using a sixty-man crew, the director mounted twenty-eight cameras strategically around the 2½-mile track to capture that in-the-car-rush.

At the Charlotte Motor Speedway in North Carolina Cruise took one of the test cars out for a spin before filming. Cranking up the revs he was being scrutinized closely by the circuit's president, Humpy Wheeler. Pulling out his stopwatch to time the car's speed Wheeler couldn't quite believe what his eyes were telling him as Cruise clocked in at 32.53 seconds per lap (166 m.p.h.) – a new track record for a non-certified NASCAR driver. Perhaps still on a high Cruise was stopped by local police for driving his own car at 66 m.p.h. in a 35 m.p.h. zone. He got off with a token fine – $125.

Paramount's insurance policy emphasized total safety, restricting the actor from gambling with his life. A total of fifty-eight cars were wasted during production, but thankfully there were no human fatalities. Jerry Molen, *Thunder*'s executive producer, described the film as being blessed. 'The miracle is that no one got hurt. The fact that there were no serious problems is just incredible.' 'They were very careful,' Cruise confirmed to *Empire* in September 1990, 'but I did more stuff than just driving around the track. I mean, I didn't do the crashes, obviously, but I had my share of stunts.' NASCAR driver Greg Sacks did most of the high-speed precision driving, while some of Hollywood's top stunt drivers choreographed a series of heart-stopping stunts and crashes. Cruise was behind the wheel for most of the rest. Indeed his enthusiasm for the sport caused headaches all round. 'One of our biggest problems was keeping him out of the race cars,' reported Bruckheimer. 'Had we let him, he would have done all the driving himself.' Rick Hendrick, owner of three of NASCAR's top teams around 1989/90, obviously knew what he was talking about when he praised Cruise's driving ability. 'In our profession, we look for drivers that have a "feel" for the car, a natural ability. Tom has that. And he has no fear in an automobile. I've never seen anyone progress as fast as he has.' It was shades of *The Color of Money* when pool champion Mike Sigel boasted that his protégé could turn professional if he gave up acting.

Filming wasn't the smoothest of rides. If the logistics weren't headache enough, foul spells of weather conspired to drag production over schedule (combined with an array of intricate stunts, including the opening smash-up. With eleven cameras rolling the stunt driver revved his machine up to 125 m.p.h., slid into a pool of water, spun, then detonated 20 ounces of nitro-glycerin tucked behind the rear axle. 'The car did six barrel rolls, and at the end of it was just this fucking shell,' remembers Scott. 'The driver came out of the car yelling, "Yeah!" with this enormous hard-on and giving everyone high fives. These stunt guys are crazy.') and soon Cruise's baby was suffering from budget blues. On *Thunder* Simpson and Bruckheimer wasted an estimated $50 to $60 million of which Cruise pocketed $9 million. The producers blamed the escalating expenditure on the studio for rushing production for a summer release, but a heap of cash simply went down the Hollywood well of excess. Such extravagances as knocking down the walls of ten rooms at a Holiday Inn to create an office prompted Frank Mancuso, Paramount chairman, to call and castigate the pair for throwing money at problems. Reportedly, an enraged Simpson and Bruckheimer roped Cruise into joining them for a half-day strike. A retreating Paramount piled up the grudges. By the end relations were so bad that when Simpson and Bruckheimer sent Barry London, co-president in charge of distribution, a *Thunder* crew jacket London contemptuously sent it back.

As filming progressed through the early months of 1990, insider talk was that *Thunder* was little more than the sequel that dared not speak its name – '*Top Gun* on wheels', as some critics later dubbed it. That both films were similarly packaged was transparent. There's the excitement of powerful, sexy machines and the special bond between men who use them (the mystique of machismo and buddy love, crushed beer cans, that gladiatorial rush. Act tough, stay cool); Cary Elwes as a hot-shot rival, a role reminiscent of Kilmer's Ice Man; the same style of love interest (Nicole Kidman, even more unlikely as a brain surgeon than McGillis's aeronautics instructor); and much the same plot – toothsome young speed freaks, peer-group rivalry. Throughout Cruise again poses and pouts his way to redemption, essaying the same insouciant young ace with a hellraising streak that threatens his own destruction (à la Maverick). Tom's top-grin cockiness is still the key component. Cruise tried to shrug off the comparisons: 'There are people who like to classify things. People who can't see things for what they really are.' Even some crew members were spotted wearing 'Top Car' caps. Tony Scott was also back at the helm. Since *Top Gun* he'd become famous as the cigar-chomping director of flashy adrenalin-charged entertainments. Though British his output is quintessentially Yank – you somehow know he's never going to make a movie for Channel Four about lesbian social workers hiking in North Wales. It had only been three years since their last collaboration yet Scott sensed a change in the actor. He'd become more relaxed and confident in what he was capable of giving as an actor, which made life easier than it had been on *Top Gun*. And more open and more responsive to improvisation (the influence of Hoffman?). Talking of older stars, on *Thunder* Cruise was up against another venerable legend, Robert Duvall, who forges the same sort of tempestuous father/son relationship as Newman, as the inevitable grizzled veteran who reluctantly takes Cruise the driver under his wing. Some critics suggested Cruise suffered more by comparison with Duvall than any of the other big names with whom he's co-starred (Duvall lends the enterprise a credibility it doesn't deserve), an observation Scott concurred with. 'You could see all the other actors saying to themselves whenever Duvall was on set – "I'd better be good or this guy will bury me" and they were right.' Duvall eclipses Cruise, who is running on auto-pilot here.

Cruise envisaged *Thunder* in very simple terms, and let's face it, it's a *very* simple film. Essentially an idolatrous tribute to the daredevils of the American stock-car circuit, its sole focus is rookie driver Cole Trickle (surely the stupidest movie hero name in history), a hick from the sticks with speed in his veins and a natural behind the wheel. His ego swells with victory. Cole's the cliché motor-racing hero who arrives from nowhere to chase the championship against all the odds. Moreover, he's the formulaic

Cruise hero – a young buck out to prove himself, be it as pilot, driver, pool player or bartender, here learning what it takes to beat the fear inside after a mind-bruising crash. The theme of *Days of Thunder* reads like Tom Cruise's career plan.

No one could believe that Paramount wanted the movie's release brought forward in time for the lucrative fourth of July holiday weekend, meaning a radically shortened post-production period. There was a frenzy of round-the-clock activity as editors tried to beat the odds and finish the movie in just six weeks – instead of the usual six months. It was a quite unprecedented time squeeze, and as it turned out a short-sighted short-cut that cost the film its box-office laurels. Tony Scott was shooting racing footage at the Daytona track just three weeks before the movie hit theatres. It was chaos incorporated and punishing to everyone. Not unexpectedly Cruise's ballistic spirit rose to the challenge, revelling, with an almost masochistic glee, in the cold-sweat pressure. He would check on the editing, loop dialogue, then take care of his office business at night: getting home at 4.30 in the morning was not uncommon. 'It's exhilarating because it really puts you absolutely to the limit.' This was the way they used to make movies, he reasoned; John Ford would shoot a movie and a month or so later it would be playing in cinemas. 'This is history in terms of what we're trying to accomplish in this time period. This isn't filmmaking, it's war.' It's not surprising that Simpson and Bruckheimer's nickname for Cruise during filming was 'Laser-head', because of his ability to zoom in on the matter at hand and dissect it until he could understand it. Perhaps this was a positive legacy from coping with dyslexia in his youth. 'I had to train myself to focus my attention. I became very visual and learned how to create mental images in order to comprehend what I read.' Cruise could read a screenplay and immediately get a sense of its visual impact – an invaluable skill for an actor to possess.

In a summer of high-profile movies (*Dick Tracy, Die Hard 2, Total Recall*) *Thunder* was among the most anticipated. On paper it looked a surefire box-office hit, given its macho race-car image and rock soundtrack. Surely it couldn't fail to play well to men under 25 – cinema's biggest audience. But industry vultures were already writing the film off; what with the successful and talented personnel involved, many in Hollywood were itching for *Thunder* to fall flat on its face. For months they whispered that the film was a disaster and virtually unreleasable, that it had become a bloated, rushed mess under the haphazard guidance of Simpson and Bruckheimer. In today's climate, where stars, producers and directors take cream percentage profits and agents healthy commissions, *Thunder*'s final box-office tally of $80 million starts to look an exposed sum; the usual Hollywood benchmark for success is earnings of roughly three times the original cost. *Days of Thunder* was going to have to perform miracles internationally for Paramount to make a profit from so expensive an enterprise. In the end the studio were lumbered with so many useless prints that they started destroying most of them, accidentally incinerating one of only two 70-mm working prints of Terrence Malick's 1978 film *Days of Heaven* in the process.

Days of Thunder's less than spectacular performance marked the first serious chink in the Cruise armour (he'd started out by refusing to do much publicity but ended up going on the Oprah Winfrey show in a doomed effort to jump-start his movie). It also perhaps signalled a sea change in audience taste, a move away from overblown action movies to dramas like *Ghost*. And the critics? Well, let's just say they didn't go a bundle on it. 'By any civilised standards, *Thunder* is a monstrosity' – *Observer*; '*Thunder* is nothing more than an exercise in dollar-sifting movie-making by numbers' – *Today*; '*Thunder* never flags as long as the cars are careering round in circles. Off the racetrack, however, the movie has the momentum of a Sinclair C5 with the wheels off' – *Sunday Telegraph*; '*Days* has a horrible cranking feel to it, reminiscent of a bloke trying to have a wank and scraping the bottom of the barrel to come up with a workable fantasy to get him going on it' – *City Limits*; 'Cruise is dull, a real comedown after his recent subtle, detailed performances' – *Independent*. After the ambitious and hard-won credibility of *Rain Man* and *Born on the Fourth of July* Cruise regresses to a role that any pretty boy could play, a cynically manufactured star vehicle. One critic took pity though: 'Cruise has never looked better. In 20 years he'll be ready for Paul Newman's crown and life achievement Oscar.' Maybe Cruise figured he deserved a break, a role of no artistic merit or challenge, one which just needed him to do what he does best – look good. The film's biggest disappointment was that Cruise had so readily reverted to type after courageously breaking the mould as Ron Kovic. Having played a crippled and impotent Vietnam veteran Cruise may have been anxious to re-establish his screen virility – a call-girl disguised as a cop grabs at the Cruiser's crotch and he has a fairly vacuous romance with Kidman. But clearly he's no fool, cleverly interspersing fluff (*Cocktail*) and formula action (*Thunder*) with gradually more demanding dramatic roles (*Fourth of July, Vampire*). *Days of Thunder* is dismal stuff – even the climactic big race lacks suspense. It is loaded with stock cars and stock characters and a script constructed from the scrapyard of old movie clichés – including the one that holds that race-car movies never work.

7   The Biggest Star in the World

'God, I hope I can stay normal.'
                                        — Tom Cruise, on fame

On 28 June 1993 Tom Cruise confirmed his immortality outside the legendary Mann's Chinese Theatre on Hollywood Boulevard. In one of the few rituals of moviedom left over from Hollywood's golden age Cruise pressed his palms into quickly hardening cement, with music from *Top Gun* blasting out from speakers. He signed his name beneath and left behind his footprints for good measure. 'Growing up, I would wonder what it would be like to come here and be asked to leave my own footprints,' Cruise told reporters. He then rushed over to shake hands and sign autographs with the hundreds of fans who'd gathered. Hollywood had honoured him before, back in 1986, with the 1835th star on the Hollywood walk of fame, despite some reservations about Cruise being too young. At least he was a human being, unlike Lassie and Mickey Mouse who have their own pavement star! Within four years Cruise's star had all but vanished – fans had been helping themselves to bits as souvenirs.

Cruise is no stranger to awards, save the one he most covets, the Oscar, though it's hard to imagine how that would make the slightest difference to an already glittering career. In 1991 he received the coveted American Cinema Award for Distinguished Achievement in film, and in 1993 collected the Actor of the Decade award at the Chicago International Film Festival. 'When film-makers need an intelligent and sincere performance, they ask for Tom,' said festival director Michael Kutza. 'At 31, he is a true movie star and there are very few of them today.' The award was given days before Cruise began work on *Interview with the Vampire*. The event featured movie clips and an onstage questions-and-answers session. Cruise looked at ease throughout, sporting his 'grunge' look: long hair pulled back into a ponytail and designer stubble. Nicole Kidman likes the Cruise hair long, as did DeMornay before her. This grunge look harked back to his *Legend* days, for normally Tom sports short hair in his films, only allowing it to grow in between film work – 'I'm not big on haircuts.' It thus serves as a barometer of how long he's been unemployed, though 'unemployed' is probably a word that is the least applicable to Tom Cruise. He's also been voted Harvard University's Man of the Year (in 1994), cheerfully joining in with the 'Rag week'-style jollity: he wore a pair of red stilettos, a university joke based on Tom's not being very tall. Cruise said of the award, 'It has nothing to do with the fact I just played two Harvard grads.'

A decade earlier Cruise was just another Brat Packer who seemed to be going nowhere in particular. Along with Matt Dillon (Brando to Cruise's Montgomery Clift) he was singled out as the American juvenile lead most likely to succeed. But a contender for greatness? Who could have foreseen that the plump, squeaky-voiced kid in *Taps* would rise to become one of the biggest movie stars of the modern age, Hollywood's sure thing – 'a recession-proof movie star,' *Rolling Stone* call him. Cruise fan or not you can't underrate his staggering achievement. Since 1983 his films have grossed over \$3 billion, demonstrating his popularity with audiences worldwide. Even his flops, and there have been remarkably few (like *Far and Away*), take more money than most other people's hits. Not surprising really, given that his output tends to be big-budget affairs, popular entertainments aimed squarely at the multiplex millions of middle America and beyond. 'I could make smaller movies,' says an unrepentant Cruise, 'but after running in the Olympics, why should I go back to High School?'

He is numbered among a select batch of top guns, fireproof stars – Schwarzenegger, Ford, Gibson, Stallone – who can virtually guarantee a film's success, in the States or overseas. An actor might open a movie in America but go down like a lead balloon in say the Philippines or Italy; stars like Cruise and Schwarzenegger are global icons, American brand names as identifiable as Coca Cola and McDonalds. In a 1989 poll for the cinema trade paper *Hollywood Reporter*, assessing the bankability of America's top stars on foreign shores, Cruise led the bunch. Though garnering most of the critical laurels, people didn't go to see *A Few Good Men* in their millions to watch Nicholson, they queued to see Cruise. 'He could get a film based on his first communion set up tomorrow at the studio of his choice,' wrote esteemed movie magazine *Premiere*, and that's no idle exaggeration. His commercial clout is such that he gets the pick of the scripts. Even when films miss the bullseye (or in the case of *Far and Away* end up missing the target altogether) Cruise's stature endures. If an actor has the mystical box-office power to lure unsuspecting punters to C-grade garbage like *Cocktail* or *Days of Thunder* Hollywood executives sit up and take note. But he doesn't come cheap. Cruise is one of the highest-paid entertainers on the planet, currently earning $15–20 million per film (that's more than the entire budget of *Top Gun*), plus a healthy cut of the profits and numerous other perks. Cruise would brag at school that he was going to be a millionaire before his thirtieth birthday. In the end that turned out to be a very modest estimation: he achieved that fifty times over.

The rest of the world's economy may be in tatters, but there's no sign of a recession when it comes to Hollywood star salaries, which have shot through the stratosphere in recent years. Today Cruise and his ilk are reaping personal fortunes that far exceed any need they may have for the rest of their lives. The more inflated the pay cheque, the happier the star, not because they need the money but because money means power. It denotes muscle. People are going to respect an actor they have to dole out $10 million for more than one that comes on the cheap. As perennially pessimistic screenwriter William Goldman once scorned, 'Today, a million dollars is what you pay a star you don't want.' Cruise could not have come along at a more propitious time. The industry, more conservative and nervous than ever in the face of escalating production costs, had never relied so heavily on stars; such economics gave those like Tom Cruise an absurd degree of power. The male movie star has become the most powerful part of the film-making process. The stars and their agents, not the studios, now call the shots: the tail is very much wagging the dog. Cruise's sudden rise to fame was indicative of just how much the male movie stars dominated the industry in the eighties, and still do. A box office name attached to a project could mean the difference between a movie getting made or getting shelved. But he reckons he's worth it. 'The people who own studios didn't get to where they are by being dumb businessmen,' he told *Empire* in July 1992. 'They aren't going to pay me one penny more than I'm worth. They wouldn't pay it if I wasn't worth it. And the day I'm not, they won't.' And there are others who think so too, such as Kevin Pollack, Cruise's co-star in *A Few Good Men*. 'This guy has a work ethic the like of which I've never seen. I can't believe I'm saying this, but this guy really works for his $12 million.' In 1992 *Movieline* magazine came to his defence, writing, 'If you're going to pay anybody too much to star in the movie you're spending too much to make, pay Tom Cruise. He's the only bona fide movie star of his generation.'

That Cruise can now command such staggering figures is a measure of his status in the Hollywood firmament. But he had to pay for it. Fame and popularity, coveted and courted by artists – even by those who deny it – was, when it came, sudden and frightening. After *Risky Business* it was a little unnerving being recognized and approached by strangers off the street. 'Things went a little crazy.' Living in New York as he did when people started gawping at him, his instincts told him that he was going to be mugged, or that maybe his shirt was sticking out of his flies. At first he was a little uncomfortable with all the adulation. Then with the release of *Top Gun* things got immeasurably worse.

How did Cruise handle fame? Was he afraid of it? Complacent with it? Arrogant with it? Creative with it? It's such a lottery, this business; all actors' careers, however seemingly secure, are subject to fate. The prospects of being successful are pretty remote and for the kind of success Cruise wanted, but never believed he could ever attain, they were even bleaker. But once he'd decided on acting there was only one direction in which he was heading – up. Somehow actors do what they can and they're chosen. It's luck more than anything else. With *Top Gun*, Cruise became the all-American male psyche on film: his clean-cut, good-guy image gave him almost universal appeal, and he became the actor every lad wanted to look like and every girl lusted after. Lucille Ball, who co-produced *All the Right Moves*, thought Cruise would score because he was the boyfriend every American girl wanted. That practically sums up Cruise's mid-eighties appeal. From nobody to *nonpareil* in five years: viewed from a distance Cruise's career can look as if it's progressed almost too smoothly, and people resented that he'd risen so fast, without paying any dues. He was a kid who bought glory with his looks. For a time he was racked with guilt about his stardom, his looks, his wealth. He knew he wasn't the norm. 'I wake up every day and know I'm a lucky guy. Then I thought: Listen, this is where I want to be. You see some people who destroy themselves because they become successful and feel guilty about acknowledging it – and then it goes away. However terrible it is, I'm enjoying myself.'

Cruise tries to lead a normal and unassuming life. As fame grew Cruise increasingly withdrew from the lifestyle he espoused on screen: he didn't go out boozing and he shunned the limelight; control and self-improvement became all. After the corrupting oxygen of Hollywood, he sees it as vital to get out there in the real world as often as possible, to get a sharp intake of reality and not hide away in his ivory tower (both he and Nicole Kidman resent the 'recluse' tag with which the press have labelled them). In particular he doesn't want his kids to miss out on anything. Cruise hasn't allowed fame to hinder him or his family from going or doing whatever they please, he and Nicole regularly go to rock concerts and the movies, not private screenings but public performances; they even go skating in Central Park at night, where the problem isn't autograph hunters but getting out alive! Since the arrival of babies, however, Cruise and Kidman have understandably grown more nervous, and his sprawling Los Angeles mansion comes complete with high walls and a hi-tech alarm system. But there are no squads of bodyguards like those employed by some over-inflated pop stars we could mention. Indeed when Tom was filming *Mission: Impossible* in London Nicole was spotted with newly adopted Connor in a park happily chatting away to local mothers.

'I don't like to put myself into situations where I get stared at a lot. On a screen, it's fine; in front of a crowd, I'll pass.' He's so normal-looking in person that it would be easy to overlook him anyway; Cruise is not as immediately identifiable a star as say Schwarzenegger or Nicholson. And because Cruise is not predominantly an action hero, a killer-machine movie star like Arnie and Sly, he attracts different kinds of fans and attention. When fans approach he doesn't see it as a threat and they're generally congenial towards him. Cruise is happy to sign the odd autograph and chat briefly with the people who after all pay his wages, unless he's otherwise engaged. 'I just treat people the way I want to be treated.' It only becomes a problem when they try to trespass, ingratiate themselves too much, or push a bit too hard. Then Cruise is the first to say: 'Look, excuse me, this is not OK.' But it's rare for people to hassle the couple. At first the attention Cruise received alarmed Nicole. 'I don't suppose I'll ever get used to seeing girls gazing at my husband lustfully,' she told the *Daily Mail* in July 1992. 'But at least they don't try to rip his clothes off.' Cruise remembers a visit to the Smithsonian Institution in Washington DC around the time of *Top Gun* when he was chased by a flock of fans. As he was with his sister and new-born niece, it unnerved him greatly. He's since learned to be master of such situations. Valerie Golino experienced Cruisemania first-hand during the shooting of *Rain Man*. She was amazed when a female fan, near to fainting, tried to kiss her hand because she'd just been holding Tom's in a scene. Stuff like that was not uncommon.

Cruise has dealt with stardom astoundingly well. He's a resolutely calm and balanced individual who has never allowed celebrity to go to his head: exploiting it rather than letting it destroy him. Director Ron Howard sees Cruise's career progress not as 'a cold, calculated lust for power; it's a journey of self-actualization and fulfilment of his potential. The actor never deliberately sought power and claims one of the few positive aspects of fame, a natural by-product of his profession, is having the clout to get any project of his choosing off the ground. In Hollywood that's some power. It means that if Cruise is unhappy with a scene he can, regardless of cost and without question, have it reshot, demand more close-ups or script rewrites. It means endless perks, everything from luxury trailer homes (Cruise's huge dressing-room trailer, lined inside with an abundance of family photographs, and customized gym travel with him to movie locations) to first-class travel. It means directors of the calibre of Oliver Stone holding up production of *Born on the Fourth of July* for nine months to wait for him, or Brian De Palma happily spending two years in pre-production on *Mission: Impossible* because Cruise wants to star in it.

Famous at twenty-one, when most of us are still coming to terms with who we are (Cruise included), movie stardom was more of a shock than a pleasure. It took time to adjust, though one feels he's never got used to losing what most of us hold dearest – privacy. What must it feel like to have the spotlight on you from the moment you walk out of your own front door to when you return?

As intensely private about his personal life as he is driven and focused in his professional life, Cruise vowed never to let himself become public property, while remaining wise to the fact that some of his inner life was bound to be stripped away by his new-found fame and celebrity status. Cruise once encountered an author who intended publishing a book featuring stars' addresses in New York – a prurient and pretty dangerous concept. The actor has had his fair share of stargazers and fruitcases loitering near his apartment. He was particularly unnerved to catch two young girls spying on him with a pair of binoculars from an apartment block across the street. Confronting their father with the evidence the star proposed a deal: he'd take his peeping daughters out for lunch on the proviso they refrain from further surveillance operations. A satisfactory conclusion, yet it got Cruise to thinking: take away teeny girls and binoculars, add unbalanced weirdo with sniper's rifle; result: front-page headlines. At the height of his early fame Cruise remembers thinking how easy it would be to lose his way, to surround himself with advisers who'd 'yes' him to death. 'When I think back on it, sometimes I wonder how I got through all that stuff.' Fellow artists are struck by how down-to-earth he is. 'My own stardom, fortunately, came much slower,' Paul Newman told *Vanity Fair* in October 1994. 'It's tough when it happens as fast as it did with Tom. He's a very savvy kid ... a very savvy man. So far he's kept his head on his shoulders, but he's one of the very, very few.' Another mentor, David Geffen:

> Tom has had the burden of being a star since he was a teenager. The only other person I know of who had to deal with it in a similar way is Bob Dylan. It's very hard to have people that focussed on you from such a young age. I think Tom has survived it better than anybody else I know who has had that kind of scrutiny and that kind of attention and that kind of adulation. It can be awful.

And Holly Hunter: 'Tom wants to please, and with someone of his stature that's pretty enchanting, since that's usually the first thing to erode in major movie stars. I couldn't speculate where that comes from. Tom is breathing rare air, and he responds to it in a unique way. He's very, very unspoiled.'

'This guy will be around for a long, long time,' testifies his

Cocktail director Roger Donaldson. 'Because he's not going to be dependent on whether or not he's popular – he's just a great actor. If he falls from grace, he'll be back with a vengeance.' That fall from grace is about as likely as a Disney remake of *Driller Killer*. On legends and staying the course, the noted film writer David Thomson in his *Biographical Dictionary of Film* drew parallels between Cruise and Clark Gable. Yet in his early thirties Gable's career hadn't even kicked into second gear – *It Happened One Night*, *Mutiny on the Bounty*, *Gone with the Wind* were still years off. Cruise, with all he's achieved, is still in his mid-thirties – the mind boggles at his future. 'If Cruise has not yet been in an unmistakably good film, he has shown a range as an actor, and a willingness, that are impressive.' This link to Hollywood's golden age has been made more than once about Cruise. *Variety* has called him: 'The Tyrone Power of his generation.' And David Shipman in his book *The Great Movie Stars* referred to Cruise as the heir to Cooper, Cagney and Gable. 'If they are looking down, you can bet they're surprised.' Indeed on public occasions Cruise and Kidman don't look unlike glamorous old-time movie stars. For a moment it's possible to believe that Hollywood is the way it used to be – when film stars truly were America's royalty.

You can sense in Cruise a genuine nostalgia for the way Hollywood was in the thirties, forties and fifties. He misses those times, even though he never lived through them. It's one of the reasons Cruise holds so much store by the Oscar ceremony: 'It's tradition.' He pines over old photographs and talks often with Newman about the days when men wore suits to work or got spruced up to go on a date. Cruise loves that kind of high style, the class and dignity it denotes. Watching crackling black-and-white movies makes him yearn for a return to the old values, when there was a real sense of community and the studios looked after you, developed properties for you. Though it is doubtful he'd have sat well in the studio system. Cruise even controls what stills a studio can release, to avoid becoming teen-idol poster fodder. Louis Mayer and Harry Cohn would rather have strangled their first-born than submit to that. Wisely Cruise is not over-sentimental about the days when actors were treated no better than pieces of meat, loaned out, sold off and exploited. 'There was such a vicious brutality to the way they sometimes treated these artists,' said Cruise. 'Ultimately, that's why the studio system had to go.' But he'd surely have enjoyed the reckless pace; back then

Cruise hangs out with the co-stars Sean Penn and Timothy Hutton during the making of *Taps*

Birth of the Brat Pack: Francis Ford Coppola's *The Outsiders*

Hitting the big time in *Risky Business* and the birth of Cruise power

Cruise as teenage heart-throb with Lea Thompson in *All The Right Moves*

Cruise as innocent: Playing Jack
O' the Green in *Legend*, not long
after the death of his father

Art as propaganda: *Top Gun* faced
criticism for its glossy depiction of
America's war machine. Cruise
took it as fantasy and it made him
a superstar

Jousting with pool cues. Two icons – Cruise and Paul Newman – lock horns
in Martin Scorsese's *The Color of Money*

First wife Mimi Rogers in Ridley Scott's *Someone To Watch Over Me*

Cruise struts his stuff to no avail in *Cocktail*

The epitome of star power – Cruise and Hoffman propel *Rain Man*, a potential audience turn-off, to mega-bucks glory

Super smooth, super cool: Cruise as star in complete control of his career and destiny in *Rain Man*

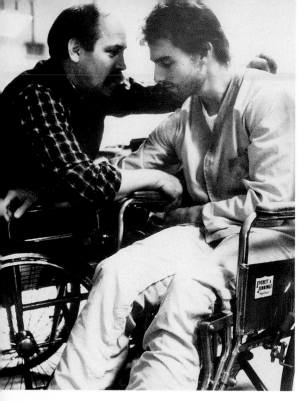

Fact and fiction merge: Cruise takes solace in the words of Ron Kovic, the man whose story he brought so vividly to life on screen in *Born on the Fourth of July*

Cruise behind the wheel of a race car in *Days of Thunder*; not the potent force at the box office many had predicted

The stunning, quiet beauty of
Nicole Kidman

Scene from *Far and Away* which
symbolizes the fairy-tale
romance that is the
Cruise/Kidman marriage

The maverick comes of age:
A scene from Rob Reiner's
courtroom drama
A Few Good Men

Looking for a way out: Cruise contemplates the meaning of life in *The Firm*

Cruise was a revelation in *Interview with the Vampire* as author Anne Rice's macabre Lestat – the most charismatic screen vampire since Christopher Lee's Dracula

Another scene from Neil Jordan's horror epic *Interview with the Vampire*

stars churned out upwards of three or four movies a year. Now Cruise is usually the guy producers go after when they're looking for a young leading male. In the past competition was fierce. Cruise must wish there were more actors vying for these same roles like in the days when Bogart, Cagney, Tracy, Cooper and Gable might be all gunning for the same parts.

Time magazine summed up Cruise's appeal:

It's a pleasure to find a movie star like Tom Cruise who radiates old-fashioned star quality. Onscreen Cruise looks life-size or a little less, his body is not so much beefy (like Schwarzenegger or Stallone) as stocky. He effuses an unselfconscious self-confidence, an anachronistic but winning spirit of American go-get. In an ideal suburbia, Tom Cruise is the boy next door most likely to succeed.

And this from *New York Times* film critic Janet Maslin:

My take on Tom Cruise is that he's a great object onscreen. The quality he radiates as an object is this healthy, glowing, all-American well-being. When he just gets out there and plays The Handsome Hunk, then he seems redundant to me. The times he has been great are the times that someone uses that healthy, handsome thing of his, yet leaves him wounded and bewildered by it – in *Born*, or in *Rain Man*, to some extent, or *The Color of Money*, and even *The Firm*. Sometimes he can give off this kind of anguish that can get right to you, and other times he's as bland as he was in *Far and Away*. A lot of the intelligence about how he comes across comes from his directors, which is, in a way, the real sign of an old-fashioned movie star.

8   *From Pool Cue to Bar Stool*

'This kid has the head and balls to be one of the great ones.
The next Hollywood legend'.

— Paul Newman

Pairing Paul Newman, Hollywood's most durable star, with
Cruise, its hottest, young bull, had to be the casting coup of the
year, the kind of dream team producers would sell their grannies
for. It had everyone salivating well in advance, and it delivered
most of the goods.

Times had certainly changed since Newman first played Eddie
Felson in 1961. The screen's foremost 'anti-hero' – filling the
vacuum created by the death of James Dean and the decline of
Marlon Brando – Newman had a blend of cynicism, moody
rebelliousness and rugged individualism that perfectly embodied
the alienation and restlessness of the period. What's more, he
possessed that traditional beauty, with his Greek god profile, that
linked him with Hollywood's glamorous, fading past. The
Newman era was dominated by pretty-boy rebels, stars like
McQueen and Beatty, who in turn gave rise to the urbanized,
ethnic actors of the seventies, De Niro, Hoffman and Woody
Allen. By the eighties the anti-hero was washed up, and
Hollywood had replaced cynicism with idealism; a flag-waving
president was in the White House and audiences wanted
nationalistic films with true-blue heroes. As the enterprising
yuppie-in-training in *Risky Business*, the high-school football star
in *All the Right Moves* and, most significantly, as the gung-ho
fighter pilot of *Top Gun*, Cruise emerged as the can-do kid of his
generation. It was emblematic of the time that Hollywood's
hottest young actor should have risen to fame as a glorified pimp

and military hero – Cruise was the perfect star for Reagan's eighties America.

It was Paul Newman who suggested Cruise for the role of pool-cue wizard Vincent Lauria to director Martin Scorsese. He'd caught the youngster in *All the Right Moves* (directed by Michael Chapman, cinematographer on several Scorsese movies) and liked what he saw. They never approached anyone else. Here, thought Scorsese, was Paul Newman as the American Icon and Tom Cruise as the new American Icon. Certainly what gives the film its special quality is observing the disparate acting styles of Hollywood old and new. Guided by Scorsese, Newman and Cruise, idols of two vastly different age groups, raise the level of each other's game.

The director called Cruise at home, out of the blue. At this time (prior to *Top Gun*) the actor was anything but major league, yet Scorsese sensed that his participation would help the project cross generational lines and thus boost box-office potential. Take a look at the script, he asked, and tell me what you think of it. And there was Cruise thinking, 'Martin Scorsese wants to know what *I* think of it.' As soon as he began reading he thought, holy shit! There's a role in here for me. Cruise loved the story, the characters and the dialogue; put simply it was the best script he'd ever read (Richard Price's screenplay is arguably the best that's ever graced a Cruise movie). He returned Scorsese's call, a bag of nerves. 'I'd like you to play Vincent,' went the voice on the other end of the line. After thinking about it for at least a micro-second, Cruise replied, 'Yes, sir, I would love to.' 'I didn't sleep for about six months after that,' he playfully told reporters. *Color*, coming on the heels of *Top Gun*, was a wonder stroke of timing, both artistically and commercially. Having made the ultimate pop movie – *Top Gun*, like *Risky Business* and, later, *Cocktail*, treats Cruise as the star of his own feature-length rock video rather than an actor – Cruise was ready to prove his mettle as a serious actor.

Certain reports suggest that Cruise initially turned down the offer, fearing he might come across as rather redundant acting alongside Newman. Director Ron Howard was having lunch with Cruise soon after *Top Gun* and asked him what he'd got lined up.

'I'm doing this movie *Color of Money* with Newman.'

Howard nodded approvingly.

'Scorsese's directing.'

'Wow. That'll be interesting, huh?' gushed Howard.

'Yeah,' Cruise replied. 'That's why I did it. I can learn so much from those two guys.' There it is: Cruise's career plan in miniature. 'I know he felt the same way about *Rain Man*,' Howard told the *Daily Telegraph* in July 1992. 'I think it's always been a part of his personality to grow as fast as he possibly could. He's just a sponge.' From the *Rain Man* script it must have been obvious to Cruise that Hoffman had the bravura role, but in the end he gracefully and intelligently played second fiddle, as he does here with Newman. It was Newman who personally pursued Cruise to take on Vincent. Cruise came to realize just how much it meant to the old timer. It's one of Newman's most personal films dealing as it does with growing old and recognizing that at some point the king must turn the sceptre over to the prince. The cocksure contender reminds Eddie of himself in his hotshot days, which seemed to have an echo in real life, with Cruise very much the heir to Newman's crown. 'I looked at Tom,' Newman said, 'and saw me thirty years ago.' By the same token Cruise clearly saw Newman as the ideal model of how an actor should build a solid career that will withstand the rigours of fame and public fickleness over the decades. 'I want to go all the way,' Cruise announced in 1990. 'Look at Newman, look at what this man has created as an actor and a human being.' You sense in their relationship Cruise as the boy king to Newman's Merlin. Since their inspirational collaboration Cruise has continued to establish himself as the Newman of his generation, a star who balances his sex symbol appeal with serious acting ambitions and a desire to become involved with weighty material.

Any actor would have given his eye teeth for the chance to work with the likes of Newman and Scorsese. Cruise, having already worked and learned from a seasoned director like Coppola, could now gain experience from an established older actor (Newman was the first in a veritable flood of elder statesman co-stars). Cruise felt blessed. 'I feel so lucky to have done what I have and made so much so soon,' he once blurted out to Newman on the set, who replied. 'I said the same thing once to George Roy Hill [director of *Butch Cassidy and the Sundance Kid*]. Know what he said to me? There's an art to being lucky.' Back in 1984 Cruise auditioned for Newman, then casting the juvenile lead in *Harry and Son*, but wasn't deemed old enough. The role was played instead by Robby Benson, of whom the world later said – who? 'I saved your career, kid,' Newman told Cruise. Lucky indeed. At that meeting in Newman's New York office the star had just seen *Taps* and insisted on calling Cruise 'Killer'. 'Listen, man,' came the reply. 'Five more minutes and I would have taken that school over.'

Upon accepting, Cruise obsessively set out to learn from scratch the game of pool, aware Scorsese wasn't going to want to fake the shots; all but one in the movie Cruise performed himself. With his professional trainer, Mike Sigel, Cruise spent nigh on two months shooting pool, working on improving his style and hanging around the seedy pool halls of New York soaking up the atmosphere. In the dizzy bravura of the pool room sequences, as poetic and powerful as the boxing montages in *Raging Bull*, Cruise's cue stick is twirled and flaunted as the emblem of his virility and skill. 'Some people pick up a pool cue and are totally helpless,' said Sigel. 'It's fortunate that Tom quickly picked up the basic form. After playing for only a few months he was able to look like a champion.' Newman was astonished, calling his co-star 'a gifted athlete. Cruise was better in six weeks than I was in five months back in 1961.' They were both out to prove something to each other. Pool tables were installed in their apartments for the duration of the production, and Cruise spent every sleepless night potting balls till dawn. In between filming they'd constantly slog it out on the green baize, a few side-stakes livening up proceedings. Newman sardonically claimed during press interviews that he 'won' Cruise's house in one bet – he didn't collect. Like a pair of schoolboys, each accused the other of moving balls while his back was turned. On occasion the kid beat the master, but most of the time ol' blue eyes wiped the floor with him.

Pool competition was nothing, however, compared to the artistic rivalry between the two stars. Both knew that when *Color* hit the screens audiences would be arguing who was the hottest hustler. Both knew it would be down to sex appeal, personality and sheer acting ability – plus, and most significantly in today's movie climate, who got top billing. In Hollywood billing is everything, proof of how much power your 'talent' commands. Cruise has learnt this lesson well; it's written into all his contracts that his name and his name alone stands above the title. Back in 1986, it was a thorny question of whether Newman or Cruise received pole position. There was also much buffeting of egos as to whose face should adorn the cover of that November's *Life* magazine, until some bright spark came up with the Mississippi compromise. On newstands west of the Mississippi the photograph of both stars lying on a pool table displayed Cruise right side up and Newman upside down, while the situation was reversed for the eastern states. Both camps declared themselves happy with the absurd arrangement; neither had won but, more importantly, neither had lost. As well as *Life*, Cruise has also graced the cover of *Time*, *USA Today* and *Newsweek*, such spaces being usually reserved for presidents, royalty, serial killers and starving Africans.

In spite, or perhaps because, of all the macho rivalry, a special relationship developed between the two men. 'On a personal and professional level they were absolutely compatible,' according to Mary Elizabeth Mastrantonio who played Vincent's hard-nosed girlfriend. Cruise shares Newman's intense pursuit of privacy and dislike of public proclamations about himself. Like Cruise, Newman had tried hard to be a jock at high school – hockey, football, skiing – but never excelling in sport until he sat behind the wheel of a car. They soon began hanging out together. When Newman turned sixty-one during filming the producers threw him a boisterous party. Cruise's surprise present was the *coup de grace*, a suspender belt and bra from a local sex shop. This camaraderie extended to the whole cast and crew; a sense of generosity and selflessness pervaded the set, giving rise to a fertile working atmosphere. Egos were left at the door and collected after hours. Newman called it one of the most creative and stimulating experiences of his career.

Cruise, who'd lost his father just two years before, found in Newman someone he could at last look up and aspire to. Indeed it's hard not to see in his friendship with Newman a hankering for the father he never really had, in addition to the more conventional mentor/protégé relationship. And for Newman, did the young Cruise help fill the void left by the tragic death (suicide?) in 1978 of his only son Scott, then aged not much older than Cruise, from a drug and alcohol overdose? Prior to his death Scott seemed actively to be courting disaster by indulging in hazardous hobbies such as skydiving, a dangerous pursuit that Cruise himself is keen on. Poor Mary Elizabeth Mastrantonio felt somewhat left out. 'We'd have dinners together and whatnot, but it was like – boy talk.' She felt as if she spent the movie being buffeted between the super-calm Newman and the hyperactive Cruise. 'I always felt like an old lady next to him, because I don't think Tom needs sleep,' she told *Rolling Stone* in November 1986.

'We treated each other as people. We weren't flirting or anything, and sometimes I thought, "Oh, this must be what it's like to have a brother. Kinda neat." ' This brotherly feel that Cruise radiates to his leading ladies – is it because he grew up with sisters and automatically takes on the role of brother in female company? – was also felt by Lea Thompson, his co-star in *All the Right Moves*. 'When we were introduced, Tom reminded me so much of my brother that it made me nervous.'

Cruise became a regular weekend visitor at the Newmans' country estate in Connecticut, where he'd sample the veteran's renowned home cooking and *that* salad dressing. On set Cruise usually lunched in the Newman trailer and often dined there too, which added to the 'family' feel of making the picture. It was a million miles from his bachelor existence back in Greenwich Village. Cruise took Newman as his role model of the perfect family man. 'Paul lives a normal life,' Cruise told one journalist, wistfully. 'He's got several businesses, a wife, a family. That's good for me to see.' On occasion Cruise brought along his soon-to-be wife Mimi Rogers (to pass inspection?). Their first public outing as a couple had been at a race meeting with Newman in Georgia soon after the launch of *The Color of Money*. Newman was a pivotal influence on the youngster overcoming his fear of marriage and taking the plunge, dispelling his fears that being a husband might somehow wreck his career: would female followers still come to his movies? Newman didn't lose his sex appeal after marrying Joanne Woodward and both continued to lead separate successful careers. It is rare, but possible.

Cruise, who always suffers terribly from nerves at the beginning of a project, found *Color* by far the worst. He'd seen every one of Newman's movies but quite rightly wasn't going to allow himself to be overawed or intimidated by knowing he was acting opposite a cinema legend. He wasn't going to be knocked off balance by the sheer wattage of the star. Newman meanwhile heaped praise on his protégé. 'Cruise just jumped in with both feet, showing tremendous actor's courage, not retreating from anything. He's got guts and great instinct as an actor. If you told him to jump into a fire he'd say he'd give it a whack.'

One of the most respected auteurs of his generation, a man who like Cruise almost entered the priesthood, Martin Scorsese is short, intense, asthmatic, and speaks with the speed of a person who is packing his whole life into the next five minutes. Many were surprised that Scorsese, the man who made *Mean Streets* and *Raging Bull*, could stoop to making a sequel – particularly a sequel to another director's work. And besides he didn't know the first thing about pool. An unabashed fan of Newman, Scorsese was sufficiently intrigued when the actor contacted him in September 1984 to volunteer his services for a project that was already a year into development. Scorsese dumped two draft screenplays, preferring to start from scratch with novelist Richard Price (*The Wanderers*), a fellow New Yorker with a fine ear for low-life scuzzballs, who was determined not to make 'Rocky with a pool cue or Top Stick'. Sitting around Newman's Malibu beach house the trio hammered out the new story, with Eddie adrift in late middle age, a jaded liquor salesman who has hung up his cue but still haunts the tables bankrolling any likely young talent that passes before his mercenary gaze. When he discovers this arrogant whizz-kid Vincent you can almost see the dollar signs light up Eddie's eyes. He takes the kid under his wing, educating him in all the corrupt and lucrative tricks of the hustler's trade. The action builds to a major tournament, with Eddie all the while perverting the kid's purity because it's threatening to him. Vincent's raw hunger for the game makes Eddie envious of his youth and reminds him of his early self. He wants Vincent to betray his gift and make money his only value; the trouble is, Vince loves the thrill of winning more than money and, as Eddie sneers, couldn't find the big time with a road map. In the process of corrupting Vince's idealism Eddie recaptures his own lost glory, and by the close the roles have reversed. Eddie rediscovers his appetite for the game, while Vince acquires the low cunning of the soulless hustler. The stage is set for a showdown, as Eddie is forced to confront the Frankenstein's monster he's unleashed. What begins as a fascinating portrayal of pool-hall low-life mutates midway into a morality play of typical Scorsesean themes – guilt and redemption.

Filming began early in 1986 after a year of endless fine-tuning of the screenplay and a cohesive two-week rehearsal period, 'with actors working,' Newman commented, 'as we used to in live television, back in the stone age'. To keep the budget within the $13 million limit set by Disney both stars took a wage cut. Scorsese briefly toyed with the idea of shooting in black and white, but backers Touchstone, Disney's adult arm, objected strongly. Scorsese shot at a spanking pace, finishing in forty nine days and ahead of schedule, a testament to Scorsese's meticulous preparation and organization prior to production. Despite the frenetic work rate it was a playful set, with Newman credited as keeping spirits light (Cruise and Newman held a competition every day on set to see who could tell the worst jokes). Cruise would deferentially refer to Newman and Scorsese as 'Sir' for the first month; though clearly a by-product of his fine upbringing it soon began to annoy his collaborators: 'I mean, I'm old,' said Scorsese, who'd resort to clobbering Cruise to make him stop, 'but I'm not *that* old!' So the story goes, Coppola was reduced to a similar strategy. Tom Cruise is famously courteous, as Tony Scott recalls: 'Tom is frighteningly polite. He's so nice he's sick' – which is amazing considering his status and wealth. 'Manners aren't developed. They're what you come from,' he once said. But you have the sense his demeanour is controlled, like everything else, well practised and programmed.

The film opened to a divided critical reception in America. Never intended as a direct sequel to *The Hustler* critics couldn't help but raise unfavourable comparisons with Robert Rossen's monochrome classic. Nevertheless, it attracted huge publicity – articles appeared in everything from women's weeklies to *Playboy* and the sport of pool suddenly came alive again across America. For Scorsese the movie proved his first commercial success since *Taxi Driver*, rehabilitating him with Hollywood after a string of stiffs. Like Felson he'd risen from the ashes to prove himself a player yet again. It's undeniably a Scorsese picture: urban – not New York this time but a succession of decaying middle American towns and their seedy pool halls, save the final showdown amid the plastic garishness of tourist clogged Atlantic City; violent – not like *Mean Streets*, for the violence is all psychological, implosive rather than explosive; and bleak – in retrospect Scorsese would have preferred to make it tougher and bleaker, but he'd achieved his most accessible picture to date without compromising his gritty style.

For Newman, for whom the movie was very much a star vehicle, it was a huge personal triumph. 'It's about time!' shrilled Bette Davis upon announcing his Oscar victory, for, shamelessly, he had been overlooked on six previous occasions. 'I was thrilled,' Cruise said later, 'when he got it for our movie.' Curiously, after all that waiting, always being a bridesmaid never a bride, Newman never turned up on the night to collect his Oscar. This wasn't the first or last time Cruise's elder co-star would steal the lion's share of the critical glory. Cruise, as always, is diplomatic and philosophical about this potentially tender issue. 'When you act with very good people, it's natural that they get noticed, and they should be rewarded. Anyone should, who does a good job.' Newman showed genuine remorse that an Oscar nomination hadn't been forthcoming for his co-star, in spite of the misguided efforts of Cruise's then publicist Andrea Jaffe to start hyping him for a supporting actor Oscar even before the film opened. In a telegram Newman offered his commiserations, adding: 'If I win, it's ours as much as mine because you did such a good job.' Cruise had the telegram framed on his New York apartment wall, though he'd have preferred an Oscar on the mantelpiece. At the 1994 Oscar ceremony it was obvious to the watching millions that Cruise and Newman had remained good friends when Tom presented his old mentor with the Jean Hersholt Humanitarian Award and in a show of genuine warmth and love, unnatural in a town as false as Los Angeles, gave the old-timer a hug.

As for Cruise, it's amusing in retrospect to see what an absolute baby he looks in his first real 'grown-up' film. By the time of *Rain Man*, the slightly chubby, gawky kid of *Risky Business* had gone, to be replaced by a new Cruise – handsome and full of confidence and inner assurance. *Rain Man* would be his graduation from the boyish image that first made him a star, but it was the image-stretching role of Vincent that first catapulted him out of the teen-movie ghetto, legitimizing him in a town that too often disposes of its young talent for the next hot star. As *Newsweek* argued, 'Anyone who doubted his seriousness as an actor will have to think again after seeing this whirlwind display.' *Color* prompted the best reviews of his so far short career: 'Cruise reveals himself to be an actor of some depth, communicating the arrogance of innocence with undeniable charm' – *Sunday Times*; 'Cruise is remarkably good. The teen dream is a real actor' – *People*; 'Cruise's is a full out, show-stopping, frenzied perform-ance' – *Cinema Papers*; 'The film's revelation is Cruise – it's a loose, surprisingly vulnerable performance. Cruise is almost the best thing in the movie' – *Village Voice*. Cruise played Vince with a subtlety and panache few believed him capable of, utterly convincing in his graduation from innocent to hustler. In the scene where he struts around the pool table high on his own brilliance, singing along and preening to *Werewolves of London* as he casually pots every shot, he's his own cheerleader. While no demonstration of great acting it oozed star quality. Yet for all Cruise's dynamic sassiness and exuberance, it's Newman you watch. Effortlessly graceful and charismatic, he is a master who even in moments of stillness commands the screen. Cruise's quest for more challenging and serious roles started here, although you wouldn't have thought so with his next choice.

'Tom was very concerned about showing his arse'
          — Roger Donaldson on *Cocktail*'s naff sex scenes

Nineteen eighty-six was *the* year of Tom Cruise; no one else got a look in. *Top Gun* opened in May, *The Color of Money* later in the autumn, and he was named America's top box-office attraction, beating Eddie Murphy and Sylvester Stallone, an honour he reclaimed the following year. Furthermore, he got married. What else was there for the man to do, save conquer Everest? Having achieved stardom he promptly vanished from the celluloid earth. It was not of his own doing, for Cruise, who committed to *Rain Man* around Christmas 1986, found himself snarled up in a script development process that dragged on for nigh on two years. The year he wasted in London shooting *Legend* seemed minor by comparison; then, at least, cameras were rolling. This time he was gridlocked in a succession of meetings, albeit with a parade of peerless pros; when you're sitting around a table with the likes of Hoffman, Spielberg and Pollack you're not entirely wasting time. This said, one of the surest box-office draws in the United States was, well, just hanging around waiting for something to happen, and for a man who is happiest when working this stalemate was driving him crazy. His patience eventually snapped and in an act of foolish desperation he decided to make *Cocktail*, a film aimed so brazenly at the multiplex millions of middle America as to be embarrassing. On paper it all seemed quite promising. Director Roger Donaldson was hot after working with Kevin Costner on the thriller *No Way Out*; Tom Hanks and Don Johnson had supposedly voiced interest in what was intended as an 'interesting little art film' (Cruise's words), a commentary on materialistic eighties values. The script by Heywood Gould (based on his own novel) had been hanging around Hollywood for some years when Jeffrey Katzenberg, believing he had an eighties *The Graduate* on his hands, pounced on behalf of Touchstone, the company behind

Color. But the blinkered Disney regime's insistence on audience-friendly movies turned a potentially interesting muck-rake on yuppie ideals, an alcoholic's *Shampoo*, into a glossy, lightweight beefcake vehicle. Shrewd and soulless instead of savage and biting, it's the cinematic equivalent of solitary confinement.

With just two weeks of preparation, Cruise threw himself with characteristic drive into extensive script revisions, working particularly hard to tighten up the film's love story. 'Tom Cruise is high-priced talent,' said producer Robert Cort, who paid his star $4 million, 'but he's fair-priced talent. There are a lot of guys getting more money than Tom who don't deserve it.' Cort, in a *Radio Times* interview in October 1989, ranked Cruise as the biggest star of his generation. 'If we had made *Cocktail* 50 years ago the actor I would have chosen for this role would have been James Cagney. I think he has that same chin-out, come-hit-me quality. And that smile. Tom is the closest thing to Cagney that exists today.'

Cruise plays Brian Flanagan, a would-be yuppie, a willing innocent seduced into a fast-track lifestyle by veteran bartender Bryan Brown. Much like Eddie Felson, he acts as mentor, teaching the ingenuous go-getter all the tricks he knows. Together they create a ludicrous vaudeville act behind the bar, flipping spirit bottles in the air and strutting to the interminable clatter of the movie's rock soundtrack. All the way through, Cruise as Flanagan does nothing more than smile and show off his suntan, sleeping with more female clients than he serves with drinks. Women really are treated disgustingly in this film. They don't even get the luxury of a raw deal. In one scene Flanagan boasts he bedded a woman for a bet. Was this a conscious attempt to make Cruise come over as less lovable? It's actually a testament to Cruise's screen charisma that his charm can transcend playing such a jerk. Donaldson takes the shallow side of Cruise's personality to the absolute limits. *Cocktail* is old-fashioned chauvinistic claptrap. As *Time Out* succinctly put it, 'If a visitor from Mars needed a crash-course in sexism, this would serve. A terrible advertisement for heterosexuality.' The term AIDS had as yet not entered the vocabulary of these film-makers. Cruise's sexual pursuits were castigated by the press for setting a bad example to his young fans.

One got the feeling that Cruise had much more fun making *Cocktail* than we will ever have watching it. Having trawled the

bars of New York for several weeks for the purposes of 'research',
he then trained properly at a bartending school with John Bandy, a
flashy Los Angeles barman. He slogged hard at making the
technical aspects of his role seem like second nature, aware that in
order to get at the very core of Flanagan's character he needed to
understand the environment in which such a man operated. Cruise
could soon pour like a pro (tossing ice cubes into a glass behind his
back was a speciality) and decided to test his prowess by
moonlighting as a bartender at a chic restaurant. 'It's like a war.
People are just all over you. You have to control the crowd –
otherwise they'll eat you alive. The end of the night after I
worked, I was wired!' Bandy was impressed with both Cruise and
Brown. 'They were pretty good. They really worked at getting it
right.' Both actors had a side bet as to who would drop the more
bottles. 'I dropped two more than Bryan. I dropped seven and he
dropped five. He won.' Cruise learned fast the finer points of bar
politics: always serve the girls free drinks – that always fills the
place with guys; if a girl's on a date, make her boyfriend feel like a
million dollars – the better he feels, the bigger the tip you're going
to get. That's what it's all about, tips – money. It's a film crudely
stuffed with eighties values, yet it embodies Cruise's favourite
theme, that of the cool jerk who undergoes a radical personality
transplant by discovering moral values that transcend personal
ambition and monetary gain. It's all so horribly predictable from
scene one: you just know that by the time the credits roll Cruise is
destined to end up with the loot, the girl (settling for a poor girl
she, surprise surprise, turns out to be an heiress), a glittering
career – and with his morals intact.

Cocktail was justifiably slated on both sides of the Atlantic.
'Cocktail has no reason for being other than to market the Cruise
charm like a cheap celebrity perfume' – Time; 'Don't even
contemplate seeing this crass star vehicle. A sobering experience'
– Sunday Times; 'Everyone plays dumb to make Cruise look like a
brain' – Village Voice; 'Cocktail is an astonishing blend of macho
posing, melodramatic cliche and bad acting. As such, it is
perversely entertaining and unintentionally hilarious' – Monthly
Film Bulletin. Indeed after sitting through Cocktail most people
were in need of a stiff drink. The film's critical lambasting was
made all the more ironic given comments made by Donaldson to
Premiere in July 1988, near the time of its release. 'I've always felt
that Tom was one of those actors whose abilities exceeded the

material he had to work with. They haven't been movies where people have said, "This guy is Oscar material." Know what I mean? That quality that makes him so magnetic to the audience hasn't been exploited in a movie where Tom was taken seriously as an actor. And I think this piece could well do that.' Donaldson's effort was later dubbed 'worst of the year' by Hollywood's Golden Raspberry Foundation and by an *LA Times* nationwide poll of critics. And yet, remarkably, the Cruiser's reputation remained intact; if anything it was enhanced by the fact that his smile alone could carry such tosh past the $70m bracket.

By this stage, however, a Cruise movie was virtually critic-proof, and in some cases that was just as well. But the film's artistic failure left him bitter. 'What were some of the mistakes of that one?' he pondered to *Rolling Stone* in January 1990. 'Those are some of my secret pains.' One can understand the attraction of this project for Tom, since he's the centre of attention throughout and is given free reign to exhibit his boyish appeal. Cruise is typically likeable and embarrassingly exhibitionistic. His impromptu poetry readings to packed bars recall the serenading of McGillis in *Top Gun* and the Y-front *Top of the Pops* routine from *Risky Business*. That isn't enough, however, to camouflage a remarkably superficial and exploitative piece of Hollywood trash. Characteristically he remained gracious in defeat, unwilling to name guilty parties and still able to laugh it off as a bad dream. Even the film's setting was ridiculous. The interiors were shot in Toronto and yet the bar is supposedly a slice of hip Manhattan. What's more, the clientele have about as much style as a kipper tie. 'I never believed I was in New York. It was just not the night scene in New York.' For someone who wields so much control on a movie set, why didn't he stand up and say something, go over to the production designer and ask if he's living on the same planet? Cruise attended an early screening with Mimi and watched squirming with embarrassment. The memory still makes him chuckle. 'You sit there and you go, "What the hell happened?" When we saw it on the screen, we go, "What the fuck is that? What the hell was that?" ' Ultimately it was just another learning experience, and it pains him that people think just because a film bombs you don't work just as hard. 'I worked my ass off on that movie.' It was a mistake, of which he's made remarkably few, a critical custard pie in the face. Maybe that's the point: you simply dust yourself off and get out there and try it again.

9 The Cruise Women

'A magnet for women'

— Tony Scott on Cruise appeal

Everybody remembers their first kiss, those awkward adolescent fumblings in the dark and their first carnal conquest. Tom Cruise's indoctrination into the opposite sex was the dream of a million teenagers. Alas, he was too sexually immature to exploit the situation.

Tom felt monstrously inadequate growing up; self-consciousness about his size, combined with an acute natural shyness, made him flustered and nervous around girls. He confided in his sisters, then approaching the age of sexual awakening. Lee Anne's girlfriends had begun experimenting with boys and needed someone to practise their kisses on – Tom was just the cutest little guy they'd ever seen. So Lee Anne invited them over to teach her brother about romance. Tom would return eagerly from school, sprint up the stairs into the bathroom where he'd sit upon the sink and be smothered with kisses. 'They taught me how to French kiss when I was eight years old. The first time I almost suffocated. I was holding my breath.' But it took days to wipe the grin off his face.

'Whatever you think, you've never arrived'
—Geraldine Page's advice to Rebecca DeMornay

The girl wore her blonde hair classically straight, framing a smooth whey-pale complexion that had never known a sun tan – beautiful enough to stop rush-hour traffic. Striding up to him she whispered secretly in his ear: 'You know what this is? This is the big chemistry test. We got to get some chemistry going fast.' Cruise laughed and asked for her name. Two hundred girls had been interviewed by Paul Brickman for the role of heavenly whore Lana by the time Rebecca DeMornay, an actress with no previous experience except a walk-on in a flop picture, came through the door. In the final touching scene of *Risky Business* Joel asks Lana where she thinks they'll be in ten years' time. Her reply is prophetic. 'We're both going to make it, big.'

Despite their torrid love scenes it wasn't until after filming wrapped that Cruise and DeMornay began a passionate real-life affair, setting up home together for two and a half years. 'During the film we did have a strong affinity for each other,' said DeMornay. 'But it was, like, not the time.' On the set both stars initially shared a love-hate relationship, to such an extent that Cruise, adamant DeMornay was miscast, apparently ordered her dismissal. Today the actress would no doubt be sent packing, but then the famous Cruise clout was just a glint in his eye. Told to get on with it and stop whingeing, Cruise returned two days later informing the producers he no longer needed his hotel room, he'd moved into DeMornay's. Problem sorted. Nice story, but not true. They didn't jump into bed straight away: what happened was a truce which led to genuine friendship and ended in Cruise's first serious romance. Rebecca had reasons, beyond the purely physical, for feeling strongly attracted to Tom. His peripatetic childhood was very like her own and both had been young and vulnerable when their parents separated. Hers was a family destroyed before she was old enough to understand the consequences – a father (Wally George, who went on to win notoriety as a right-wing TV talk-show host) who deserted them, and a mother who remarried only to be widowed within three years. Rebecca had lost a second father before she'd reached her sixth birthday. 'There's definitely something different about kids who come from broken homes,' DeMornay told *Rolling Stone* in June 1986. 'They have this sort of searching quality, because you're searching for love and affection if you've been robbed of a substantial amount of time with your parents. I think that's true of Tom.'

Born in 1962 in California, but raised just about everywhere else, DeMornay's mother, whom she has described as 'sort of a bohemian vagabond,' loved to travel, whirling her children through Germany, France, Italy, Romania, Mexico (where Rebecca almost died from a bleeding stomach ulcer), Hungary, Greece, Jamaica and England for sojourns of varying duration.

Sometimes a school was found for Rebecca, sometimes not. Akin to Cruise, the legacy of all this was lifelong insecurity (little wonder she was in therapy for much of her twenties). Forever on the move but desperate to fit in, she'd strive to adopt the language, accent, style and clothing of whatever country they were passing through. It's curious that whereas Cruise is always on the move and dislikes being in the same place too long, for DeMornay the effects of her nomadic childhood had the opposite effect. 'I seek stability all the time and I'm very rooted to my home.'

Rebecca's unorthodox education got going with a few terms at the radical boarding school Summerhill in Suffolk in the late sixties, a time when anarchist liberalism ruled over common sense. The premise was complete freedom without licence. One did whatever one wanted, so long as nobody got hurt. There she enjoyed sexual liberty and personal responsibility. She remembers one afternoon in the art room when boys and girls tore off their clothes, threw powder paint at each other and ran out into the sun naked. The mind boggles at what they got up to in biology. Aged twelve, Rebecca was enrolled at a college in Kitzbuhel, Austria, where no one spoke a word of English. She graduated *summa cum laude* in philosophy, mathematics, Latin and spoke fluent German and French. Rebecca returned to England, alone this time, determined to make it big as a pop singer in London. She lived in an Acton bedsit, supporting herself in the classic actor's tradition by working the graveyard shift at an all-night café.

After a year of failure the eighteen-year-old retreated to Los Angeles, feeling a foreigner in her own country after so many years away, but determined to become an actress. While studying at the Lee Strasberg Theater Institute she responded to an ad which read, 'Zoetrope seeks unusual people'. It led to an apprenticeship with Francis Ford Coppola and one line in the disastrous *One from the Heart*. Then came *Risky Business*.

Cruise's fledgling fame and the intrigue of his relationship with DeMornay fanned the flames of public curiosity. *Paparazzi* stalked them outside their New York hotel, their names regularly peppered the gossip columns and *People* magazine asked if they'd pose for a cover. In the league table of Hollywood's most glamorous young couples, they were coasting it. 'He is a lovely guy,' gushed DeMornay. 'He is everything you see up there on screen and a whole lot more. A very decent guy. I like virtue in a guy, who at the same time is mischievous and passionate.' But when Rebecca wasn't wearing her rose-tinted spectacles the obvious was staring her in the face: they'd fallen victim to that common Hollywood disease – professional rivalry. Both were driven and ambitious people, and their relationship was always going to be a hostage to friction and clashing egos. Tom insisted on putting his career first and Rebecca refused to sacrifice hers. 'He had this habit of treating you like a princess one minute and then like a piece of furniture the next. We had a lot of trouble living with two egos under the same roof. I don't think he's got that problem solved yet.' The romance survived through the months of *Legend*-enforced separation, but on Cruise's return there was an explosive bust-up. 'Like everything, people get to the point where you go your separate ways,' revealed Cruise. 'I was just going in a different direction. When you care about someone deeply it's always difficult splitting up. But it wasn't ugly or anything.' According to DeMornay, however, their parting was hardly amicable, and she blames the fact that they weren't mature enough to cope with their problems. It was a classic case of too much, too soon. 'We were both so young,' she told the *Mail on Sunday* in September 1993. 'I did my best to make the relationship work, but our careers were always in the way. Our parting was not a friendly one. I burned the bridge named Tom Cruise. Now we have no contact.'

Eminent critic Pauline Kael had compared DeMornay to Veronica Lake, but mirroring the personal turmoil after the break-up, Rebecca's career, on a high after *Risky Business* took a dramatic nosedive. A series of dud movies followed: *The Slugger's Wife* (rock singer marries baseball player = cure for insomnia), Roger Vadim's notoriously awful remake of *And God Created Woman*, *Feds* and *Dealers*, Britain's answer to *Wall Street*. With such a cheap and tacky c.v. she wasn't even on producers' lists of people they didn't want. Her love life, too, followed in the same tragic footsteps as her film career. After Cruise she mostly dated actors before walking blindly into a disastrous marriage with screenwriter Bruce Wagner that lasted all of ten months. 'It was like two meteors colliding,' she says of it today. 'Very explosive, very painful. Luckily, we are both still alive.' She found solace in the arms of dirgeful crooner Leonard Cohen, some three decades her senior, whose own mournful take on life echoed her own. Famous as the nanny from hell in *The Hand That Rocks the Cradle*, DeMornay's undoubted looks and talent might – or might not – launch her into the same league as a Julia Roberts or Sharon Stone.

After his romance with DeMornay Cruise became the topic of much idle gossip, and was linked with some of Hollywood's sexiest starlets. His name was a permanent fixture on eligible bachelor lists on both sides of the Atlantic. The shy retiring sort, Cruise grew accustomed to the press having declared open season on his love life. 'I don't hide from cameras or anything,' he told *Interview* in May 1986. 'It doesn't bother me. I don't seek out press for the women I'm dating, but if it finds me, it finds me.' Cruise learnt to take this obsessional intrusion into his affairs with refreshing good humour. 'I don't know why people think I'm running around with everybody. A friend told me, "I hear you went out with Daryl Hannah." I said, "I did? How was I?" '

One intense affair involved Heather Locklear. The steamy romance began in 1982 when Cruise met the blonde newcomer at a Hollywood cocktail party. Locklear was struck by the physical charms of Tom and astonished when he asked her out on a date, as she still suffered from insecurity over her gawky schoolgirl looks. Once Cruise made the actress stare at herself in front of a mirror. 'Take a good look,' he said. 'You are beautiful. You have nothing to be insecure about.' Locklear was truly smitten with Tom; he was her first, 'real' love. The couple used to have dinner at each other's apartments, purposely not going out much so they wouldn't be seen. Eventually it was Cruise who called things to a halt, leaving Locklear devastated, but ultimately feeling no animosity towards him, primarily because of what he'd done for her self-confidence. 'I'm sorry it didn't work out, but I owe Tom a lot. I'll always love him. I think you always feel that way about your first,' reminisced Locklear. 'I really figured we could have had something good going. But I lost out on the cutest guy in the world.'

Never one to date the latest bimbo actress or model for cheap publicity or instant sexual gratification – he's monogamous by nature – the Cruise of the mid eighties was still the same loner he'd always been but for very different reasons, his lifestyle then epitomized the yuppie philosophy he so often espoused on film, the pursuit of wealth and success above happiness. Cruise had all the trappings of fame but no one to share them with. Contrary to the stereotype of the hot-blooded young Hollywood star, he would spend evenings alone watching his favourite movies on video

(*Casablanca, Annie Hall*) or cooking pasta or Chinese food, rather than rushing into casual relationships just for the heck of it. Coming from a childhood filled with positive female role models, Cruise respects women too much to indulge in meaningless one-night stands and treats them the way he'd like his sisters to be treated. Once he did succumb, with near disastrous consequences. Tanked up with beer, Cruise was dancing at an LA nightclub with this bombshell of a beauty. It was when he started whispering suggestions in her ear that she pulled the gun out and started waving it in his terrified face, all the time screaming and swearing. Cruise's friends had the good sense to haul him outside quick. Was it a temporary lapse caused by being unduly 'into' the character he was then playing – Woody the teenager in *Losin' It*?

Tom Cruise was twenty-three when he met 39-year-old Cher at a fund-raiser for dyslexia in 1985. Here we see again Cruise latching himself on to partners who've suffered comparable childhood woes. Cher only learnt of her own dyslexia when a doctor diagnosed both the singer and her daughter, Chastity, as being sufferers. There was an instant attraction. 'Have you ever seen a man with a face like that? And a body like that?' Cher reputedly gushed. The tabloids had a field day, with cruel taunts that Cher was old enough to be Tom's mother, and the couple's fondness for very public exhibitions of devotion only made matters worse. Embarrassed perhaps by the toy-boy jibes, Cruise denied the affair. You'd think a star on the make, a friend of one of the world's most glamorous women, would advertise the fact – in bright neon – but tacky self-promotion isn't what Cruise is about. The relationship didn't last long, just three months, and never looked like being serious. After the break-up, however, stories circulated of a crushed Cher who never came to terms with Tom's desertion and now compares all her boyfriends with the Cruiser.

The appeal of Mimi Rogers wasn't altogether different, in that she was another mother figure. Their chance encounter at a dinner party occurred at a propitious moment for Cruise, who was on the verge of stardom with *Top Gun*. The precocious Brat Packer had the world at his feet, but inside, the insecurity of adolescence still held dominion. Dubbed Hollywood's new blue-eyed wonder boy, Cruise lacked confidence and feared how he was going to cope with all the pressures and pitfalls of his new exalted status. Mimi Rogers was to play a motherly role, a guiding hand while the rising actor found his feet. Six years Cruise's senior, Rogers was an already established actress, a sophisticate who had just finished a long relationship with actor Tom Selleck. But Cruise's rise was meteoric, and when he rapidly eclipsed her limelight Rogers felt increasingly pushed to the sidelines. From the moment she started to be known only as Mrs Tom Cruise the marriage was staring doom in the face. Even after the divorce for years she had to contend with being referred to as the ex-Mrs Tom Cruise. She was still harping on about it in 1992. 'I'm waiting for the moment when I don't have to talk about that fucking name anymore. I've had it welded on to mine for too many years now.'

The daughter of a civil engineer and a dance and drama teacher, Mimi Rogers was born in 1956 in Coral Gables, Florida. An exceptionally gifted child, excelling in science and maths, she graduated from high school just prior to her fifteenth birthday to spend the next five years selflessly dedicated to community service – counselling drug-addicts, working in hospital volunteer programmes for the mentally ill and veterans of the Vietnam War. Acting was simply one of many interests (she had childhood ambitions to become either a geologist, a chemist or a physicist) until she joined a theatre group and fell in love with the performing arts. One of thousands of young, ready-to-be-exploited pretty girls who flock to Hollywood every year, Mimi's bewildering ignorance of the difficulties inherent in becoming an actor certainly played to her advantage. The majority of budding thespians have nurtured this passion to act since their formative years, whereas Rogers had been involved in other arenas; she hadn't been through years of lust and desire, of waiting and wanting. 'I don't think I was even aware that millions of people walk into LA wanting to be actors,' she disclosed to *Interview* in December 1987. 'It's probably good that I was so naive. Had I known the odds against me, it might not have worked in my favour.'

That elusive first break arrived in 1981 when Rogers, who had still to land her first professional assignment and didn't even have an agent, won a screen test for Lawrence Kasdan's *Body Heat*. Although she lost out to fellow newcomer Kathleen Turner the audition did wonders for her career. All the agents on whose doors she'd been pounding began returning her calls. When some unknown quantity is suddenly tested for the lead in a major movie everybody in Hollywood sits up and takes note.

A series of cameos on a variety of TV shows (*Magnum, Hart to*

Hart, Quincy), a starring role in ABC's flop TV pilot *Paper Doll* and the evergreen *Hill Street Blues* led to her film debut opposite Harry Hamlin in *Blue Skies Again* (1983), a mediocre baseball-cum-romantic comedy that made no impact at the box office. The actress passed similarly unnoticed in Ron Howard's culture clash comedy *Gung Ho* (1986), though revelled working alongside Michael Keaton and as journalist Christopher Reeve's girlfriend in *Street Smart* (1987).

Rogers had already been through one messy divorce (she married young, aged 21, taking her acting name from her first husband a Scientology counsellor named Jim Rogers) by the time she met an equally emotionally scarred Cruise, who was still smarting from his failed romance with Rebecca DeMornay and clinging to bachelorhood like a lifebuoy in choppy seas. Marriage seemed the furthest thing from his mind. Indeed, he once candidly admitted having never been truly in love before Mimi Rogers and leading a 'pretty lonely' life until his marriage. This view was confirmed by Nancy Armel, a school sweetheart. 'He was always determined to make it to the top. He always said, "I'm never going to get married, my career will always come first." ' And now that that career was taking off, he wanted no distractions, no ties. Having come from a broken home, and witnessed his own parents' failure, he felt cynical about the institution – marriage to him was just a piece of paper that meant two people owned each other. Sadly, at his first attempt, he was proven right. But Cruise was entranced by Rogers, admiring her strength, intelligence and physical beauty, detecting events in her life that mirrored his own. Both were products of broken homes and nomadic childhoods. Rogers was just seven when her parents split up. She and her brother went to live with their father, whose job dictated moving home every year – Detroit, Washington, Miami, Arizona. Each time she had to adapt to new environments, adopt characteristics that would make her feel like she 'belonged', as Cruise had done. Finally the family settled in California when Rogers was in her mid-teens.

As with DeMornay before her, it must have been like attracting like. Cruise and Rogers took their privacy seriously and were shy of the attention they excited. Both called their wedding 'the Project' until it happened quietly and without fuss on 9 May 1987. 'Completely normal,' said Rogers, 'which is what we wanted.' Normal! Scarcely a soul was informed of this impending union, and fifteen or so guests, mostly relatives, who showed up at the house in Bedford, upstate New York, that the couple were renting thought they were attending a party, only to be told at the door it was actually a wedding. It was all rather like a covert military operation to keep the *paparazzi*'s noses out of it and for once the press were caught napping. Even Cruise's own publicist Andrea Jaffe was kept embarrassingly in the dark.

The ceremony was an intimate affair, officiated by a Unitarian minister. Emilio Estevez was best man. Tom and Mimi partially wrote their own wedding vows: even the wedding cake was homemade, baked by one of the Cruise sisters. The honeymoon, if it can be called such, was a business-*cum*-pleasure trip to Los Angeles. It was obvious right from the start that Cruise had no intention of easing up on his career plans. As he later admitted, 'My need to achieve was really great. It took its toll on the marriage.' When news of the marriage broke some girls reportedly wore black armbands to school. Mimi exhibited good humour about being the woman who 'pissed off an awful lot of teenaged girls.' She continued, 'I can't resist kidding them, saying I can get his autograph anytime. You know, "come on, honey, wake up and sign this!" '

They knew from the start they'd have to survive the strains that two ambition-fuelled careers were bound to impose. There was sincere early talk of doing everything possible not to shoot movies at the same time, so that they didn't spend too many months apart, or if that wasn't possible to visit each other's locations. Mimi was by Tom's side throughout the making of his toughest two films, *Rain Man* and *Born on the Fourth of July*, and he admitted he might not have come out the other end of Kovic's life without the keen support she showed. It was going to take planning and foresight and not a little work – this applies to all showbusiness marriages, many of which flounder under the mistaken notion that a relationship can survive constant and prolonged separations. 'We are an 80s couple, we have separate careers,' Rogers gushed to any reporter who'd listen. 'We're determined to make it work that way.' Certainly some things were easier being in the same business. 'Mimi is very secure in herself and very, very understanding.' Business hours in this profession are so erratic it was handy having someone at home who understood, who didn't yell: 'Why do you have to work fifteen hours a day? What do you mean you have to get up at 5.30 in the morning and you're not coming back until midnight? What do you mean you've got to do that with a girl?' 'She is very cool about it,' Cruise said.

They seemed the ideal couple. *Cosmopolitan* 'honoured' them with a frankly unwanted 'Couple of the Month' award in late 1987, and Tom was telling everyone how much he enjoyed married life. They seemed to complement one another, Mimi's sexy exuberance and sparky personality counteracting the conservative image of Tom. And they shared a great passion for green issues, serving on the board of the Earth Communications Office, an environmental group that includes the obligatory roster of celebrities, visiting the Amazon jungle in Brazil to witness first hand the depletion of the rain forest, even limiting the water pressure in their sinks and toilets. In 1990 Cruise committed himself to doing a voice-over for an animated Ted Turner TV show, *Captain Planet*, later backing out due to schedule conflicts: it was an environmentally motivated career move unlike his role as a fossil-fuel-burning race-car driver.

But cracks were appearing – hairline at first, though by the end they were big enough to fly an F-14 Tomcat through. There were heated rows and major differences; Mimi was upset that Tom intended to stay put in his $3 million New York apartment (situated on East 13th Street, one of the most sought after blocks in the city with fab views and rock star neighbours like Keith Richards and Phil Collins) rather than move out to Los Angeles where she felt more comfortable. But there were more fundamental differences: Mimi was a party animal who enjoyed club-hopping with best friend and fellow actress Kirstie Alley, while Cruise, the old soul in a young man's body, preferred spending his evenings at home. Reports began circulating about Mimi's irrational jealousy concerning her husband's horde of young female admirers and sexy film scenes – and US tabloids got a kick out of romantically linking Tom with his leading ladies, which didn't help matters any. At the time Cruise would never have done anything to jeopardize the marriage, but Mimi's unfounded jealousy was undermining it. The couple laughed off such claims, Cruise even hanging one headline he found particularly amusing on the wall of his LA office: 'WIFE JEALOUS' it read. I doubt if he did the same for another headline which appeared not long after: 'DIVORCE FOR TOM CRUISE'.

Not long after the marriage, it seemed Rogers might follow in the wake of her husband's meteoric success, when Ridley Scott offered her the role of a Manhattan heiress stalked by a psychopath in his glossy thriller *Someone to Watch over Me*: it made up for losing out on *the* female role of that year, Norman Bates's unhinged sister in *Fatal Attraction*, which went to Glenn Close. For about ten days she was the hottest thing in Hollywood. Industry insiders were tipping her as the star for the nineties, intelligent, beautiful, classy, cultured and discreetly sexual, a lady-in-waiting for the Michelle Pfeiffer/Kim Basinger roles and heiress to Meryl Streep. Alas the movies that followed, most of which were dire made-for-TV affairs, did nothing to advance her career, and she finally resorted to the Hollywood equivalent of the elephant's graveyard: a fitness video, this one for expectant mothers. It was at the video launch in August 1994 when Rogers announced she was expecting her first baby at age thirty-nine by long-term boyfriend producer Chris Ciaffa.

Shoved to the sidelines Mimi watched as her husband's career took off like a jet fighter, while hers came to resemble a runaway golf cart. Was she jealous of Cruise's success? Certainly she detested living in his shadow. Fiercely independent, she promised that her fame would come from merit and not his connections. Rogers dreaded the humiliation of hearing some producer say, 'Wow, we're really interested in Mimi for this movie – and, hey, Tom would be great in the lead' – 'I was armed and ready to rip out the throat of anyone who tried to do that.' Relations between them became increasingly strained, and rumours of heavyweight rows made good copy. Despite occasional attempts to revive the once ardent commitment and showbiz friends like Newman and Estevez urging the couple to kiss and make up, the marriage was frankly and firmly imperilled. The final death blow came in the autumn of 1989; Cruise met and fell in love with Nicole Kidman. Racked with guilt, Tom would occasionally move out of their LA mansion to stay with friends, but always returned, at least for the time being. US tabloids painted a different picture, claiming it was Mimi who booted Cruise out after one blazing row too many. By now it was obvious to those close to the couple and Hollywood at large that what had been deemed the perfect union was irretrievably in jeopardy – not even marriage guidance counselling, arranged by Scientologists, worked. Their age difference was never an issue, for Cruise preferred more mature women who were emotionally in tune with his older-than-his-years personality, and who, given his disrupted upbringing, offered security and comfort. But when the callow, uncertain youth of a

few years before became a man, confident, talented and at home
with his success, it seemed he outgrew the wife who'd played such
a significant part in that change – the wife who, Cruise said, had
given him the emotional strength to take bigger risks with his
career. It had been a relationship based on the shakiest of
foundations – a mother complex. 'I can't help but compare all
women to my mother and sisters,' he once admitted. 'I've always
looked for their qualities and strength in other women.' And the
Cruise perfect woman? She's got to be sexy, in mind and body,
intelligent, independent, and strong enough to stand up to him, to
be an equal not a dependant. His chaotic childhood taught him to
be self-sufficient and Cruise has always admired women who
pursue their own careers. 'I don't want someone living for me and
depending on me for everything.'

Tom was not with Nicole when he and Mimi decided on a
divorce. They had drifted apart and finally realized their lives
would be better if lived separately. It was a cold and clinical end to
three years of marriage. Cruise would never stay together for the
security, in relationships or even in business. If something's not
working you've got to face it and have the strength to move on. It
was a heartbreaking decision and left him emotionally in tatters.
Yet to the press Cruise remained stupefyingly upbeat and
enthusiastic about Mimi. 'I couldn't imagine being without her or
being alone. I care about my wife more than anything in the world.
She's my best friend. I love her.' Thus he spoke to *Rolling Stone* in
the same month he filed for divorce (January 1990). Or this to
Time magazine in the month he officially separated from Mimi
(December 1989): 'The most important thing for me is I want
Mimi to be happy' – all of which sounded like the last words of a
condemned man.

In the face of tabloid tales of an imminent split Tom gamely
continued denying there was anything wrong in the Cruise/Rogers
homestead right up to the bitter, sticky end. But journalists don't
take kindly to being made fools of and the editors of the magazines
in question were livid over Tom's misleading behaviour. What
Cruise tried to do, of course, was conserve some modicum of a
private life. But he should have come clean earlier and the US
media rapped his knuckles for it. *Newsweek* even ran a piece
entitled 'The Great Tom Cruise Cover-Up', which said it all.
Gossips claimed the split was caused by the couple's inability to
have children and that both had undergone intensive fertility

treatment. Was that true? Mimi waited three years before having her say, declining a good few tempting offers to spill the beans earlier because her divorce settlement included a silence clause. In the March 1993 issue of *Playboy*, she broke her silence sensationally, mouthing off about her ex-husband while displaying so-called artistic snaps of her body. 'Tom was seriously thinking of becoming a monk. It looked as though our marriage wouldn't fit into his overall spiritual need. And he thought he had to be celibate to maintain the purity of his instrument. Therefore it became obvious that we had to split. My instrument needs tuning.' Not ideal PR for Hollywood's hottest sex symbol. Rogers hastily claimed on TV's *The Tonight Show* that it had all been one big joke. She even wrote to *Playboy* informing them that her remarks were 'totally playful and completely in jest'.

At the time of the divorce in 1990 Cruise issued a press statement saying: 'While there have been positive aspects to our marriage, there were some issues that couldn't be resolved, even after working on them for a period of time.' The clinical words suggested a certain amicability to the divorce. Understandably family life, for a kid whose own family disintegrated, is crucially important. 'You can have everything in the world but without the love of a family you're a pretty empty person,' he philosophized. It's a particularly bitter pill to swallow, then, that his own marriage should suffer the same fate as his parents'. And the price of love? Rogers bagged the house in Brentwood, west Los Angeles, and a multi-million-dollar jackpot settlement. Just as well money doesn't matter to Cruise. Asked for his feelings on the subject today, Cruise's reply came ready-frozen. 'It was a long time ago. I really don't think about it.' And Rogers is equally frank. 'It's like talking about chalk: dry and boring.'

'Do we smoulder together? I should hope so!'

—Nicole Kidman

A private screening of the blistering Australian thriller *Dead Calm* would change Tom Cruise's life. He couldn't keep his eyes off the bewitching image of the tall, willowy, frizzy-haired female lead, and strayed only to lean across to his companion and ask, 'Who is that girl?' His friend offered no clue. It didn't matter; Cruise's mind was settled that he'd track her down wherever she was. As his gaze returned to the screen he said with sparkling seriousness, 'I want to make a film with her.' Nicole Kidman was in Sydney, oblivious of such astral machinations, when her agent called with the news that Tom Cruise wanted her in his next film. Kidman's immediate reaction was natural: 'Oh, sure – I don't believe it!' Kidman had seen both *Risky Business* and, more recently, *Rain Man*. 'I thought he was fantastic, an actor I'd love to work with,' she disclosed to *Today* in April 1990. 'If you had told me that not long after that I would actually be working with him I'd never have believed it. I would have laughed at the idea.' Then Tom Cruise was simply a face on the cover of a magazine, a face she thought very attractive. When the offer turned out to be genuine doubts still remained, namely height and the star's world-famous lack of it. Kidman went into the audition thinking, 'They always want the leading actress to be a lot shorter than the leading man and I don't stand a chance with this.'

She was the proverbial ugly duckling, the girl who couldn't get a boyfriend; at school she was considered a shade freakish due to a height that scuffed the heavens and weird, frizzy hair that resembled a storm-ravaged haystack. At age thirteen, Kidman was her present height – 5 ft 10 in – earning her the unfortunate nickname 'Stalky'. Balking at the revolting images she swore mirrors threw back at her, Kidman confided to her equally lofty mother, who tried to console her daughter. 'Don't worry, men like tall women.' Local males preferred the petite and curvy, tanned and blonde type, not pale, carrot-topped bean-poles. 'Who cares about men?' Kidman hit back. 'I'm interested in boys.'

At the age of fourteen, she phoned every agent in Australia until one agreed to represent her. Kidman had already decided on an acting career, discarding previous notions of becoming a lawyer or a barrister or working in journalism, her teenage awkwardness evaporated on stage in the persona of another person. 'Theatre, that was a place where I could go and just be somebody else,' Kidman told *Movieline* in March 1994. 'I was like, "I hate who I am, I hate how I look. I hate how I feel with all these hormones racing through my body." ' But she remained fearful of rejection because of her tall and gangly frame, an insecurity which threatened to poison her adult life. Born in Hawaii to Australian parents – Dr Anthony Kidman, a biochemist and author of self-help books and Janelle, a nurse and literary editor – Kidman was raised in Sydney's affluent northern suburbs and studied ballet from the age of three, on her own initiative. As an impish five-year-old she made her theatrical debut as the innkeeper's wife in the school nativity play. 'I was one of those terrible kids who said everybody else's lines,' she recalled to *Premiere* in June 1992. 'I auditioned all the time and never got parts.' – on account, even then, of her height. She recalls auditions for the eponymous *Annie*, where they measured you at the door; you couldn't be taller than Daddy Warbucks. Not to be outdone she gatecrashed the following year's Christmas pageant in the made-up role of an unruly sheep. 'I wore car-seat covers. I bleated through the whole show, and I got my first laugh. When Mary is rocking the baby Jesus, I went baaa-baaa-baaa – this stupid kid trying to upstage the baby Jesus. I got a laugh, and that was it: "Wow, this is fun!" '

With adolescence came the bonus attraction of meeting boys, and if you were really lucky kissing them onstage. At fourteen one of the drama tutors unknowingly cast her opposite a sixteen-year-old she had a 'major crush on' in a production of Frank Wedekind's *Spring Awakening*. It was in this play, a sustained attack on sexual repression in the late nineteenth century, that Kidman saw her first penis. Girls had to share the dressing room with boys, some of whom were two or three years older, and they had to change in front of each other. One scene involved a group of naked boys whipping themselves with towels, all of whom were totally embarrassed, while the girls were just plain fascinated. 'That's how I first saw a guy naked. It was thrilling! All of us girls would peek at them, laughing. Every night, I looked forward to going to work. I also had a scene in petticoats where I was begging this boy to beat me. It was amazing for me to be dealing with all that stuff at that age.'

Roles in various theatre productions got her spotted by a casting director, which led to feisty participation in a couple of kids' movies now best forgotten: *Bush Christmas* (1982) and *BMX Bandits* (1983). The producers of the latter did, amazingly, tip her for future stardom. She continued her studies in between domestic movies, which came along with reassuring regularity. Making *Windrider* (1986) Kidman fell in love with her co-star Tom Burlinson, an affair which ended after two years when Burlinson suggested marriage. There were no regrets, but 'I wanted to establish my own independence first without having to depend on a man.' Such films were trivial, unmemorable and, luckily for her, scarcely seen outside Australia. She earned far greater applause on television. The critical and popular success of the mini-series *Vietnam*, in which Kidman plays a student who becomes an anti-war protester (shades here of Cruise's Kovic role), resulted in the public voting her the year's best actress and bagged Kidman the Aussie Oscar. She recaptured the same award the following year with one of her most accomplished performances, as a heroin addict in *Bangkok Hilton*. It wasn't long before she was being hailed as Down Under's answer to Sigourney Weaver.

The freckle-faced waif had blossomed into an astonishingly beautiful, intelligent young woman. Her slightly pinched features, thin lips and petite nose, are off-set by her crystal-clear eyes, porcelain complexion and endless legs. Her talent stole the attention of notable luminaries of a flowering Australian cinema like George Miller, director of the violent *Mad Max* series. 'Nicole is not just acting for stardom. She is deadly serious,' Miller told the *Sunday Express* in November 1989. 'When I first met Mel Gibson fresh out of drama school, I had this same gut feeling about him. He had this presence on film one couldn't stop watching. I feel that quality in Nicole.' It was Miller and fellow indigenous director Philip Noyce who gave Kidman the role of Sam Neill's terrorized wife in *Dead Calm*. Her valiant performance as a timid, vulnerable girl-woman haunted by nightmares from her past who uses cunning and true grit to foil her psychopathic opponent proved to be her international breakthrough. A move to Hollywood was almost inevitable, reinforcing a striking independence that was established when the seventeen-year-old overrode well-meaning opposition from her academically inclined parents by leaving school to backpack alone across Europe. She announced one day that she was getting on a plane to Amsterdam. She'd met a Dutch guy and proposed living there with him, strictly platonically; she would share his bed but it was understood from the start that sex was taboo. The 'relationship' lasted on and off for six months. 'My parents are pretty cool. Things were never bad with them, I just said, "I'm doing this. See you later." But it was a big deal because I was so close to my mother.'

Two weeks after the Cruise call Kidman found herself in an audition room with the star, along with the producers, director, the writer and the casting director, all sitting in a row, waiting. She cracked a joke about there being only men in the room: no one laughed. The part in *Days of Thunder* Cruise had in mind for her was that of Dr Lewicki. In a film that treats women as accessories –

there's not much room reserved for them in a sport that's as macho as a beer commercial – she's the obligatory love interest. Her highbrow profession serves as a sop to feminism, and she pops up now and then to put the female point of view, calling Cruise and his ilk infantile egomaniacs. Kidman picked up the script, or the mindless scribblings that passed for dialogue, and began reading, doubtless gritting her teeth. Her strong reading convinced everyone she was right for the part, save Cruise who knew already. 'She was just impressive, very powerful.' Before the day was over, much to Kidman's surprise, she'd got the job – and stolen the heart of the world's biggest movie star: not bad for an afternoon's work. In the flesh, as opposed to celluloid, Cruise viewed Kidman as 'amazingly sexy and stunning. It grew into love and respect.' In the July 1995 article in *Vanity Fair*, he continued: 'I say to myself, thank God I made the right choice in marrying her, and was fortunate enough that she said yes. I knew she was it for me. I absolutely knew – I just knew it. I just knew I couldn't live without her. It's the best decision I ever made.' The instant physical attraction was genuinely reciprocated. 'I thought he was the sexiest man I'd ever seen in my life,' says Kidman. 'So it started on lust.'

Cruise was sure he'd found the person with whom he wanted to share the rest of his life. There are innumerable reasons why it's not easy being the biggest movie star in the world; for one thing it's tough knowing who to trust. In Nicole Tom sensed he'd found a true friend and ally. Kidman's effect on Cruise was to be profound. Her unpretentious, fun-loving, try-anything-once approach to life complemented Cruise's more intense, guarded nature; in her company he seemed to lighten up a bit, not take life so seriously. Cruise has a reputation for being earnest and it's not difficult to see where it comes from, as Cruise explained to *Today* in December 1994. 'Nothing makes you more serious than when your parents get divorced. When you have to watch your mother asking friends for money so you can eat, it's not the most pleasant experience. It leaves a lot of scars on you and you become determined never to let anything like that happen to you again. You see the world differently. That's why I can't let up.' The star of today was forged on the anvil of a tough childhood. In the past he'd never been able to relax or find contentment in anything but his work, defining his life purely in terms of his career – working non-stop, jumping from one project to the next, cracking

off twelve pictures in a relatively short career. At that rate he was
going to burn himself out before reaching his thirties. Even at the
start of his career he was an obsessional workaholic, just as intense
and focused. Now it was as if a whole new life had opened up, as
Kidman's stabilizing influence helped to lessen the angst brought
on by his once overpowering quest for perfection in everything he
did. Indeed she's overtaken Cruise in being the more prolific
worker in the partnership, but then she's still establishing her
career. Even when all the domestic distractions came along
Kidman never lost sight of her own priorities. Mimi Rogers was
the complete opposite, deferring to her husband in the career
department and making it known she'd pass on a big movie if that
meant a long separation. Such strength of independence, far from
turning Cruise off, was one of the qualities he found so attractive
in Kidman.

By close of filming on *Days of Thunder* Cruise and Kidman had
become lovers. Keeping their romance secret from the
ever-inquisitive tabloids wasn't easy, and reports were soon
filtering back of them sneaking off the set for romantic afternoons
alone. Once, after reporting sick, they were later spotted together
at Disney World. In interviews Kidman was cagey about their
relationship, no doubt at Cruise's behest, and scoffed at the
rumours of impending marriage, condemning them all as rubbish.
Yet she milked every moment and every rumour during *Thunder*'s
release in a bid to launch her Hollywood career. Shortly after close
of filming the pair retreated to the Bahamas, out of the glare of the
spotlight, to spend a fortnight alone sleeping romantically in
hammocks, walking hand in hand along deserted beaches and
swimming in crystal blue waters. Their first notable public
appearance together was at the 1990 Oscar ceremony held on 26
March. 'Would you mind going with me?' he asked, not having a
date for the evening. Imagine that, Tom Cruise without a pretty
girl on his arm. At first Kidman refused, no doubt thinking of all
those popping lights and wagging tongues, but then thought, Oh,
what the hell, you only live once! He's my friend, he's nervous and
I'm going to support him. Cruise was up for best actor for *Born on
the Fourth of July*. Everyone, including himself, expected him to
win. His self-confidence was so high that he was the last star to
arrive at the Dorothy Chandler Pavilion in Los Angeles holding
his mother's hand while Kidman held on to his other arm. 'When
he lost I said to him, "So what? You've got the film, you don't

need a statue on your mantelpiece. The film is what is gold. And in twenty years time your children can look back and watch that and an Oscar won't mean anything at all." '

One of Cruise's favourite Hollywood occupations is attending Oscar night. The following year the Cruise and Kidman double act showed up again. Cruise was there to present the best director award. Introduced by Billy Crystal with the words, 'Some people say there are no real movie stars anymore. I say they're wrong. Ladies and gentlemen, Tom Cruise,' Cruise announced the winner as Kevin Costner for *Dances with Wolves*. Cruise and Kidman didn't start dating seriously until after their romance was publicly acknowledged on that first Oscar night. The Hollywood gossip machine was quick to put two and two together; that appearance was all the Tinsel Town tattlers needed to insist the pair were 'an item'. It was all very lovey-dovey, but there was a problem: his name was Marcus Graham and he was Nicole Kidman's lover. They'd met a year earlier in a play and had begun an intense relationship, moving in together. A former soap star Graham watched his career hit the skids, while Kidman was already setting her sights on conquering America. Oblivious of the encroaching Cruise upon what he presumed was his vulnerable and lovelorn Nic, Graham continued their affair via long-distance telephone until the truth of what was happening struck with the force of a hammer when he saw Kidman and Cruise hand in hand at the Oscars. As part of a secret trip Nicole made to Australia to introduce Tom to her parents, the actress made a point of visiting her ex-boyfriend's home, to catch up on how he was doing. Graham refused even to speak to her, however – hardly surprising seeing Nicole had insisted on bringing Tom along.

For the first few months of Tom and Nicole's very public courtship, home was the Hotel Bel-Air in Los Angeles. Now it's a luxury $5 million mansion in Pacific Palisades, California (Arnie and Sly are neighbours), an apartment in Manhattan and a 77-acre estate in Colorado. Not to mention the home in Australia, close to Sydney so that Nicole's parents can spend time with their grandchildren and so that the actress can visit whenever she misses her native land and family, which is two or three times a year.

The couple married on Christmas Eve 1990 at the remote Colorado ski resort of Telluride in conditions of secrecy befitting a tryst between spies. Determined to avoid the media circus his pal Sean Penn's marriage to Madonna stimulated back in 1985 (at least Cruise didn't scrawl FUCK OFF in the snow as Madonna did on a sandy beach to the hovering *paparazzi*) Cruise set aside a month for meticulous pre-planning. Kidman's parents, discreetly couriered out of Australia for the formal 30-minute ceremony, sat tearfully alongside Mary Lee and her daughters as Tom and Nicole, then only twenty-three, exchanged their self-written marriage vows. He was dressed in a black tuxedo and Nicole, with her baby sister as bridesmaid, was resplendent in a white gown.

Evidently Telluride holds a sentimental significance for the couple. Cruise especially considers it a special refuge, and recently has taken steps to become more involved with the local community, attending charity benefits and the like. On their fourth wedding anniversary Cruise flew his wife's parents, with whom he has a good relationship, from Australia for a family skiing holiday at their hideaway lodge in the hills of this celebrity-laden winter wonderland. He spared no expense in treating everyone to private ski lessons and even hired out a whole restaurant for a private slap-up seasonal feast.

'Before I met Tom, I was never going to get married. Never. But he was just the most incredible, unusual man I'd ever met.' At that first meeting on *Days of Thunder* a connection was forged – 'that special connection,' offers Cruise, 'when you recognize your soul mate.' Truly he was smitten, blushing deep red and going all puppyish, observed one journalist who met the star on the set of *Far and Away*, at the very mention of Kidman's name. As Cruise and Kidman toured the world on their perpetual honeymoon roadshow, (soon after the wedding Cruise announced: 'Officially, we will be on our honeymoon for the rest of our lives'), their public displays of affection became well known; necking in movie theatres like love-struck teenagers is a favourite. Cruise's awesome devotion to his wife is also well documented. He simply dotes on her whether it's blandishing her with top designer clothes, sending bouquets of flowers to her trailer on the set of *Billy Bathgate* or buying her a red Mercedes or the odd piece of antique jewellery. Conscious no doubt that a marriage takes work, Cruise is determined not to take his role as husband for granted this time, placing far more emphasis on being together than before. If the couple are apart for more than two weeks at a stretch they'll fly anywhere to spend at least an evening in each other's company. 'Life's too short to endure months of separation,' says Kidman. They work, too, at keeping the relationship fresh and stimulating, refusing to allow parenthood to turn them into premature fuddy-duddies: they still enjoy partying all night or jetting off to Las Vegas on a moment's notice, sharing in everything and forging common bonds all the time. The only inequality concerns their careers, and the general discrepancy between male and female stars' wage packets is highlighted by how much more Cruise earns than Kidman.

Kidman was shrewd enough to realize the double-edged effect her marriage would have on her career. Her association with Cruise right from the beginning resulted in welcome fame, but she worried that, for instance, people would think she got the role in *Far and Away* because of him. Until the marriage, her only American film, *Billy Bathgate*, had been a dud, which doesn't usually qualify you for a starring role opposite Tom Cruise let alone one with equal billing. Michelle Pfeiffer could demand it but for Kidman it was a courtesy. These days, of course, she'd warrant equal billing in her own right. People chose to forget or were plain ignorant of the solid reputation she'd earned in Australia as a dramatic actress. As Mrs Tom Cruise her undoubted abilities became less relevant, and malicious gossip bitched that she only nabbed the big roles because of her husband's star power. The irony is that she probably would have made it without his clout and influence, but by marrying Tom she simply hitched a short-cut ride to stardom. To get the *Bathgate* role, with or without Cruise's help, Kidman spent four hours a day for three weeks studying with a dialect coach to perfect an upper-class New York accent. 'I've been acting since I was fourteen years old,' she defended herself in *Premiere* in June 1992. 'I fell in love with someone who happens to be very famous, and I got married to that person because I love him – so if I can get through this difficult period, then hopefully it will be a bit easier.' While shopping in London once an assistant at Harrods addressed Kidman as 'Mrs Cruise'. Nicole informed him that her name was in fact Kidman. Sympathetically, the assistant asked when they had divorced. The reply he received was Nicole's back as she promptly left the store. Kidman used that wonderful actress Anjelica Huston as a role model: her famous father (director John) and her well-documented affair with Jack Nicholson made it tough for her to be seen as her own person. Kidman seeks and deserves to have her own star identity, even if she has the added distinction of being successfully married to a superstar, much like Joanne Woodward. For too long she was famous for being just Mrs Tom Cruise but eventually she managed to carve out her own niche, moving into contention for top roles without the influence of her powerful husband. She's every bit as driven and focused in the career department as Tom; breathtakingly ambitious, she has always pursued her goals with the relentlessness of a heat-seeking missile. And with that same need to constantly court new challenges, Kidman quickly recognized that she had to push herself as hard as she'd done before in Australia – that's why she made *Malice* and *My Life* back to back and why she hosted *Saturday Night Live* even though the prospect terrified her. Aware that marriage can breed laziness, and the urge to ease off the career pedal, Kidman's out to prove that she's her own woman, with a separate career from Tom. In 1994 they were offered the chance to be on the cover of *Vogue* together; it would have been the first time a couple had graced the fashion bible's cover. 'We've never even done a photo shoot together,' Kidman explained to *Movieline* in March 1994. 'The *Vogue* cover was not of interest, particularly for me because then it looks like I'm riding on his coat tails. I'm over-defensive about it. Which is why we haven't done a movie together since *Far and Away*.' Cruise has always been supportive of her career, and was intensely proud when she won the female lead in *Billy Bathgate*. Hoffman called her personally with the good news. 'Tom was hugging everyone,' Kidman remembers, 'and jumping around the room. He said it was just as if he had got the part.'

They share a kinship for adventure, the pursuit of all things 'outdoors' and to be one with nature. Kidman surprised Cruise by being fully conversant with the kind of macho sports that normally leave women cold, such as boxing and football. In Australia she'd indulged in horse-riding, tennis, wind-surfing (a pursuit Cruise excels in), even kick-boxing. As children Nicole and her sister performed push-ups every day at the behest of their father, a habit she's never grown out of – 'I can do about 50.' Both pursue a full sports life, going on hikes together, swimming with whales off the South American coast, even skydiving. They began skydiving for fun on *Days of Thunder*. For Cruise the pastime dates back to childhood when as a four-year-old he tried skydiving from his roof using sheets as a parachute. 'Buried myself in the mud,' he says. Cruise gifted Kidman a series of skydiving lessons. They've even kissed freefalling, where tabloid camera lenses dare not go. Both find an intense exhilaration hurtling to the earth from 16,000 feet.

'It's an amazing sensation – not as good as sex, but almost,' said Kidman to *Vanity Fair* in July 1995. 'It's like before you go onstage opening night, when you're almost dizzy from adrenalin. I love that feeling.' It's the closest thing to flying. It's also the closest thing to dying – though being Cruise one feels in the presence of somebody to whom nothing bad could possibly happen. Once Cruise was returning from a rafting trip (a Hollywood male-bonding ritual), and his party were making their way to three helicopters they'd chartered to airlift them back to civilization. This one man was terrified of them but reasoned, 'I'm going to get in the chopper that Tom Cruise gets in, 'cause God isn't going to kill him.' That's the way Kidman thinks, too. 'He's got that feeling about him as a person. Even when you get in a race car with him. Or in a plane.' Kidman admits to sharing Cruise's love of that adrenalin rush. 'Tom thinks it's cool that I'm willing to jump out of a plane just to be with him,' but she doesn't share his enthusiasm for racing, even though he taught her how to ride his treasured Harley Davidson. Now that they're parents with responsibilities they have both tried to curb their shared love of danger.

After her forgettable role in *Thunder* Kidman won praise for her edgy, physically uninhibited performance as Dutch Schultz's moll in *Billy Bathgate*. The film flopped big time, enhancing her prospects not one jot. After further sex scenes in *Malice* Kidman surely possessed the most widely seen posterior in Tinsel Town. Some were shocked, at this apparently unmotherly exhibitionism. Kidman couldn't care less; she has no qualms about disrobing for the cameras (she'd done it in *Dead Calm*), providing it's not gratuitous, 'not some director or writer getting his rocks off'. She's been exploited before in a film as a budding actress in Australia and vowed it would never happen again. However, she was a little shocked by how long the camera lingered on her pert behind in *Malice*. Kidman's frank attitude towards nudity is sharply at odds with an increasingly prudish Cruise, then drastically curtailing his on-screen bedroom activities, probably in a bid to jettison his sex-symbol tag and be taken seriously as an actor.

* * *

Ron Howard's face speaks of ice-cream sodas and apple pie, America's boy-next-door (as Cruise himself has been described). Chiefly remembered as the ginger-haired goof from *Happy Days*, he's actually one of Hollywood's major players, having directed a string of hits – *Cocoon, Parenthood, Apollo 13*. Howard's boyish demeanour and charm remain; he is cheerful and spectacularly decent, a man who actually married his high-school sweetheart. Asked why Cruise wanted to work with Howard the first thing out of his mouth was, 'I heard he was a really great man.'

Sure as the Moon, as Howard originally wanted to call his pet project, (other rejected 'chocolate box' titles were *Distant Shores* and *The Irish Story*. On the film set a board was put up on which the crew proposed their own titles. Somebody scrawled 'Tom and Nicole's Excellent Adventure') was a decade in the making, staggering as that might seem given the end result. His idea was inspired in part by the peregrinations of his great-grandfather who'd participated in the Great Land Rush of 1893. Cruise's own great-great-grandfather emigrated to Louisville from Ireland in the mid 1800s. And both Tom and Nicole were to fall irrevocably in love with the country during their stay; returning to Dublin in 1993 to attend a New Year's Eve party at Neil Jordan's home, accompanied by rumours the couple were thinking of buying a property in the area. Originally planned as a low-key Gaelic romp that was to have been made on a minimal budget, Howard started thinking 'big' when Cruise was cast. In the end the film cost $60 million, $12 million of which went into Cruise's pocket.

Howard was in the middle of a shot on *Backdraft*, deep in the heart of Chicago's Chinatown with his cast of fireman studs perched atop a fire truck waiting for him to call 'action'. The phone rang; it was Cruise. 'I gotta take this call,' he yelled over at them. Kurt Russell, the cast's natural spokesman, who'd been playfully giving Howard grief from day one, scented the chance for another swipe. 'Oh, yeah? Who is it?' 'It's Tom Cruise, all right?' said Howard, trying his damndest to look nonchalant. 'Oh, Tom Cruise,' Russell sarcastically hit back. 'Let's everybody take ten, shall we?' Picking up the receiver, Howard didn't believe what he was hearing; Tom Cruise wanted to be in his movie. The actor had always been his prototype for the role of poor Irish tenant farmer Joseph, but as he'd become a bigger and bigger star Howard saw his chances of securing him diminish with each hit movie. Over the years they'd got to know each other quite well and Howard promised himself that if he ever got around to making the movie he'd give Cruise first crack. Seven months after turning down a

role in *Backdraft* Howard sent him a script. Cruise was on the
look-out for a strong romantic vehicle and another joint project for
Nicole and himself. A response was not long in coming. 'I really
love this script. It's magical,' said the actor. 'I'm so thrilled to hear
you say this,' was all Howard could offer. Now came the crunch,
the Cruiser's ulterior motive. After asking Howard who he was
thinking about for the female lead he said innocently, 'Are you
familiar with this actress, Nicole Kidman?' Excited Howard called
his friend and business partner Brian Grazer. 'Wow,' he began,
'Tom really likes this movie, and he mentioned Nicole Kidman.'
Howard acknowledged the fact he didn't know who she was, but
promised to familiarize himself with her work, when Grazer
butted in with an audible sigh. 'If you just turn on the TV or read
the paper you'd see that Tom and Nicole are the hottest couple in
Hollywood!'

True to form Cruise attacked his role, courageously plunging
head-first into tackling a British accent. Beware all American
actors who enter here: Dick Van Dyke's infamous cockney accent
in *Mary Poppins*, three decades on, is still held up to ridicule and
Kevin Costner's Robin Hood was more Hollywood than
Sherwood. That said, English actors can be just as feeble at
impersonating Americans; Kenneth Branagh's Yank in *Dead
Again* was about as convincing as Bob Hoskins's private dick in
Roger Rabbit; and Michael Caine's southern drawl in *Hurry
Sundown* could be seen as England's revenge for Dick Van Dyke.
Prior to rehearsals Cruise opened up to both Ron and Nicole. 'I
just have no idea what I'm doing,' he told them. Cruise felt
embarrassed to be attempting an Irish accent in Ireland. It was
Howard's insistence on intensive rehearsal time that allayed
Cruise's concerns, and he brought in a dialect coach who spent
months working with Cruise to perfect Joseph's west Kerry lilt.
And some weeks before shooting, to set the mood, they flew over
to Ireland to soak up the culture. Still fearful, Cruise insisted on
hiring an additional on-set dialect coach at his own expense further
to hone his accent – or, rather, to perfect middle America's idea of
how a nineteenth-century Irish tenant farmer talked. Universal
were extremely concerned that the film be intelligible to a broad
spectrum of the US audience. In spite, or perhaps because, of all
this vigorous lingual manoeuvring, Cruise's accent, or lack of one,
was gleefully hammered by the critics. It must have galled him,
considering the who-can-ride-faster fiasco, more of which later,

that Kidman scraped through the ordeal relatively unscathed.

'Never work with your wife,' Howard once advised. Apart from the fact it reeks of nepotism, working so closely with your partner is apt to cause friction. If you start to bring your private life into your work life there's a danger of muddying the waters. It was always going to be a challenge to direct a couple so obviously in love that they could barely keep their hands off each other. *Far and Away* was in many ways a honeymoon project, a togetherness movie. Modern Hollywood marriages haven't been properly exploited until newly-wed bliss is sanctified by making a movie together, despite the fact it became their *Shanghai Surprise* – co-starring in a historical epic could well become grounds for divorce in southern California. 'Ron Howard centres on the spectacle of Cruise and Kidman flirting and jockeying for the camera. It's like a Burton-Taylor vehicle retooled for teenyboppers' – *New Yorker*. The passion and freshness of their relationship was tailor-made for Howard's Irish fable, sometimes too much so. Their ardour was at such a fever-pitch that one of the crew suggested dousing them with a cold bucket of water. Howard certainly used the couple's intimacy to his advantage. 'When Tom is looking at Nicole,' the director told *Empire* in August 1992, 'It is very easy for him to remember the first time he really sensed her beauty or her magnetism and I think the same thing is true for Nicole of Tom.' One of Kidman's concerns was whether she and her husband could maintain the required sexual tension for two hours. How was their big screen kiss going to spark off the desired fireworks when the public knew they were lovers in real life? Howard came up with the D-Day plan of stopping his star pair kissing for twenty-four hours; in the end they just went ahead and shot the scene with some of the crew standing by the video monitor giving marks out of ten.

Early on Howard approached both of them, warning about pressures the marriage would be under by working together. 'Maybe you ought to work through me as much as possible,' he said. 'If you've got something you think about the other person, whisper it to me.' Howard the mediator often saw himself cast as Howard the marriage guidance counsellor. The last thing he wanted was for Tom and Nicole to go off playing married couples, directing each other and cat-fighting. He did witness, however, the extraordinary rivalry that existed between the newlyweds. Cruise's obsessive competitiveness, demonstrated by his willingness to take

punches from beefy and very, very tough stuntmen in the boxing
scenes. Cruise described *Far and Away* as one of his most
physically exerting films. As a bare-knuckled fighter Cruise beats
seven bells out of every opponent thrust in front of him, despite his
medium stature, without so much as a broken tooth. Not
surprisingly burly stuntmen were wary at first to let fly at Cruise;
they were all looking at each other with expressions that said, 'I'm
not going to be the one who breaks Tom Cruise's nose.' Close-ups
were essential if these moments were to carry any impact, but
through the lens it looked plainly obvious that fists were missing
the Cruiser's head by a mile take after take. Finally the
exasperated star seized the initiative and demanded that the
stuntmen knock him about for real. 'Look, hit me and let's just get
the damn thing over. Just stick it in there once and we move on.'
Cruise took a brutal pounding. A squeamish Kidman could
scarcely watch from off-camera, at one point pulling Howard aside
asking for it to be stopped. For ten days afterwards his body was
racked with pain. Cruise's innate rivalry let up not one jot. Even
when dealing with his wife; if anything it increased, particularly
during the shooting of the land rush sequence, which involved
riding. First-timer Cruise, who had only had five lessons before
climbing into the saddle, would ask the animal wranglers how fast
seasoned rider Nicole went. 'About thirty-five miles an hour,'
they'd reply. Kidman rode past him and said in his face,
'Thirty-five!' Then it was Cruise's turn and he went hell for
leather, asking the wranglers on his return, 'How fast do you think
I was going?' They'd mutter, 'You must have been going about
forty miles an hour.' His face looks as if he's just won an Olympic
gold; turning to Nicole he shouts, 'YES!' Kidman, having lost her
own fear of speed, responded in kind by cranking up the horse
power and badgering the wranglers about how fast she clocked in
at compared to Cruise. This competitive spirit is at full blast all the
time. When they play games together (chess, backgammon – 'I
whip his ass at backgammon,' hails a proud Kidman) it's not for
the pleasure of it but for the winning. Kidman taught her husband
how to play squash; three months later he'd mastered it and was
trouncing her on the court. Perhaps this is one of the reasons why
the Cruise/Kidman marriage always seems so fresh and alive.
Howard, though, found himself marvelling at their mental com-
posure. 'They were remarkable. How'd they do it? Especially
newlyweds, when they're sorting out all this stuff: I don't think they

really lived together particularly, and they got married. Only on a couple of occasions did I have to sort of be Uncle Ron, you know, "Now, now, kids." '

Far and Away marked the beginning of Cruise's Greta Garbo period, a reclusiveness that looks like lasting a long time. Crew hands went to inordinate lengths to keep Mr and Mrs Cruise out of the public gaze during their eight-week Irish sojourn. Aides had orders to keep the stars' movements secret, as if this was some papal visit. Actually the couple were warned they might make a tempting target for terrorists, so an understandably shaken Cruise reluctantly agreed to have three bodyguards, two of whom were ex-SAS, shadowing their movements. Most of their time was spent inside a huge customized trailer (valued at some $750,000) complete with a fully furnished living room, kitchen, king-size bed and satellite television. Huge black screens were put up to shield a set in the centre of Dublin, and for filming at Kilruddery House in County Wicklow an eight-foot-high brick wall was constructed around part of the vast estate to block the top-secret doings within from passers-by. In Dublin two girls who climbed on to a roof with a video camera had their tape confiscated, and Cruise himself was involved in a row with a pair of students who tried to get autographs and pictures as he was driven on to the set. 'The driver got out and remonstrated with them.' An eyewitness told reporters, 'At one stage Cruise left the car and joined in the argument.' Usually the Irish are quite blasé about stars, 'because they're used to living with big literary names like Yeats and Joyce,' said Irish production manager Seamus Byrne. 'But everyone was interested in Tom and Nicole. There was that bit of the prince and princess about them.'

Cruise plays a turn-of-the-century potato-picking peasant, sporting a gymnasium-trained torso and gleaming teeth. A rebellious spirit, he tries to take a potshot at the English landowner who is responsible for his father's death – only to run off to the United States with the old villain's headstrong daughter. After the botched assassination Joe winds up receiving medical attention on a bed in the posh nobs' mansion, stark naked and unconscious, with a chamber pot covering his modesty. The feisty Kidman can't resist taking a peep, just out of curiosity. 'I saw a rough cut with an audience,' boasted Cruise to *Premiere* in June 1992, 'and they just howled: they were like "Oh, is she ... she's gonna look!" ' Asked what it felt like to have his wife check out his genitals beneath the glare of a seasoned Hollywood film crew, the

Cruiser replied, 'Ahh, the actor's life for me. You got to do what you got to do – anything to make the scene work.' The vital Cruise area was actually covered with a cloth, but on the final take Howard persuaded Tom to remove it, as a laddish jape. When Nicole looked this time her surprised reaction was judged perfect and that's the one Howard used in the movie. When asked later what it was she saw beneath the chamber pot, Kidman replied, with a barely repressed chuckle in her voice, 'Something nobody else will ever see!'

Unquestionably the film's highlight and the only thing that warranted the expense of Panavision Super 70 mm, save the odd panoramic glance at Irish bogland, is the climactic Oklahoma land rush (actually shot in Montana). In this passage the lovers stand up to hundreds of other settlers in the hope of staking a claim to some acreage on the newly plundered Indian territories – how fitting that *Far and Away* was released in the year of the Columbus quincentenary. Howard had trouble sleeping the night before fretting about the safety of his cast and crew, not to mention 800 riders and extras. Fortunately there were only a few minor casualties, though everyone was given little more than these inadequate instructions: 'Get on those horses and just go in that direction. Don't hit anybody and don't get hit. And go as fast as you can.' What an exact science film-making is.

Post-production was arduous, not least three weeks of laborious looping in New York. The sheer technical demands of looping – synchronizing new line readings to the lip movements already caught on camera – are frustrating for any actor. A total of 1,595 separate bits of dialogue needed to be revoiced, a combination of poor volume, on-set noise, some rather dubious accents and Cruise's desire not to overplay his scenes.'As much of a pain in the ass as it is,' he says of the process, 'you do have the opportunity to go back and make the performance better.' The mood in the studio was lightened considerably by games of basketball Cruise would play and win against Howard.

Not even the Cruiser's participation was enough to prevent *Far and Away* joining the other summer blockbusters (*Alien 3, Universal Soldier, Boomerang*) in their lemming-like plunge down the American box-office charts. It says much for contemporary Hollywood values, however, that a film can gross $60 million in the States and yet still be regarded as a turkey. The first indication that Howard's baby was in deep trouble came when it was unveiled at

Cannes in May. Celebrity lustre was supplied by Cruise, who descended upon the festival with Kidman in tow for a memorably dull press conference; he also acted as master of ceremonies at the closing prizegiving bash.

Universal, who squandered millions on a fruitless advertising campaign, made a serious tactical error by releasing *Far and Away* opposite the big guns of *Lethal Weapon 3* and *Batman Returns*. It didn't stand a chance. Almost unanimous critical animosity didn't help either. 'Hatched by folks who take *Doctor Zhivago* very seriously' – *Village Voice*; 'The film lasts 140 minutes, a long time to hide under the seat for fear of seriously damaging your brain cells' – *Guardian*; 'A bland, misguided, well-upholstered bore' – *The Times*; 'A real bimbo of a film, easy on the eye, but a space the size of Wembley Stadium between its ears' – *Daily Mail*. Sheridan Morley of the *Sunday Express* was in a minority of one when he said: '*Far and Away* is the greatest film that John Ford never made. This is one of those great outdoor adventures that remind you what they once built cinemas for.'

Flying in the face of popular trends Howard's foray into period romance was an almighty gamble. The hope was that it would prove an attractive alternative to the staple summer diet of action/fantasy blockbusters, and that a bare-chested Cruise in 70 mm would raise some serious blood pressure among female punters. But did audiences want to see real life husband–wife teams or an unconvincingly healthy Cruise as an impoverished peasant lad? 'It's like watching Tom in a \$60 million school play, where you never forget that he's really the star quarterback and the class president,' wrote one journalist in *Premiere*. His apparent box-office infallibility was going to be put to the severest test. The answer was a resounding no: the cinema-going public didn't want to see old-fashioned historical codswallop. With so much of himself invested in this epic-that-wasn't Cruise's judgement stood in question, though his personal appeal remained untarnished. Cruise would become testy whenever interviewers brought up the less than ecstatic performance of *Far and Away*, even taking time out to hit back at Madonna, who claimed the movie sent her to sleep. 'I don't care what she thinks,' Cruise responded. 'She doesn't like Kevin Costner, she doesn't like me. At least I'm in good company.' Cruise has said he'd like to make another film with Nicole, providing the script was right. In the summer of 1996, Cruise returned to London to star in *Eyes Wide Shut* with Kidman, an erotic thriller about sexual obsession and jealousy directed by Stanley Kubrick. An 'event' picture if ever there was one.

Curiously, after the *Far and Away* débâcle Kidman's career went from strength to strength. The big-budget gangster movie *Billy Bathgate* was essentially a failure, but earned her a Golden Globe nomination as best actress; *Malice* and *My Life* (with Michael Keaton) which might have destroyed any other burgeoning career seemed to slide effortlessly off her slim shoulders. Recently she's become a force to be reckoned with. When Meg Ryan pulled out, Kidman leapt at the chance of playing a murderously ambitious TV anchor woman – 'a Barbie doll gone wrong' in Kidman's words – in *To Die For*. Gus Van Sant, the director of such counterculture movies as *Drugstore Cowboy* and *My Own Private Idaho*, cast Kidman against the wishes of the studio who feared the actress couldn't handle black comedy. Far from it: it was a genre in which she excelled (*Dr Strangelove* ranks among her favourite films). She proved a wonderful comedienne, garnering admiring nods from the critics. And joining in the all-star fun of *Batman Forever*, she played the caped crusader's latest love interest. The offer came quite out of the blue, and so tantalizing was the prospect of playing what is by far her glitziest role yet that Kidman postponed a planned visit home until after filming.

Recently Kidman has taken on the potentially career-making role of free-spirited and high-minded Isabel Archer in a grandiose version of the Henry James novel *Portrait of a Lady*. The film could well propel her from the B-list of Hollywood's most-wanted actresses – the Winona Ryders and Bridget Fondas – into the A-list of $5 million-per-movie divas like Julia Roberts, Michelle Pfeiffer, Sharon Stone and Demi Moore. These are the kind of big-star actresses who in the past got offered everything and whose rejected scripts trickled down to Kidman. She'd read for *Thelma and Louise* but was passed over; the same with *Silence of the Lambs* and *Sleepless in Seattle*. She did her own audition video for *Ghost*, sending it over from Australia, but inevitably lost out, though its screenwriter, Bruce Joel Rubin, cast her later in *My Life*. With Jane Campion (who made 1993's *The Piano*) directing, *Lady* seems destined to become a prestigious movie. As it happened Campion had been waiting for an opportunity to work with Kidman and had already decided to choose her above any other actress. The two met when Kidman was fourteen and had been cast in an amateur movie that Campion (then in film school) was making. Alas her exams were looming and Kidman was forced to pull out. Prior to beginning work on *Lady* Kidman was rummaging around in her parents' house and uncovered diaries that she'd kept from age twelve onwards. Inside one of them was a postcard from Campion that said: 'I think you made the right decision and I hope one day we will work together. Be careful with what you do, because you have real potential.' Cruise may be the world's most popular film star, but I fancy Kidman's the family member with the lion's share of the talent. On screen she seems to possess the maturity of an actress who's been in the business for years. Philip Noyce, who directed her in *Dead Calm*, predicted her rise to international fame, and that was prior to Tom Cruise. And Robert Benton, her director on *Billy Bathgate*, commented after working with Kidman, 'She was just astounding. She's an astonishingly gifted actress, even more so when you consider how young she is. She's truly one of the most amazing actors I've worked with.' And this from a man who directed both Meryl Streep and Sally Field in Oscar-winning performances.

10   The Tom Cruise Rumour Factory

'When I started out, I'd think, "Those mother fuckers – I am going to go out and get every one of them!" '
— Tom Cruise on his relationship with the press

Part of the burden of fame is suffering incessant rumourmongering, so you can't actually blame Cruise for wanting to control the press as far as he can and in the manner he does it. When so much shoddy reporting goes on, little wonder he's a control addict, managing every tiny detail of his career and personal life. But on the other hand by restricting or severely denying press access don't they just make things up out of spite or frustration? He believes that for the most part the press treat him fairly, or at least as fairly as any other big-time movie star. He figures, if the tabloids get things right 10 per cent of the time he's a happy puppy. Misquoted or inaccurate journalism is not a big concern of his. The media will always be curious about the private lives of stars – stars whom these very tabloids have helped create – and Cruise almost always has far more pressing problems to sort out. When they overstep the mark, however, Cruise never hesitates to take severe action. It galls him that such people can print almost anything they like. As a frequent victim Cruise is somewhat justified in claiming that celebrity journalism has got out of hand. The higher the profile the more the rumours fly. Everywhere they go Cruise and Kidman are under the closest scrutiny. Being among Hollywood's most glamorous couples, they live under intense pressure. After the marriage, Kidman found the press intrusion into her life almost unbearable. Tom's depth of experience in media matters proved invaluable, and he taught Nicole never to read a review or a report about herself. It's still a burden, but it's something she has learned to tolerate. Unlike her husband Kidman tends to be more forthcoming when interviewed. From his earliest years Cruise has mistrusted the media. It irks him that people blindly believe all the rubbish they read about him. Here are a few examples.

In March 1989 British tabloid journalists reported that Cruise had collapsed while promoting *Rain Man* in Paris and was rushed to hospital. Fleet Street scrambled for the medical dictionary to look up some truly wonderful ailment it might be fun to strike Hollywood's biggest star down with. Was it some deadly tropical virus, picked up in the Far East while battle-hardening himself to play Ron Kovic, that doctors claimed had reduced him to a vessel of pain, barely able to move or speak? The reality turned out to be a savage bout of flu, but that would have made for boring news; the truth invariably does.

Since their marriage in 1990 Tom and Nicole have had to contend with stories that they are so protective of each other that they turn up on movie sets to make certain their love scenes stay within the bounds of decency. Cruise did indeed visit the set of *Billy Bathgate*, and why not? but in an interview for *Movieline* in March 1994 Kidman dismissed the rumour that Tom put the screws on the producers to tone down some of the film's raunchy moments.

> I'm not the kind of person who would allow that, anyway. He showed up on the set, occasionally, and was hanging out with Dustin, but not when we were doing those kinds of scenes. On *Malice*, Tom also occasionally came by (again gossips claimed Cruise arrived one afternoon unannounced to watch his wife film a passionate clinch with actor Alec Baldwin and allegedly complained they were too suggestive and too long). But, he's such a strong force that I don't like to have him on the set. It distracts me and it's bad for the other actors. You can't have your spouse there twiddling his thumbs, watching. It makes me too self-conscious.

Kidman claims that her husband understands such requests because he works the same way. You need to be focused and concentrated, and can't be chinwagging with your other half between takes.

Nicole is apparently just the same as Cruise, making herself very visible when the script calls for her husband to indulge in a love scene. Like when he cavorted on a beach with actress Karina Lombard for *The Firm*. Lombard allegedly complained that throughout filming Nicole watched her like an eagle and even flew out to the Cayman Islands on the same flight as the actress and caught the same flight back again to Los Angeles. However, Kidman's Australian publicist, Wendy Day, denied the reports. 'Nicole and Tom just think the whole thing's a huge laugh.' US tabloids reported that Cruise insisted Lombard be banned from *The Firm*'s press launches. Certainly her ego was bruised by the lack of attention accorded her. After every take production staff orbited around the stellar presence of Cruise while she was largely ignored. But what did Lombard expect?

The one rumour that has been a constant thorn in Cruise's side is that he's homosexual, but he has always strenuously denied this. Indeed he has successfully sued those making such unwarranted statements. Cruise has found it difficult dealing with the rumour that he's gay – not because he is homophobic, but because it calls into question his marriage to Kidman. 'Let me make this very clear' he told a reporter from *Première* in July 1996. 'If any person is so fucking cynical to think that ... You know what I say about that – basically, that it's attacking my relationship. It is a hard-line cynicism, and I think it's absolutely disgusting that someone would say it. It's ridiculous, it fucking pisses me off. Personally, I have nothing against that at all, but this is my relationship and I'm being called a liar about it. I've called lawyers. I say, "You want to say that? Fine, go ahead, you fucking prove it." '

John Stockwell, an old acting and drinking buddy, recalls a Cruise who was anything but gay during their time together filming *Losin' It*. He behaved 'like any normal young male would in the same situation, where booze and women are in prodigious supply'.

In stark contrast to Mimi Rogers's slur on the Cruise manhood, Kidman has been very public in proclaiming the quality of their romantic life, describing Cruise as the best lover she's ever had. 'I can assure you my husband's no monk. He's a very sexual guy.' When asked why she thought people kept insinuating that Cruise was gay, she replied mischievously, 'He's mighty fine-looking, and he's worth having a fantasy about.'

McCall's magazine was forced to admit they had totally fabricated insinuations about a 'staged' marriage, and Kidman used an interview with *Vanity Fair* in July 1995 to hit back, in justifiably strong language.

> I did not marry into a marriage of convenience. I would
> never, ever do that. You marry for love. We're both
> heterosexual. We have a lot of homosexual friends, and
> neither of us would shy away from having a homosexual role.
> He played the vampire Lestat and didn't give a shit. But I
> take offence if people say I would marry into a marriage of
> convenience. I think that's very sexist, because they're
> saying, "She married for fame and money.' It's bullshit. I'll
> bet all the money I've ever made, plus his, that he doesn't
> have a mistress, that he doesn't have a gay lover, that he
> doesn't have a gay life.

Some of Cruise's biggest movies have been littered with
homoerotic references. In the cinema of Cruise the star is usually
surrounded by phallic props – planes, pool cues, liquor bottles,
racing cars – while he himself has a peculiarly boyish quality that
critics have identified as the source of his appeal. For such a big
box-office star/sex symbol the Cruiser is a remarkably asexual
actor – even contriving to co-star in a romantic epic opposite his
wife (*Far and Away*) but rarely kissing her. Even when his films
are propelled by heterosexual romance Cruise can come over all
passive, especially in recent years. In *Risky Business* DeMornay's
prostitute teaches the boy Cruise about sex and money; in *Top
Gun* it's McGillis not Cruise who makes her violent confession of
love first; and in *Far and Away* Kidman makes all the 'right' moves
peeking at his naked body. In *Days of Thunder* Cruise is groped by
a female cop; *A Few Good Men* is conspicuous for its lack of a
triumphal sex scene; while in *The Firm* the Cruise is near-raped on
a beach by a prostitute hired as a blackmailing tool by his enemies.
Cruise embodies wholesome, squeaky-clean maleness. For all his
heart-throbbing screen persona the characters he plays are almost
always more comfortable bonding with other males – with his
co-pilot in *Top Gun*, the bartender in *Cocktail*, his nocturnal
partner in *Interview with the Vampire* or paternal figures –
Newman, Hoffman, Duvall, Hackman.

From the outset Cruise's body was at the centre of his success.
He was one of the original Brat Pack pretty-boy studs who didn't
need much encouragement to strip. As he danced in his underwear
in *Risky Business* cheering audiences were turning Cruise into a

star. *Top Gun*, which solidified his fame, is a relentlessly macho locker-room fantasy – even the girl is called Charlie. We have oiled and muscled bodies posing in locker rooms and on the volleyball court, male-bonding rituals, the phallic power of the fighter jets and pilots who look like Calvin Klein models. Pushed to these extremes machismo teeters embarrassingly into homoeroticism. '*Top Gun* may well be the most brazenly eroticized recruiting poster in the history of warfare' – *New York* magazine; 'The movie is a shiny homoerotic commercial' – Pauline Kael. You also have Quentin Tarantino's vigorous assertion in the movie *Sleep with Me* that *Top Gun* is the ultimate celluloid gay fantasy. And obviously there's *Interview with the Vampire*, described by the *Independent on Sunday* as, 'The most candidly gay movie to come out of mainstream Hollywood.' The film capitalized on the sexually ambiguous nature of Cruise's screen appeal, and was based on a book, written before AIDS, which celebrated bisexual promiscuity. There was even the suggestion that the homoerotic content of the film was being toned down to the point of invisibility to protect Cruise's image. It is quite unbelievable that Neil Jordan, the man who made *The Crying Game*, would have compromised so drastically for Cruise or anyone else. Indeed Cruise revels in this, his most daring persona yet, camping it up gloriously as the effeminate Lestat. A journalist from *Vanity Fair*, on seeing the film, told Cruise: 'You've created a whole new male screen icon: the bitch god. You're frighteningly bitchy in this.' To which Tom replied, 'Good! A bitch god! I love it!' The sight of Tom hovering lasciviously over Brad Pitt's neck is one of the most explicitly homoerotic images ever served up by a major Hollywood star.

Hollywood and the press have always enjoyed a relationship of incestuous collusion. In the heyday of the studio system this meant planting stories in compliant publications, hungry for gossip. That doesn't happen anymore, we are reliably informed; today stars control their own lives, or the hordes of PR consultants they hide behind do. Their availability is carefully controlled, and they tend to meet journalists – the bridge between stars and their public – only in situations of the least peril, the utmost manageability. All stars sensibly guard themselves against inevitable sorties by the press against their much valued privacy, but with very few exceptions Cruise is the most obsessive. He even insists on blocking friends and family from talking to newspapers. 'You wanna talk to my sisters?' he told one reporter doing an 'authorized' feature on him in *GQ* magazine in 1992. 'No! They don't want to do interviews! They're not interested in it.' He also does his damnedest to stop childhood pictures from surfacing; perhaps they bring back too many painful memories. Not without reason has he been branded a control addict; why else do most profiles of the actor go under the tiresome inevitable banner: 'Cruise Control'.

The Cruise rarely commits himself to be interviewed one-on-one and these occasions have scarcely been known to last longer than one hour and are shrouded in the kind of damage control associated with presidential news conferences. He's generally polite with reporters, if sometimes a little terse and noncommittal, especially when questions swing towards such personal matters as his religious beliefs. Interviews make him nervous, and journalists are viewed as an assault course to be tackled without suffering too many cuts and bruises. But he believes in doing publicity: 'I want each film I do to reach its audience.' Cruise is not averse to phoning reporters with whom he's just spoken to alter a word or phrase. After an interview with *Rolling Stone* in 1988 Cruise called the journalist to change a single word – 'surreal' to 'real'. It had been an unusually long meeting – three hours – and the reporter had no idea in what context the word in question had been uttered. But Cruise did, and this is so typical of the man, this need to control the situation. Cruise is in a class of his own about how much or how little he cares to reveal about himself. He's well known for laying down the law when it comes to reporters, imposing strict conditions before he'll even open his mouth. For example, he makes them sign binding contracts stipulating where and when certain articles can be published. Journalists who refuse to go along with this 'game' are denied access to the star. All of which can breed bitterness and resentment. Promoting *Cocktail*, Cruise, on learning that a journalist who had once been critical of then wife Mimi Rogers was attending his press conference, allegedly threatened to boycott the event unless the offending hack was barred. Is it a coincidence that Cruise control hit maximum overdrive (during the press junket for *Far and Away* in 1992) in the same year he signed on at the public relations firm of PMK, one of the biggest PR firms in Hollywood, run by Pat Kingsley, Cruise's personal press representative? He also insists on having the final say on which publicity stills are distributed. This is perfectly reasonable; artists are exploited enough and we must applaud actors who reach the status where they sometimes get to call the shots. As an actor still very much maturing there's a danger of him being over-exposed; he's merely protecting himself from a public backlash if his smiling face appears too often on magazine covers.

Publicity hype for movies nowadays tends to be these awful press junkets that take place in extremely expensive and sterile hotels within the sphere of Tinsel Town control, where reporters in groups of eight or twelve are only allowed to field the kind of bland questions that wouldn't tax a five-year-old: 'Tell me Tom, what did you learn about life playing this character?' ...

'Did you find it difficult learning an Irish accent?' ... *ad nauseam*. But in recent years Cruise has even stopped attending these. You can't really blame him, as they're deadly-dull affairs. This is in direct contrast to Arnold Schwarzenegger, Cruise's only other box-office rival, who when he has a new product to plug – you just try keeping him away. Though he did deign to be interviewed several times on US television for *The Firm* providing the stations played by his rules, each item had to be introduced with a mention of the movie's name, the interview could only be broadcast in conjunction with said film's release and the videotape of the interview had to be turned over to the star after it had been conducted, no doubt for approval. In the case of CNN, Cruise's publicist, Pat Kingsley, demanded to see a tape of the reporter before consenting to sit down with him.

11 Tom Cruise: the Finest Actor of His Generation?

'I don't pretend to be the character, I am the character.'
— Tom Cruise

It's ironic that the actor who became the predominant screen icon of his generation by portraying characters who simply ooze self-confidence should himself start each new film sweating and shaking with an overriding fear he'll forget how to act. 'Every single time I go to start a picture, without fail, I feel as if I don't know what I'm doing,' he told *Premiere* in June 1992. 'There's a moment where I go, "I don't know how to do this anymore. I don't know how." ' Does his talent come in a mysterious way he cannot fathom, or is he just too afraid to analyse his ability in case it leaves him? Does his acting come from intuition? People have talked about gut-driven instinct. According to Dustin Hoffman, 'Tom doesn't have an intellectual idea of what he wants to do – he's coming off his gut, and that makes him a pleasure to work with.' Perhaps that's why he relies so heavily on research and a character's physical appearance, the technical aspects of acting, and not the mysticism of performing. Cruise physically inhabits every role, reshaping his body to suit each character – soft and heavy in *Risky Business*, muscular and toned in *Top Gun*. Each time it's different.

Every day, either working on a script or performing, the Cruise perfectionism rears its head to spotlight his inadequacies and pushing him on to impossible-to-reach goals. Moments enter his life when everything just clicks and it all seems so easy. But then tomorrow inevitably arrives, those feelings are gone and all is dead. 'It's never that I wake up, get out of bed and it's an easy day,' he explained to *Empire* in October 1993. 'But it's the challenges of life that I love, you know? They bury me and depress me and make me feel excited about life. When the scene comes in and you read it and it works, it's just life – wow! But Jesus, all the hours and days of sweating over, "I know nothing, I'm terrible...." '

Acting theories are irrelevant when you're talking about Cruise, though his celebrated single-minded determination to get the smallest details of his characters just right – from pumping iron for months in beefy preparation for *Taps*, refusing to shower during the making of *The Outsiders*, digesting legalese for *The Firm*, to painstaking immersion into the world of the handicapped for *Born on the Fourth of July* – smacks of the Method, an acting technique originated by Stanislavsky and developed at the Actor's Studio in New York during the fifties. Each film is approached as a new experience, and while preparations differ, certain ground rules are observed. Cruise must find himself in the character and bring to life aspects of his own personality relevant to the role. That's the framework. He believes in complete immersion. 'He can act younger and more innocent than he really is,' noted Lea Thompson. 'He can play a crazy kid in *Taps*, a slick kid in *Risky Business*. That's the mark of a terrific actor – how you pick up on one aspect of your own personality and use it for the role.' The best way to get a character together, though, is to make sure he's in good shape. 'I can't concentrate unless I feel good and clean. I can't act when I'm tired.' Cruise keeps to a strict diet, refusing to touch fatty foods, and drinks water prodigiously with every meal after a doctor informed him that 'flushing out' his body after eating would help prevent cancer, the disease which claimed the life of his father. He gulps great handfuls of vitamins, has a medical check-up twice a month and every morning launches into a rigorous one-hour work-out. Discipline is paramount. He rarely drinks now or smokes. When Newman heard Cruise was going to play a barman (*Cocktail*) he sent him a six-pack of beer with a note telling him to take the weekend off and learn how to drink it.

Despite holding his own against major league icons like Newman, Hoffman and Nicholson, his detractors, and there are many, argue that Cruise is merely a movie star pretending to be an actor.

This is the problem facing Cruise and it's one unique to a star of his stature – eighteen films down and no one can decide how good an actor he really is. It's accepted that Schwarzenegger couldn't act his way out of a paper bag; you can visualize Cruise giving Shakespeare his earnest best but Arnie? What is indisputable is that the camera adores him. The Cruise presence lights up the screen, and he is blessed with the alchemical power of turning even the most turgid dross into gold. But it is precisely the fact that this highly desirable gift has been tested (sometimes sorely) more often than it should have been that puts a question-mark over Cruise. Time and again he's proven himself a poor judge of material. There are actors who become stars, though not in the box-office sense (Pacino, Hoffman, De Niro are all hugely popular, but who do the masses queue up to see?) and there are stars who are never properly considered actors. Just which one is Tom Cruise?

David Puttnam called Dustin Hoffman a 'worrisome American pest,' and it is true that he is the most notorious perfectionist in Hollywood, obsessive, monomaniacal and the scourge of directors, producers and screenwriters. He once phoned Puttnam asking if he'd cast him in his movie *Agatha*. He arrived in England with his own writer and his cameo was expanded into a co-starring role. A furious Puttnam quit from his own project. It was not a happy ship. Hoffman and Vanessa Redgrave scarcely spoke to one another. He wouldn't join the PLO, goes the gag. *Tootsie* was also notoriously no fun on the set. Hoffman and Sydney Pollack's standard means of communication on set was screaming. Crew members reported that the diminutive one was much more amenable in drag.

Rain Man, a project that became controversial before even a single frame was shot, about two middle-aged brothers, one a con man, the other autistic, seemed to promise more of the same. His career in the doldrums with *Ishtar*, Hoffman was deemed perfect casting as the sleazy sibling, but desired instead the showier role of the disabled man. He wanted Bill Murray as co-star. CAA head honcho Michael Ovitz, one of the most powerful executives Hollywood has ever known and the man then steering Cruise's career to new heights, suggested his new number-one client. When Barry Morrow, the script's initiator, argued that the Cruiser was a good twenty years too young for the role he was politely asked to close the door behind him.

Hoffman knew little about Cruise, save that Jennifer his daughter had a teenage crush on the star and desperately urged her father to work with him. They had first met a few years before. Cruise had just got back from finishing *Legend* and was dining with his kid sister at a swanky Cuban restaurant on Columbus Avenue, New York. He saw she was wearing a smile a mile wide after returning from the toilet. She'd passed someone on the way back. 'It's Dustin Hoffman,' she pointed, 'over there.' He was in the Big Apple wowing audiences on Broadway in *Death of a Salesman*. Cruise knew the play closed that weekend and that tickets were like gold dust. Usually shy when it comes to approaching the famous, especially those he admires. (Endearingly, there's an air of ingenuousness – a streak of shy humility unexpected in an actor of Cruise's stature. He seems to have a genuine reverence for Hollywood's elder statesmen. 'If you tell a kid, nineteen years old, "You're going to work with Paul Newman in a year and a half, and then you're going to work with Hoffman and Hackman and, oh my god, Nicholson ..." I sat in a dark theatre as a kid watching their performances and I've seen them on video hundreds of times and been just amazed at what they've done,' Cruise told the *Radio Times* in January 1995. 'And now I actually get to see them work.') Cruise made an exception in this case. 'Hey, Mr Hoffman,' he bellowed. A flicker of recognition crossed the star's face as he turned round. 'Cruise.' They got chatting. 'Look,' said Hoffman. 'We've got the last performance coming up. Why don't you and your sister come by into my dressing room and watch me get made up for it?' Hoffman certainly knows how to treat guests: not only did he rustle up top seats but took them with his family for a meal afterwards.

Four directors (including Steven Spielberg and Sydney Pollack), six writers, eight producers, two cinematographers, one crew change, the screenwriters' strike and an eighteen-month period in limbo ensued. *Rain Man* supplied Hollywood doomwatchers with material for months. It was a fight all the way to the screen, with Hoffman calling the shots, repelling studio executives who wanted to shelve the picture, and Cruise hanging in, his commitment to the project never waning. It was this unlikely bond that held *Rain Man* together when outside forces threatened annihilation. 'There were some people,' said Cruise, 'who said, "Look. Two jerks in a car going cross-country. Who's going to want to see that movie?" They just don't get it. They just don't get it.' The uncertainty was murder for a hotshot Cruise itching to supply new product for the masses; he'd rather succumb to the filmic disaster of *Cocktail* than twiddle his thumbs. There were times when he thought, Oh, God, is this ever really going to happen? In times of nervous exasperation he'd phone Hoffman for reassurance. The conversation would follow this familiar path: 'Listen,' Cruise would say, 'it doesn't look good.' Hoffman, stifling a yawn, would reply. 'Listen. If we want to make this film, we'll make it. You wanna make this movie?' Cue Cruise. 'Yeah, like I want air, I wanna make the goddamn movie.' 'Then, don't worry. We will make the movie. Just sit tight. We are going to get through this.'

First Martin Brest, the original director, wasn't happy that Cruise would be on screen fifteen minutes before Hoffman showed. 'My God,' Hoffman retorted, 'Tom's the biggest star in the world, he can hold a movie for two reels!' Brest walked out, branding Hoffman a 'micro-surgeon' for his intense attention to detail. The director had wanted the Raymond character to develop mentally, to work towards the Hollywood curse – a happy ending. Hoffman didn't. And medical opinion was on Hoffman's side; autistic withdrawal is irreversible. Unfortunate as it may seem to audiences, Raymond would not advance out of his shell (well, not until the sequel perhaps. It was reported in mid 1994 that Hoffman wanted to recreate his role in a possible '*Rain Man Returns*' and hoped Cruise would sign up, despite the star's known aversion to sequel work.) *Rain Man* won both credit for authentically tackling a hitherto little-known and unglamorous disability and flak for exploiting it – using autism as a dramatic gimmick that lends an off-beat quality to a stale genre, the buddy/road movie. But the film manages to be touching without overdosing on sentimentality and funny without derision or condescension. There is, though, something morally suspect about actors in full possession of their faculties aping the physically and mentally handicapped as a means of winning fancy awards. Strange how after being tipped for an Oscar nomination for *Rain Man* but losing out and seeing his co-star collect his that Cruise should next play a disabled man, and, surprise, surprise was rewarded with a nomination, only to be beaten by another actor in a wheelchair.

Raymond Babbitt is an autistic savant who has spent most of his life cocooned in a respectable mental asylum. Withdrawn and wary of human contact; in the film Cruise and Hoffman never once face each other. Raymond's head is permanently sunken as though afraid to face a world that he doesn't understand and that doesn't understand him. Hoffman warned Cruise that he wanted to avoid

the intimacy of eye contact, making Cruise's performance all the
more admirable in that he was acting to thin air. And yet the
by-play between the actors is pure delight. Babbitt, from a quirk of
neurology, is capable of astonishing feats of mental agility,
working out mathematical puzzles in a matter of seconds and
memorizing numbers – something that comes in handy during
some of the movie's brightest moments at the gaming tables of Las
Vegas. Hoffman took typical pains to absorb autism's decidedly
unromantic reality, passing the time waiting for production to start
by talking to specialist doctors and autistic sufferers. He and
Cruise got additional pointers by going bowling on a double date
with an autistic man and his brother.

Barry Levinson was a hot ticket with *Good Morning, Vietnam*
riding high on the box-office charts when the shop-soiled *Rain
Man* landed in his lap with just seven weeks to put it together –
location scouting, script revisions and so on all had to be done in
record time. Out went some of Raymond and Charlie's more
absurd cross-country mishaps, like getting involved with the mafia,
running foul of a motorcycle gang, meeting a hooker and landing
in jail. It was a virtuoso rescue job. Then after sticking with *Rain
Man* through two years of development hell it was Hoffman who
threatened to quit just a week into shooting. 'Get Richard
Dreyfuss,' he told Levinson after watching early rushes. 'Get
somebody, Barry, because this is the worst work of my life.' He
was persuaded to stay and the first five days of footage were
re-shot. Thereafter it was relatively plain sailing. Levinson shot
the whole thing in under three months by imposing a tough
working schedule – six-day weeks and long hours – altering the
screenplay as he went along, and encouraging his actors to
improvise all the time. Levinson wasn't married to the script in the
way some directors are. For instance, when he heard the
impassioned way in which Cruise talked about cars it was decided
to change Charlie's occupation to that of a car salesman, a brash
wheeler-dealer facing financial ruin. There's that memorable
moment when Raymond realizes he's not wearing his K-Mart
boxer shorts and refuses to let up about it. Cruise and Hoffman
expanded the dialogue as if it were a comedy routine, making it
funnier with each take. Another unscripted contribution, this time
solely from Hoffman, arrived, unfortunately for Cruise, in the
cramped confines of a phonebox. Reading the scene Hoffman
suddenly broke wind. 'I like to fart when I'm among my men

friends,' he boasts. 'This one was a good one, a cracker!' Cruise said, straight out. 'Did you just fart?' The exchange played beautifully and was retained in the finished print. Humour was to play an important function; the subject matter was potentially so depressing that a lightness of tone would rope the audience into the story, make it more accessible. Cruise himself saw the film in terms of a comedy.

Though from different acting backgrounds Cruise and Hoffman got along famously and within a short period became firm friends. You can't fail to sense the special rapport that existed between the two men, the larkish rivalry coming from Hoffman and the hero worship of Cruise. 'It was the first time I was ever working on a set where I was just anonymous,' Hoffman said of the ego-levelling experience. 'As far as the crowds were concerned it was "Tom, Tom". It was like a nightmare.' This from an actor who has worked with Steve McQueen, Robert Redford, Warren Beatty and Sean Connery. Like Newman before, Hoffman couldn't help but see a little of himself as a young actor in Cruise, all that crystalline energy. 'He's a demon,' he told the *Sunday Express* in February 1989.

> He gets up early, he works out, he goes home early, he studies, he works out again at night. He watches his diet as though he's an old fart like me. He doesn't drink. He doesn't smoke. He's very spartan while making a film. And he always wanted to rehearse. It affected me emotionally, being in his presence.

Compared with his edgy, energetic young co-star Hoffman's manner seemed almost sedate and expansive.

Cruise, who'd been too young to catch Hoffman's early movies until they made it to television, was daunted by the prospect of working with the man who made *The Graduate*. 'Meeting him was intimidating. Sometimes I'd be watching the rushes and I'd just sit back and say, "Wow! That's Dustin Hoffman." But Hoffman's not pretentious. He doesn't remind you he's a genius.' Cruise learnt much from working and observing the old hand, principally where best to focus his energies. Cruise has a tendency to overdo his research, preparing for roles by immersing himself in everything about them. The problem is that you can get so much information you don't know what to choose. Hoffman was just more specific in the questions he asked. Basically, Hoffman taught Cruise how to cut corners.

Despite the inspired casting of box-office champ Cruise with critic's favourite Hoffman, Hollywood felt that a road movie *cum* voyage of discovery about a slimeball and his mentally retarded brother would be an audience turn-off. Nobody expected it to make much money, including Levinson, who on opening night drove past one of the theatres, which was half full. OK, he thought, it'll do reasonable business. When the first weekend figures were published they surprised everyone, and the second week was even better; word of mouth had turned the picture into a monster hit grossing $173 million ($500 million worldwide). Only *Batman* and *Indiana Jones and the Last Crusade* made more money that year. Not bad for a picture executives said nobody would want to see. 'The fact that *Rain Man* turned out to be the overwhelming success it was has to be looked at as one big fluke,' Levinson told *Empire* in April 1991. 'For some reason it just took off. It's a complete mystery to me.' *Rain Man*'s success offered proof that despite a plethora of hi-tech diversions the public could still be drawn into intimate human dramas.

At the time of *Rain Man*'s release United Artists (the project's backers – Warner Brothers, to whom *Rain Man* was first offered, passed in part because it already had their own 'idiot man/child' vehicle in the works, *Forrest Gump*) was a studio in need of a good life-support machine. Levinson deliberately held only one preview, keeping the result a secret from the studio as it had been a decidedly mediocre one. The audience resented the fact there was no happy ending. One man even told Levinson, 'I thought the little guy was going to snap out of it at the end.' There were complaints, too, about Charlie's callous behaviour towards his brother, calling him a 'fucking retard,' and that he should have been a more agreeable character. Hungry to be accepted as a serious actor, Cruise had taken on a risky role, daring to appear initially unsympathetic. Charlie is a louse, treating his girlfriend with off-hand insolence and his father's death with greedy nonchalance. Levinson refused to pander to the whims of a public weaned on simplistic soap-opera banalities; his intention had never been to make a piece of mass entertainment. Who cares if they couldn't see the art.

As well as striking a mysterious chord with the paying public *Rain Man* also proved an Oscar-strewn phenomenon with eight nominations. It eventually won five, including Best Film and Best Director. That year the Oscars were held at the Shrine Auditorium. The double act of Cruise and Hoffman was presenting the award for best actress (Jodie Foster for *The Accused*). Hoffman apologized for neglecting to mention Cruise or even Levinson in his earlier best actor acceptance speech (instead he'd thanked and praised Ovitz). 'Tom, thank you very much. I love you very much.' They embraced. Later members of the in-crowd gathered inside Spago, where *the* hot party was taking place. *Women's Wear Daily* observed that, 'Tom Cruise must have liked the roar of the crowd outside, because he made not one but two entrances.'

Although Cruise claims he can never judge in advance whether a film will be a hit or not, he did feel confident about *Rain Man's* chances of success. Hoffman, on the other hand, was astonished by its reception. Indeed, the fact that a simple drama about two men who can't relate, with no sex, violence or conventional happy ending should have fared so well around the globe was little short of miraculous. In February Cruise and Hoffman attended the film's royal premiere in London. Fergie, then the Duchess of York, was wheeled over to the West End. The Wapping hacks delighted in eavesdropping on her irrelevant 'showbiz' chatter. 'Your haircut really suits you,' she commented on the crew cut Cruise was wearing for *Born on the Fourth of July* and told both actors she thought they looked just like brothers, saying, 'I'm convinced of it.' This was the big question: could Cruise and Hoffman pass muster as brothers (the age gap was twenty-eight years) or was it taking suspension of disbelief too far? (Apparently *Rain Man* is the Princess of Wales's favourite film, autism being one of her charitable concerns.)

On the whole critics applauded the film, but there were dissenting voices, some louder than others. 'This film is a mess – an overlong, poorly acted and pointless embarrassment. The talentless Tom Cruise fails even when faced with an undemanding role' – *New Musical Express*. But is Cruise any good in it? Well, yes and no. He certainly received some of the best notices of his career up to that time, a welcome change from the critical rancour that greeted *Cocktail*. Here at last was a meaty role he could really sink his teeth into. 'Charlie's the most complex character I've ever played and this is the best role I've ever had,' Cruise offered up as part of the pre-release hype. 'Tom Cruise proves what a resourceful actor he has become, despite a script that requires too abrupt a change in his character' – *The Times*; 'No one can argue that *Rain Man* is Cruise's quantum leap, but he holds his own with the masterly Hoffman' – *Los Angeles Times*. Pauline Kael, the *New Yorker*'s eminent film critic, had this to say, however: 'Cruise as a slimeball is just a sugarpuss in Italian tailoring. He doesn't even use his body in an expressive way. His performance here consists of not smiling too much – so as not to distract his fans from watching Hoffman. Cruise is an actor in the same sense that Robert Taylor was an actor. He's patented: his knowing that a camera is on him produces nothing but fraudulence.' Other than that she loved it! 'It's her opinion,' Cruise said when shown the quote, 'and she's entitled to it.' He needn't worry, for Kael used to lambast John Cassavetes and Meryl Streep, so he's in fine company. It should be made clear that Kael was never one of Cruise's biggest fans. While the great majority of critics praised his performance in *The Color of Money*, here's what Kael thought: 'Cruise tries, he really works at it, and he's certainly a more active presence here than he was in *Top Gun* – he goes through the motions of a real performance. But there's nothing underneath his motions, and they don't mean anything to us. He's so wholesome and harmless he's like a cheerleader's idea of a De Niro flake.' He's had his fair share of detractors, of which Miss Kael is the most noted. Anne Billson of the *Sunday Telegraph* launched this attack on Cruise in her review of *The Firm*. 'If Cruise ever had any acting cards up his sleeve he exposed them to us long ago. But one has to admit he exudes earnest boyishness and a certain pimply star-power, and, even if he is one of the blandest film stars ever born, at least this enables him to blend seamlessly into material such as this.' Vanessa Letts launched this attack in the *Spectator*. 'Tom Cruise has a short neck, short arms and a short arse. Add slabs of muscle all over the place and he starts to look rather freakish.' And Adam Mars-Jones writing in the *Independent*: 'This actor is surely ripe to be superseded as a star, since he continues to represent what he has always represented, eagerness and determination. He has the will to charm, rather than the thing itself. His warmth is no more than grin-deep.' Cruise's revenge is that he rarely reads reviews; after all, it's only their opinion. No kid ever grew up wanting to be a critic.

Criticism is a fact of life when you're a movie star. The bigger the target the more people want to take pot shots at you – even more so when you're a teen heartthrob determined to leave behind the gossip columns, ignore the screams and be taken seriously as an actor. 'I'm still finding my footing,' Cruise said at the time. 'The trouble is, all my experimenting has to be done in the public eye.' His performance, though excellent, could have been equalled by any number of his contemporaries just as Penn, Dillon, Estevez and so on could have taken on *Top Gun*'s Maverick. As famed screenwriter William Goldman put it, '*Top Gun* would have worked with Rob Lowe in it. *Top Gun* would have worked with any pretty kid'. The praise lavished on Hoffman left little room for proper recognition of Cruise's contribution, but there can be no argument that his presence attracted a vastly wider audience than the film otherwise would have reached. His role was not as cinematically flashy as Hoffman's and therein lay the problem. The spiritually 'autistic' Charlie – like Raymond he's locked up in himself, coldly using and manipulating the people around him – is callow and materialistic. On discovering his curmudgeonly father has willed $3 million to an older brother he never knew he had, Charlie kidnaps the brother, effectively holding him to ransom. Furthermore, Charlie is emotionally stunted so that overall he is by far the more complex character. Where Hoffman finishes the film on the same monotonous note he started Charlie matures from selfish yuppie to caring nineties man. It's actually Cruise who makes the whole film work, who propels it forward. Unable to relate to Hoffman, audiences are forced to identify with Cruise, whose indifference towards his brother mirrors our own horror and morbid curiosity of the disabled. As he grows more responsible and devoted we too develop a deeper compassion. The relationship becomes increasingly touching in later scenes, notably when Charlie teaches Raymond to dance. Cruise's dilemma was that he couldn't play the emotion until the last reel – which is fine, except that a better actor could have hinted at what Charlie is holding back. Cruise doesn't, playing it as monotonously as Hoffman, only louder. Cruise even blows the big emotional finale by faking it behind a pair of sunglasses. Charlie, who has learnt more about life in a week from his brother than he has in his whole life and has formed a protective attachment to Raymond, realizes how helpless he is in the outside world and reluctantly returns him to the institution. But how can we see what he's feeling? Never in a film has Cruise's penchant for wearing shades been so irritable and misplaced; it's as though his performance has been sponsored by

Ray Ban. What makes it doubly disappointing is that the film struck such a personal chord with Cruise. 'I can see some of myself in Charlie.' While Hoffman interviewed every autistic expert on the planet, Cruise needed to look no further than himself for his own research, peering behind doors he'd rather have remained locked. 'It was painful confronting parts of my life that I'd shut down. I found out a lot about myself, some things quite disturbing, and it really did change me.' The experience left him dwelling on his troubled childhood, his parents' separation, the death of his father and his own emotionally barren, edgy, reckless younger self.

Tom Cruise came to *Rain Man* with a considerable reputation behind him. Rocketed to early stardom on the strength of a string of phenomenally successful but risibly lightweight movies, Cruise moved away from the mainstream with *Rain Man* and into the world of serious acting. The role was an accumulation of everything he'd learned so far – one he'd never have been able to tackle, say, three years earlier, immediately after *Top Gun*. That was a measure of how far he'd progressed. Never again would anyone doubt his abilities as an actor, even though they were not limitless. If it hadn't been for his development on *Rain Man* it is doubtful he'd have had the confidence to tackle *Born on the Fourth of July*, which marked the first occasion Cruise carried the full weight of a 'message' picture. And one must applaud his desire to tackle more serious subjects. The direction of Cruise's career into more dramatically credible and substantial roles suggested a realization that such films as *Top Gun* and *Cocktail* represented the easy option. Most agreed that the absence of his name on the Oscar nomination list was a glaring omission (Barry Norman, when he interviewed Cruise for the BBC, told the actor he thought he should have won instead of Hoffman). His $5 million fee, plus the further $5 million he made from his share of the profits, was a consolation of sorts. If he was bitter about Hoffman stealing all the thunder, Cruise hid it well. Hoffman was highly admiring of his co-star's performance and dedication; it isn't often he meets an artist with the same zealous perfectionism about their craft. 'Tom and I, right from the beginning, formed a kind of club which reminded me a little bit of what took place between Voight and I on *Midnight Cowboy*,' Hoffman explained to *American Premiere* in December 1988. 'We never stopped working.' Both would drive to the set together, using the time to rehearse, then spend most of the day in each other's trailers going over scene after scene. Theirs was a thorough and creative working relationship. 'Tom was always knocking on my door saying, "Why don't we do it this way?" He'd do my lines so well, he could have played my part. He would have been terrific as Raymond.'

'If I had been drafted, I probably would have gone.'

— Tom Cruise

It is June 1965, and eighteen-year-old Yale dropout Oliver Stone arrives in Saigon, school books not a rifle in his hand, dispensing pencils not bullets to kids in a classroom. The war is still in its infancy. Then it all seemed rather grand, a military safari with plentiful supplies of sun and sex for the restless invaders. The streets of Saigon were more like those of Dodge City, thought Stone: soldiers with guns, no curfews, shoot-outs in bars and whores on every corner. Restlessness crept in and Stone shipped out with the merchant marines, undergoing a queasy crossing of the north Pacific to Oregon. Two years later Stone was back, this time as a grunt with a rifle.

'There is nothing prouder, nothing finer than a United States Marine.' The words of high-school recruitment officers still rang in the ears of Ron Kovic as he set out for Vietnam from the small town of Massapequa, Long Island. Movies had made war heroic for young Ron until a Vietcong bullet shattered his illusions. As Kovic and his platoon were pinned down by intense artillery and mortar fire a bullet blew off his heel as he struggled to reach a wounded colleague. Then, as he played out his own John Wayne movie, screaming, 'Come on, you Commie bastards!' a second exploded through his right shoulder shattering his spine. He came home in a wheelchair paralysed from the chest down and impotent, a fact which obsessed him more than his inability to walk.

In 1967 Oliver Stone volunteered for the draft, fired, like Kovic, by youthful verve and patriotic fervour. He firmly believed American involvement to be correct; Vietnam was going to be *the* war of his generation and he didn't want to miss out. On that first day in Vietnam Stone realized he'd made a terrible mistake. His season in hell lasted fifteen months. Stationed near the Cambodia border he'd been hit within a fortnight. In a fire fight on a night ambush, paralysed with fear at the sight of the enemy, he was wounded in the back of the neck. Another inch higher and he would have been dead. The man beside him had his arm blown off. A month later he received some shrapnel in the leg and buttock. On New Year's night of 1968, Stone's battalion came under heavy attack. Stone was decorated for his do-or-die charge and for lobbing a grenade into an enemy foxhole. Today, however, he shrugs it off. 'Something went crazy in my head. I was pissed off,' the director told *Rolling Stone* in January 1987, ' 'Cause I knew the guys that had been killed, and I had been smoking a little dope that morning.'

Kovic returned from Vietnam to an uncomprehending United States gripped by peace protests. Flags weren't being waved anymore, but burnt. Kovic still loved his country but it didn't want to know him. Scorched with anger that he'd become an impotent cripple, his life ruined, the all-American boy metamorphosed into disillusioned war hero, then warrior for peace. He became an emblem for the passion and outrage of the sixties. Getting ejected from the 1972 Republican convention for heckling Nixon was a far greater achievement than anything he'd done in Vietnam. Four years later his speech at the Democrat convention on behalf of the Veterans against the War made prime-time TV. The world was beginning to listen.

Both men exorcised their demons. Stone made *Platoon*, an unflinching depiction of the savagery and insanity of this most hopeless and needless of wars. It won the Oscar for best film, ignited a storm of political debate, purged the nation's guilt and saw Stone achieve volcanic maturity. In a heartbroken evocation of American innocence betrayed, Kovic committed his own harrowing experiences to paper – a scream of rage about how he was mutilated and neglected.

There was an immediate rapport between the two veterans as they worked together for eighteen months on a screen adaptation of Kovic's autobiography. Then disaster. With Al Pacino cast as Kovic, the project collapsed just days before shooting was scheduled to begin in 1978. Was it the spineless backers who got cold feet, or was it Pacino? 'If Pacino had really hung in there, it could have been done,' Kovic still believes. 'It was a heartbreak,' confessed Stone. 'I became semicomatose, and Ron became a complete basket case.' Stone promised Kovic that if he ever made the top flight he'd return to the project. The success of *Platoon* led Stone, after discounting a sequel based on his own post-war experiences, to call Kovic. 'Ronnie, I'm ready.' Universal president Tom Pollock had greenlighted the picture after practically everyone in Hollywood had been turning it down for fifteen years. 'We don't care if it's Al Pacino or Marlon Brando,' said one film company executive. 'It's not the kind of movie that can make a dime.' The proviso was that it had to be made on the cheap ($18 million), with a major star. Hence Cruise and not Sean Penn, Charlie Sheen or Nicolas Cage, three early candidates.

Cruise was conversant with Stone's reputation as America's most controversial and politically forceful director, dubbing him the Van Gogh of film-makers. 'His films are intense, vibrant, explosive, unrelenting – just like he is,' Cruise told the *Los Angeles Times* in December 1989. 'Watching him in action is like seeing Bruce Springsteen live for the first time.' Returning from Vietnam 'very mixed-up, very paranoid' with a Purple Heart and a Bronze Star for valour, Stone enrolled in New York University's film school studying under Martin Scorsese. 'He helped channel the rage in me.' Writing eleven scripts in six years, courting failure and penury, Stone took odd jobs like cab driving and drifted in a druggy haze, remaining so stoned that he didn't mind living in a crumbling apartment where snow sometimes drifted into his bedroom. 'Many times I looked in the mirror and had the razor out.' Everything changed when he wrote the screenplays for *Midnight Express* and *Scarface*, and then directed *Salvador*. Stone has since proved with *Platoon*, *JFK* and *Natural Born Killers* to be one of the most ferocious and unrelenting cultural critics of our time.

With Pacino now too old for the part and past his box office peak, Stone wanted Cruise from the kick-off, believing he was as close to Ron as anyone of his generation could be. He and Kovic shared working-class backgrounds, Catholicism and even high-school wrestling (we first see Cruise in the sweaty throes of a wrestling bout). As Stone shrewdly observed, both men were motivated by a desire to be the best, to prove something. 'Like Ron, Tom is wound real tight.' And he sensed that the darkness in Tom's past, his own dysfunctional and pressured upbringing, might help in his struggle to play the role. In some small way, too, Cruise related to Kovic's disability because of his own dyslexia. It was actually Stone himself who bore the most resemblance to Kovic. Both were the product of upbringings that instilled unquestioning allegiance to the flag. Both volunteered for action having swallowed the 'better-dead-than-red' cold war propaganda and received Bronze Stars for bravery. Both returned home injured and alienated. They were one another's alter ego. 'My story and that of other veterans is subsumed in Ron's,' said Stone, who viewed him as a kind of emblem of the Vietnam generation. Cruise viewed Kovic in purely heroic terms. What the director shared with Cruise was that he too was from a broken family; Stone's parents divorced when he was sixteen. Cruise had been angling to make a movie with Stone for some time when Paula Wagner dug up the dog-eared script of *Born*. After ten pages Tom knew it was going to be tough to refuse – from an actor's point of view it was an incredible story. 'I could feel the script in my balls. I felt Ron could have been me.' Only one day separated their birthdays.

Stone just had a hunch about Cruise, just as he did in choosing Michael Douglas for *Wall Street* when everyone else said he was too lightweight to carry the movie. Martin Bregman, who in 1978 had vainly put up $1 million of his own money to get *Born* off the ground, voiced doubts that Cruise could ever better Pacino and was convinced that box office was the overriding factor. 'Tom Cruise was an interesting choice, but not a brave one. Given his popularity with the youth audience, Tom Cruise could do Tom Pollock's Bar Mitzvah picture and it would do well commercially.' Pollock had already publicly supported his director over the choice of Cruise, and not only because of his box-office clout. In any case there's always a risk in using a big movie star: will the public accept their idol attempting something so radically different? *Born* demonstrated Cruise's eagerness to appear in an unglamorous, albeit still heroic, Oscar-seeking role. 'Tom Cruise is America's all-American boy. The film's journey is more powerful when it is made by the maverick from *Top Gun*. It's not only Ron who goes through this wrenching story, it is Tom Cruise – our perception of Tom Cruise.' Strong words, but Universal Picture's actions didn't back them up. The studio fought a pitched battle with Cruise's representatives to stop them from releasing stills of him in a wheelchair for fear of scaring off the star's 'traditional' audience, those who flock to see him in stereotypical heroic roles. Would they accept Cruise as an embittered, dishevelled invalid? In one scene he violently yanks loose his catheter and sits sodden in his own urine – not a pretty picture and a long way from the sexually magnetic roles in which Cruise became a star. Could he carry the role off? was the talk of Hollywood. 'The thought of Cruise in a wheelchair is terrifying,' wrote one journalist. 'It's almost as if his crony Sean Penn were to take the lead in *Gandhi 2*.' Cruise would suffer *déjà vu* five years later when everyone said he was miscast as a vampire. Ironically, however, the two roles for which he was deemed most unsuitable have turned out to be his most accomplished.

Cruise's aggressiveness is what first impressed Stone. He wanted to shatter the golden boy image and create a character which would shock Cruise's fans. Did Stone, who deplored *Top Gun*, deliberately cast Cruise to deromanticize his hero war image as Maverick? Casting Cruise was a brilliant tactical coup, perhaps the most significant casting decision of the decade – as Cruise's Hollywood persona then typified the reactionary cinema of the Reagan era. *Born* calls into question the all-American values that Cruise's earlier films so fulsomely embodied. Stone messed up the Cruise image to such a degree that the star's gaunt look and weight loss achieved for the part fuelled speculation that he had everything from cancer to jungle fever. But in the process he extracted a career performance-best. Laid bare, *Born* is a conversion of Cruise's *Top Gun* image; you're number one, the best of the best, but what happens, Stone is asking, when you get blown out of the cockpit? The kid becomes a man. As a result of the film a part of Cruise passed from youth to middle age. Just as *Platoon* sucked something out of Charlie Sheen, it was going to be hard for Tom to claw back his innocence. He would always carry around Ron Kovic. This was one role he was never going to be able to lay to rest in the closet with his other costumes. 'I think he passed out of his youth truly into early middle age,' Stone revealed to *Rolling Stone* in January 1990. 'He'll never be the same boy that he was before. He knows too much now.' After filming, star and director travelled separately through South-east Asia, their paths crossing in Thailand. 'You've done a great job, Tom,' Stone informed him one night. 'You should go out and just be young and enjoy the autumn of your youth. Because it's gonna go. Go out now and have a fucking ball.' Cruise couldn't help but agree, taking time out to unwind, holidaying in Europe with Mimi, but was soon charging headlong into another project. *Born* became the ultimate Tom Cruise rite-of-passage movie – a secular parable of fall and redemption – and Ron Kovic his Hamlet.

Kovic had severe doubts about cinema's golden boy portraying him ('I wondered if he had the depth and passion to play me'), arguing long and hard with Stone over the choice. He never went to see *Top Gun*, so appalled was he at the message it preached. But the power of that universally known Cruise image might be more properly served here, thought Kovic. Even if the performance proved mediocre, Kovic hoped that the millions of young people who'd see the movie, lured by the Cruise name, might be forced to re-evaluate their view of war. For them Vietnam is blurred history, and Kovic wanted to undo the dangerously seductive images presented in films like *Rambo* and *Top Gun*. In the process maybe they could stop new generations of young boys being shot to hell and by doing so give meaning to his own suffering and to what he'd sacrificed – turn tragedy into triumph. When they eventually met in February 1987 Cruise ran to embrace the veteran as an old friend or lost brother. Both talked for hours. Cruise went through his books, watched old home movies, all the time explaining how he really wanted this part and wasn't going to let Ron down. At one point Kovic burst into tears. 'I felt like a burden was lifted, that I was passing all this on to Tom.' The old veteran looked into the eyes of the Hollywood star and found reflected there a mirror image of himself when he went to Vietnam in 1965. He recalls thinking, 'He's so full of life. He's so sure. He's so representative of America before the war. I was thinking, "He's about to go through this hell and he doesn't even know it." I was convinced he wouldn't be the same when he came out of this.' There was an instant rapport with Cruise that Kovic never experienced with Pacino. 'I had never really felt that Pacino connected with me as much as Cruise or that he understood what we had been through,' Kovic told *Premiere* in February 1990. 'I was touched by Cruise. Cruise understood.' After that first meeting Kovic was convinced the youngster could pull it off.

The two were to become best buddies: on the last day of filming Kovic presented the actor with the combat medal he'd won in Vietnam that had been languishing in a wooden box next to his bed for the last twenty-one years. Cruise was incredibly touched by the gesture. He'd been in his dressing room ready to climb into his wheelchair for the last time when Kovic came in and gave him his Bronze Star. Both men hugged tightly, and a weeping Cruise was reluctant to let go. In his own words Kovic had, 'finally found the person who deserved this medal. I told him it was for his heroic performance. He took the romance and glory out of war and replaced it with the truth.' Surely there can be no greater accolade bestowed upon any actor.

Cruise would spend hours at a time with Kovic, peppering the veteran with questions, soaking up the man's life. He also visited VA (Veterans Association) hospitals. At one in Long Beach, California, Cruise was besieged by veterans clamouring for autographs. It took two hours of constant signing by Cruise, whose reputation for being the most courteous 'major' star seems well founded, before he agreed to leave. At rehabilitation centres, he got to know paraplegics, digesting every detail about the effects of paralysis and life as a disabled man. The most shocking images, which newspapers gleefully reported Cruise fans being repelled by, were reserved for the hospital scenes of helpless veterans lying among vermin and their own excreta. Stone, not the most subtle filmmaker, is like a rhino charging at his subject, sparing no stomachs. He is a poet of excess, battering you into emotional submission. The *Village Voice* called *Born*, 'a vast oozing wound of a movie,' full of in-your-face shots. Kovic lived in pain and pain to Stone has to be seen in close-up. Cruise found researching the film the most painful he'd ever undertaken, particularly coming face to face with people not much older than himself suffering from the most dreadful injuries. He drew strength from their bravery. 'The kind of courage that these people have makes you realise what the human soul is capable of in terms of surviving,' he said. At that first meeting in Kovic's LA home Cruise insisted on bringing a wheelchair. Later in the backyard he whacked himself while attempting to do wheelies; even in a wheelchair Cruise can't resist taking it to the limit. From then on he persisted in going through entire days as an invalid, although unlike Kovic, Cruise could always walk away from it. Arriving for an interview with *Vanity Fair* in his chair and wearing Kovic's dress of cheap jeans, checked shirt, baseball cap and stubble, Cruise hung around the door of a restaurant in a Dallas shopping mall before confronting the surprised journalist with the words, 'Hey, I guess it's working.' And at the end of each stressful day he'd wheel right up to his bed and clamber in beside Mimi as if he were actually paralysed. He'd often bomb around with Kovic in matching wheelchairs, rarely being recognized, encountering a good deal of prejudice along the way. Once he was browsing with Kovic in an electronics store when a girl assistant came over to say, 'Excuse me, sir, I'm sorry, but could you please stop rolling around on our carpet, or I'm going to have to ask you to leave.' A bewildered Cruise inquired why. 'Your tyres are leaving marks.' Now the centre of attention Cruise, uncharacteristically losing his temper, screamed at the woman about how he had as much right to be in the store as everybody else. Outside Cruise turned to Kovic and asked why the veteran had not exploded at the woman himself. 'You've only had a month,' he replied. 'I've had twenty years of this discrimination.'

At one point Stone talked Cruise into injecting himself with a solution that would paralyse him for two days. This is taking method acting a little too far. The insurance company agreed, stepping in to stop the lunatic scheme – there was a slight chance he might end up permanently crippled. The point is, Cruise was willing. Stone pushed Cruise, sometimes almost to the limit. 'I put a lot of pressure on Tom, maybe too much,' he told *Time* in December 1989. 'I wanted him to read more, visit more hospitals. I wanted him to spend time in that chair, to really feel it. He went to boot camp twice, and I didn't want his foxhole dug by his cousin.'

For Kovic, who came to the set most days, seeing himself portrayed was painful, sometimes unbearably so, particularly the moment where he drunkenly heaps vitriolic abuse upon his god-fearing mother over his damaged sexual organ. Cruise wanted Kovic to relive the trauma, so in rehearsals asked him to read his own part. After a few run-throughs the emotion became too much. Gripped by a sudden urge to escape Kovic hightailed it to his car and ordered to be taken home. A Jeep pulled up beside him, with Cruise inside. Kovic rolled down his window in time to hear the actor yell, 'God, what are you doing to me, Kovic? Why are you putting me through this?' Kovic starts cursing. 'Fuck you. You're making me depressed.' Cruise returns fire. 'You're making *me* depressed.' It's easy to visualize them as Cruise and Willem Dafoe in the film, arguing the toss on a Mexican dirt track with all the frustrations draining out amid laughing and cursing, shouting and screaming. 'I suddenly realized I wasn't alone,' Kovic told *American Film* in January 1990. 'Tom was agonizing over this part and he didn't know if he could go on, either. I realized that Cruise understood, that I had a brother, I had a friend. We were in this till the end no matter what.'

It was imperative that Cruise understood what it was to be a marine. In the sixties to be a marine was, for kids like Ron, to be the best. It was the job of Dale Dye, a former marine captain, to instil in Cruise that creed – 'which wasn't too difficult, given Tom's nature,' remarked Stone. Dye led Cruise and other actors on two separate week-long training missions, one in Texas, one in the Philippines (which stood in for Vietnam and Mexico); they trained with weapons, dug their own foxholes where they'd sleep and went on long marches. Dye found that the cast 'came together very quickly,' absorbing in a short time the equivalent of twelve to thirteen weeks at a real camp. For the young Tom Cruise Vietnam didn't mean very much (he was six when Kovic won his Bronze Star, still in high school when Pacino was up for the role), but he recalls seeing blurry images of news footage on his television. He also remembers that famous *Life* magazine cover of a girl hit by napalm, running naked in the streets. Sometimes he overheard his school mates arguing in the playground over who won the war. 'We got our asses kicked in Vietnam,' one would say. 'Oh, we won Vietnam, we're America,' offered another. While there was always one little urchin who'd ask, 'What is Vietnam?' Even in high school no one was educated about it (and that was before Hollywood tried to rewrite history with *Rambo*). Probably the closest he came was a friend who wore a copper bracelet for her Green Beret brother missing in action, and then later as a senior in high school going to see *Apocalypse Now*.

Playing Kovic physically and emotionally wrecked Cruise. Stone would work for twelve or thirteen hours at a stretch, and by the end the actor had nothing left; he was burned out. But that feeling of closure and accomplishment, after overcoming obstacles, is Cruise's drug. Artistically it was the most challenging and complex role of his career and a mighty gamble, one he readily admits he could never have handled five years earlier, before having served his self-assigned apprenticeship with Newman and Hoffman. *Born* was Cruise's chance to sustain the new-found maturity and critical acclaim that he'd established in *The Color of Money* and *Rain Man*. Mixing drinks and sleeping around in *Cocktail* wasn't in the same dramatic league as a screaming match with Dafoe, brawling over who killed more babies in Vietnam. Nor did it touch the self-loathing carcass Kovic became, lost in the tequila-drenched degradation of a Mexican brothel before his frustration, self-pity and all-embracing rage transformed into politically active anger. Kovic and Stone were left marvelling at the sheer stamina and courage of Cruise, especially during the harrowing hospital scenes where he'd be strapped into a revolving medieval-like torture device for hours on end. The pressures were sometimes immense, but Cruise took each day at a time, giving the role everything he had. 'If I looked at the mountain, it was just too high.' There had been concern early on about the Cruiser's cocky attitude – he reckoned he could handle anything. Stone expressed healthy scepticism, for he knew that the youngster had bitten off a lot, more than he'd thought. Cruise's performance was ropy at first (behind the confident façade Cruise was apprehensive. 'Oh, man, I just don't want to blow this,' he worried. At the end of it all he didn't want to hear Ron tell him, 'I made a mistake, you shouldn't have played me.') but they shot in continuity as much as possible and Cruise gradually got to grips with it. His regular routine before each tough scene involved skipping rope like a prize boxer to get his adrenalin charging and then proclaiming, 'OK, let's rock n roll!'. Kovic recalled to *Empire* in March 1990 the moment he and everyone else realized that Cruise was going to make it work. 'We were watching the dailies and the place was packed. A crew member leaned over and whispered, "He's doing it, he's doing it." We all knew then something special was happening. Cruise is the great surprise of the film. He gives the performance of his life, going to the ragged edge, at great risk to himself.' In the Philippines the strain, not surprisingly, took its toll. Suffering exhaustion and sick from dehydration, he was prescribed a plethora of medicines by local doctors that served only to compound his illness.

'I could have compromised by backing out of the film, or by being less brutal and gruelling on the people around me, or by not insisting on the right make-up or the right performance,' Cruise related to *Premiere* in February 1990. 'Sometimes Oliver would say, "Okay, we've got to move on to the next setup," and I'd say, "Wait, let's do one more take." Or I'd say to Oliver, "Look, man, I'm lost. You've got to help me. What would you or Ron be thinking in a situation like this?" ' On occasions he'd lose it altogether, and just couldn't make it happen. 'I don't know where I am,' he'd admit. 'Oliver, I'm sorry, man, I just don't have it. It's just not working.' Stone would turn on his star. 'You are Kovic, just don't think about it. Just do it, man, do it.' Most of the time Cruise didn't need to think, as inspiration came naturally. He was inhabiting a role as never before. As Kovic himself said, 'I truly believe he actually becomes me.'

Stone wrapped after a 65-day shoot, tracing a script that

spanned three of the most turbulent decades in US history. It was the toughest he could recall, and nine months of editing still stared him in the face. It was soon obvious that the film was too long – the first working version ran eleven hours! Drastic cuts were needed, especially in the opening sequence in which the young Kovic is played by child actor Bryan Larkin. It was felt that Cruise was absent from the screen for too long. 'We've got to get to Cruise a lot faster,' said Joe Hutshing, the film's co-editor. 'Not this little kid with the puffy cheeks who looks like a squirrel.'

For the second time in a row Cruise had turned a movie Hollywood swore wouldn't make a dime into a box-office bonanza ($70m gross in the US) and in the process notched up his best ever reviews. They won't come any better than this. 'Cruise gives the outstanding performance of his brief, lustrous career' – *Sunday Times*; 'No longer the gormless, grinning ingenue of old, the US airforce endorsed dummy of *Top Gun*, Cruise finishes the movie a changed man, possibly the finest actor of his generation' – *New Musical Express*; 'This landmark performance is in every way the equal of Marlon Brando's in *The Men* and will surely be rewarded with a Best Actor Oscar' – *What's On in London*; 'Cruise displays a depth and range never previously even hinted at in a remarkable performance' – *Empire*. Cruise adorned the covers of *Premiere*, *Rolling Stone* and *Time*, which proclaimed, 'He carries the film heroically, like a soldier bearing a wounded comrade across a battlefield.' Roger Ebert, a stateside version of Barry Norman, wrote, 'Cruise is both a genuine star and a genuine actor, although not always at the same time. His work in *Born* was one of the more amazing performances in recent American movies. Few others with his star appeal would have had that depth and range.' Critics were of one voice over the Cruiser's performance, though he himself felt slightly annoyed that only now were his talents being duly recognized; 'it's not like all of a sudden I can act, for chrissake, I've been bustin' my hump for years.' Cruise scoffers went a bit quiet, save Pauline Kael (again!) who thought him 'negligible' as Kovic. The film itself was less joyously received, especially from right-wingers who attacked Stone's anti-Americanism.

Unquestionably *Born* was the most historically honest and incisive indictment of US folly in Vietnam, made with conviction and evangelical verve. Its impact was lessened only by the veritable conveyor-belt of Vietnam cinema, with Hollywood recognizing the war's status as an eighties media event. Audiences were becoming Viet-numb and tired of the usual clichés. Yet *Born* still remained an 'event' picture, its main failure being that Stone so self-consciously constructed it to be a 'Nambuster' – the Vietnam movie to end all Vietnam movies. Like *Platoon*, moreover, it peddles the myth that the real victims of the war were the invaders, not the countless number of hapless civilians wasted. Stone redressed the balance later with *Heaven and Earth*, but predictably no one in the West cared as much.

Kovic paid more than most for the sins he committed. His Vietnam baptism was a confused nightmare of casual carnage during which his unit carelessly slaughtered a village of women and children and Kovic mistakenly killed a comrade. The guilt builds so that when Kovic is himself shot it almost becomes an act of penance. His purgatory ends with a purifying confession to the family whose son he killed. The film contains a strong Christian motif – the theme of redemption. The hero can only become a man after he's been absolved of his sins, and in the process tread the path from innocence to enlightenment.

Awards were showered on the production, but alas for Cruise, not the one he wanted. The omens had looked good. The Golden Globes ceremony, the precursor to the Oscars, happened to fall on the twenty-second anniversary of Kovic's paralysing injury. *Born on the Fourth of July* swept all before it, winning best picture, director and screenplay. Proudly holding aloft his award Kovic, fighting back his emotion, said, 'No matter how difficult it may get, believe in your dreams.' The smart money in Hollywood was now riding on *Born* to clean up again on Oscar night, and Cruise became the bookie's clear favourite to snatch the top acting prize. He had already defeated among others the original would-be cinematic Kovic, Al Pacino (in the doleful *Sea of Love*), to win the Golden Globe for best actor. Despite this being Cruise's first ever award the *New York Daily News* were proclaiming that, when it comes to the Oscars, 'the Best Actor race is already over, in the eyes of many critics and insiders'. But to become the youngest actor ever to triumph in his category Cruise had to beat Morgan Freeman, Daniel Day-Lewis (for *My Left Foot*) and Kenneth Branagh. Martin Grove of *ShowBiz Today* guessed he wouldn't triumph, since 'most Academy voters don't earn $9 million for a film like Cruise, and they may express their jealousy'. David Edelstein of the *New York Post* mused that Cruise and Day-Lewis might split the wheelchair vote, leaving the prize for Freeman. But it was *Newsweek* who spoke for the masses in its stern belief that Cruise would prevail over Day-Lewis because the 'Academy likes *American* handicapped people better'.

Everyone was expecting Cruise to win (Barry Levinson tipped him for the Oscar), and no one more so than himself. Cruise attended the ceremony with his mother and future bride Nicole Kidman (and the usual entourage). The whole gang were in high spirits. Stone was there, wearing that public smile of his that looks as if it's been produced with a hammer and chisel. Ron Kovic was tearing around the concourse in his wheelchair introducing his parents to the crowd, the press and anyone who was interested. Clearly the organizers hadn't read the script, because it was the sentimental *Driving Miss Daisy* that won best film and Daniel Day-Lewis, not Cruise, who stepped on to the stage to accept the award and bask in the adulatory applause. Slight compensation came when Stone, in his acceptance speech for best director, saluted Cruise, 'for making Ron's dream come true'.

Industry analysts informed the post-Oscar world, as if it actually gave tuppence, that *Born* and Cruise had peaked too early. What made matters worse for Cruise was knowing that it was going to be tough achieving such an inspiring performance again. The likes of Spencer Tracy, Marlon Brando and Paul Newman have, say, half a dozen great performances in them; actors such as Cruise, despite his unrivalled global popularity, are lucky to reach such peaks once in their careers. Ex-girlfriend Cher offered Cruise genuine commiserations on his Oscar loss. 'He deserved it so much! But I got one eventually – and so, I'm positive, will Tom.' He could prove us all wrong, though; his bravery in tackling the role of Lestat (which, ironically, Daniel Day-Lewis turned down) bodes well. What must also be irksome is the fact that two of his co-stars – Newman and Hoffman – have won Oscars on the same bill as Cruise, while his own performance in both cases went largely unnoticed. 'But, as they remind me,' Cruise has said, 'they weren't even started at the age I am now.' This is no exaggeration. Newman was thirty-one when he made his breakthrough film *Somebody Up There Likes Me* and Hoffman was thirty when he made *The Graduate*. Both had hardly got going by the age Cruise became conqueror of Hollywood.

Did Cruise feel he was feted as a star before he was acknowledged as an actor? Almost *en masse* critics, around the time of *Rain Man*, seemed taken aback that Cruise could actually act. Barry Norman said to Cruise's face that it wasn't until *Rain Man* that he realized what a powerful actor he could be. Arguably if Cruise had been a little less beautiful he'd have acquired some of that recognition a little earlier. But the industry itself cottoned on to the Cruise talent long before the critics. When they were dismissing him as a teeny pop idol he was getting telephone calls from Ridley Scott and Martin Scorsese to be in their movies. And with each film, audiences adjusted their estimation of him – from Brat Packer most likely to succeed, to all-American dreamboat, to serious actor. Where next?

12   Director

'I want a director who expects a lot of me, because I expect a lot myself'

— Tom Cruise

Now well into his thirties, Cruise can look back at these last few years with a healthy amount of satisfaction. His most recent outings – *The Firm, Interview with the Vampire* and *Mission: Impossible* – not only saw him broadening his acting range and appeal but also made a tidy packet at the world's box offices. Buoyed by a life enriched by a wonderful marriage, Cruise has now set his sights on another cherished professional goal: the hands-on development of his own projects – to star in and, possibly, direct. He's already taken on the producer's role (*Mission: Impossible*). As someone who enjoys working with other actors it does seem that directing is the next logical step. In the summer of 1992 Cruise set up his own production company with agent Paula Wagner from CAA, one of his closest, most trusted Hollywood confidantes whom he affectionately calls 'Wags'. She shoulders the primary business responsibilities for their company, giving Cruise the freedom to concentrate on his film roles. Next on the list is *Jerry Maguire*, a comedy directed by Cameron Crowe about a conniving sports agent, originally written with another Tom in mind, of the Hanks variety. Was this leading man megalomania or genuine ambition? The star production company has become the new symbol of power in Hollywood. In Cruise's case he got an exclusive multi-picture deal with Paramount. His production company is a plush suite of offices once occupied by Howard Hughes, and on the wall inside hangs a poster from the classic movie *Sweet Smell of Success* signed by the stars. Burt Lancaster has scribbled, 'You got it, Kid' and below Tony Curtis offered, 'To T.C. from T.C.'. These star production outfits, usually headquartered on a major studio lot, multiplied like rabbits in the early nineties, with Hollywood majors desperate to forge closer links with their audience-drawing stars. What, above all, do they have in common? Dumb and obscure names. Kevin Costner's company is called Tig Productions. Why? Because he used to call his grandmother Tiggy. Cher's is called Isis, after the Egyptian goddess of fertility. Patrick Swayze's goes by the name of Troph Productions, a shortened version of his high-school nickname, Trophy, so called because he was always winning one. And Cruise named his production company Odin, after the king of the Viking gods, which really speaks for itself.

To say Cruise has always been ambitious would be an understatement. From the early days it was on the cards he would ultimately be seeking the kind of role carved out by Warren Beatty – that of producer, director and star. As early as 1986 he spoke of his desire to direct, though conceded he was far from ready. Some might argue that the Cruise control he exerts over each of his productions – script approval, casting approval, power of veto over the advertising campaign – amounts to him already having half-directed his movies. Such power is usually the domain of the director and the studio, and because Cruise knows moviemaking is essentially a director's medium, that's one of the reasons he's so keen to join up. To the star it's never been just a matter of control, but of contributing his utmost to produce the best possible picture. 'Tom didn't just sit in on the marketing meetings. He made the meetings,' says *Far and Away* producer Brian Grazer. 'He had a point of view about everything – the posters, the trailers, the distribution pattern. He's always testing you. But I don't mind it because it isn't about his ego. It's about the movie.' Cruise commits himself to projects to the point of obsession, because he cherishes the responsibility of giving his fans the best possible entertainment for their dollar. 'He's a very driven guy,' explained Ron Howard in July 1992's *Telegraph* weekend magazine. 'And you have to wonder what it would be like directing a guy like that. But Tom really wants to be a central part of the team. He expects there to be a team. And it was easy to say no, if I didn't agree with something he suggested.' This aside is enlightening, for one naturally assumes it is the director who calls the shots on a movie set, but such is the potential power wielded by a star of Cruise's box-office clout that even a director of Howard's standing needs to tread carefully in his presence.

Once you've reached a certain career plateau it becomes almost mandatory to try your hand at directing. Having worked with some of the finest modern film-makers Cruise has got to see a variety of different styles, to make notes and compare. Scorsese is renowned as the actor's director. Roger Donaldson's way of working is to convince the actors that this movie is worth their best work; he will incorporate the cast's own ideas but will be resolute in making them do take after take. Paul Brickman was the first director who allowed Cruise creative input on a picture and it taught him that an actor's best work comes when he's really communicating with a director open to suggestions. When Cruise ultimately takes up the director's cap he has these depths of wisdom to draw from; he can pick and choose his style from the very best – people like Oliver Stone, Ridley Scott, Francis Ford Coppola. One of the most satisfying things about being an actor, for him, is the opportunity it affords to meet great directors. If Cruise has enjoyed their movie he'll call them up or send them a note of congratulation or maybe, for future reference, will ask, 'How did you do that? How did you make that work?' Cruise recalls sitting and chatting with Scorsese about *New York, New York* and *Raging Bull* (a film he and Sean Penn saw numerous times while shooting *Taps*), and with Rob Reiner about his career. On the set of *The Firm* Sydney Pollack remembers Cruise hovering behind him, 'so he could eavesdrop on everything that was said'. Cruise was doing his homework, studying the director's role. 'I've always wanted to be in a situation where I could have more control over what I do as an actor. And I like challenges.' It's never much of a surprise when movie stars voice a desire to direct, though few actually get around to it, and fewer still do the job well. Kidman keeps urging her husband to try his hand at it, but Cruise still believes he's not quite ready for the big leap. A proposed deal for him to direct *The Firm* fell through. 'They wanted the picture to go quickly and I didn't feel that I had enough time. The first time you're directing, you need time.' A lesser man would have jumped in regardless of the consequences. By holding back, Cruise demonstrated great maturity and common sense. But there's no underestimating his eagerness to direct a feature film one day.

On the set of *Far and Away* Ron Howard was asked whether Cruise was capable of taking on such an enormous responsibility. 'Without a doubt. Whether he will like it or not, that's another story. But as an actor who became a director myself, I can see that

Tom thoroughly understands the process.' Once Howard invited Cruise over to his home and played him *Deed of Derring-Do*, his first ever movie, made in Super 8mm, which he had entered for the National Kodak Teenage Filmmakers Contest (it came second), and a couple of other early experiments. 'And he suffered through them,' Howard told the *Independent* in March 1992. 'But he was very flattering and kept saying you could see a connection with my later work – an offbeat quality. He was trying to make me feel I was an auteur.' Don Simpson believes Cruise can achieve just about anything he puts his mind to. 'Tom sees the big picture, not just his own part. I have no doubt that he'll end up directing a film.'

Cruise edged closer to achieving his cherished goal by directing an episode of television's *Fallen Angels*, a series of six half-hour *films noirs* co-produced by Sydney Pollack's Mirage Enterprises and premiered on the US channel Showtime in the summer of 1993. Cruise was offered the pick of several scripts and chose Jim Thompson's short story 'The Frightening Frammis', having fallen for the central character of Mitch, a hapless con artist. Cruise chose his cast carefully: Peter Gallagher and Nancy Travis as the lovers and Isabella Rossellini as the classic forties *femme fatale*. 'I was incredibly flattered. Tom called me personally and he called my agent personally,' said Rossellini. 'My agent almost had a heart attack.' On location in California Cruise was a little self-conscious: how would everyone react to this big star coming down and calling the shots? But he jumped in with the appropriate sense of humour and soon got into the swing of things. The cast actually felt secure in having Cruise directing them; being an actor himself he was on their side, though his experience in mega-movies hadn't prepared him for the shoestring budget of $700,000. He had only six days to film his episode. And how did Cruise's effort compare with those of *Fallen Angels*' other directors like Steven Soderbergh and fellow novice Tom Hanks. 'I was deeply impressed – and depressed – by how good Tom's film was,' Pollack told *Premiere* in August 1993. 'I hate it when these actors like Redford and Eastwood turn out to be such good directors!' That's rich coming from Pollack, one of the few directors who has made successful inroads into acting.

Throughout his career Tom Cruise has made a hallmark of stretching and challenging himself, seeking out partnership with directors and actors from whom he can learn; he's barnstormed his way to the top by taking risks and working with the best. Directing a feature film is the greatest challenge Cruise can assume at this stage in his career, the only mountain left to conquer. Or is it? like many of his fellow actors Cruise has become increasingly politicized in recent times. Making *Born on the Fourth of July* and working with Oliver Stone must have greatly influenced Cruise. His beliefs are a million miles away from those espoused by the film that made him famous and for which he will always be remembered – *Top Gun*. Certainly if Cruise ever decides to turn his political aspirations into reality, as Hollywood insiders believe he might one day consider, it wouldn't be long before banners proclaiming CRUISE FOR PRESIDENT will be replaced by those urging FOUR MORE YEARS. Cruise was among the elite of showbusiness who flew into Little Rock, Arkansas, to celebrate Bill Clinton's presidential election victory. It's interesting how the actors that Cruise has followed into directing (Eastwood, Redford, Beatty) are also the more politically conscious in Hollywood – perhaps they channel their politics into their filmmaking.

But film remains his first love. As a kid he'd save up the money he made from odd jobs for a trip to the cinema (his passion for movies began in earnest the day he saw *Star Wars* – he went back and saw it a further 13 times) and still gets a kick going to the opening weekend of a big new release. He's equally at home at glitzy premières or in his local cinema, guzzling popcorn with Kidman like two love-struck teenagers on a first date. Whatever career choices come next Cruise has ambitions to conquer every known movie genre. He's already done teen movie, fantasy, war, romantic epic, sport movie, courtroom drama, thriller, horror, action adventure – is a western on the horizon? Cruise, the cowboy, could convincingly take the Alan Ladd part in a remake of *Shane*. There have been ominous rumblings, too, about possible New York theatre work in an effort to hone his acting skills further. Cruise on Broadway ... Is there a theatre big enough to accommodate the crowds who'd want to see that one? And Cruise has yet to make an outright comedy – *Cocktail* and *Far and Away* provided their fair share of unintentional guffaws, but don't really count. Kidman has been trying to push him in that direction. 'The thing that people don't know about Tom is that he's so funny,' she says. 'When he's in a totally relaxed mood, he's hysterical.' But, as always, it's a question of waiting for the right script to come along. Even though he claims not to choose movies for their commercial potential, or for financial reward, the great majority of his output have been out-and-out money-spinners. *Top Gun*'s success stuck him with a reputation as an actor who's drawn only to the cinema mainstream. Has Cruise ever made even a faintly 'art house' film? Most stars make at least one 'small message movie', but even a cursory glance down the Cruise filmography reveals a veritable army of summer blockbusters. Cruise rightly claims that every movie, whatever its high-profile credentials, is a risk; no one can predict what will make money and what won't, but Cruise seems to possess, more than most, the knack of scenting out hit after hit from the Hollywood stockpile of no-hopers. If he wasn't already the most successful actor alive he'd make a fine studio executive; he'd be running the company inside a month.

13   Hollywood Religion

'I think it's despicable that Tom Cruise or anybody – celebrity or not – should be held up to ridicule because of their religion.'
— Lisa Goodman, Scientology's press representative

Out of the blistered earth it rises like a mirage, a ship that's seen no sea, no wind billowing in its sail. This is Scientology Central. Shaped like a nineteenth-century sailing clipper, the building dominates the 550-acre site, with its manicured grounds, at Gilman Hot Springs in the Californian desert. There are sports facilities galore: a soccer pitch, basketball and tennis courts, a swimming pool, a golf course and a man-made lake. Religion pays. And the whole place is surrounded by metal fencing, heavily secured entrance gates with video monitors and special pass keys.

According to its official description, Scientology is an applied religious philosophy. Its goal is to bring an individual to an understanding of himself and his life as a spiritual being and in relationship to the universe as a whole.

In 1955 'Project Celebrity' was launched with all the precision and cunning of a military campaign. Essentially a printed wish list that included Walt Disney, Orson Welles, Greta Garbo, Danny Kaye, James Stewart, Darryl F. Zanuck, Cecil B. DeMille and so on; followers were given detailed instructions for hunting them down:

If you want one of these, write us at once, giving the ONE celebrity you have selected. We will then allocate this person to you as your game. Having been awarded one of these celebrities, it will be up to you to learn what you can about your quarry and then put yourself at every hand across his or her path. [The brief concluded ...] These celebrities are well guarded, well barricaded, overworked, aloof quarry. If you bring one of them home, you will get a small plaque as a reward.

From the beginning, then, the netting of 'stars' has been part of Hubbard's strategy for success. But it wasn't until after his death, in 1986, that Scientology really hit the Hollywood big time. The roll call of celebrities extolling the virtues of Hubbard's teachings is impressive: John Travolta, Priscilla and Lisa Marie Presley, Anne Archer, Juliette Lewis (whose former boyfriend Brad Pitt dabbled for a while then dropped out), Karen Black and Kirstie Alley. There's something immediately unnatural about a religion that's seemingly out to grab as much money as it can. One needn't single out Scientology here but all religions, including the traditional ones. What was it that Jesus did to the money lenders? There's someone called Tom Cruise, too, undoubtedly the religion's biggest catch and ally in Hollywood, who is deeply involved on a day-to-day level (apparently progressing high up the ladder of the church's numerous and varied 'courses') and a powerful lure to new recruits. Like other star disciples Tom does all he can to help the church and spread the word. Photographs of Cruise, Travolta, Archer and others were displayed outside one of Scientology's New York centres along with the slogan: 'I Am A Scientologist ... Come In And Find Out Why.'

Scientology plays down its star-festooned ranks, insisting it does not cash in on its links with Hollywood. However, it calls one of its many in-house magazines *Celebrity* and its physical presence in Los Angeles is considerable, with offices on Sunset Boulevard and Hollywood Boulevard. And then there's the Celebrity Centre (whose purpose was, in Hubbard's own words, 'to forward the expansion and popularization of Scientology through the Arts'), a plush mock-Gothic château on Franklin Avenue. There Hollywood artists and professionals receive their religious services and attend seminars on such topics as 'how to make it as a TV writer' or 'how to succeed in the music business'. Advertisements for the Celebrity Centre regularly appear in trade bibles *Variety* and the *Hollywood Reporter*. The one-time hotel, built in 1927, counted Clark Gable, Errol Flynn and Bette Davis among its guests; now stars like Cruise and Travolta reside there, finding spiritual solitude away from the hubbub that their fame fosters outside. Hundreds of artists take courses at the Celebrity Centre, the great majority claiming its teachings have helped them both spiritually and in pursuit of their careers. However, a journalist from British magazine *Sky*, incognito as a rock musician, was far from impressed: 'During my two-day visit I had L. Ron Hubbard shoved so far up my ass it made my ears bleed,' he wrote. With its belief-system of overcoming doubt and ignoring rejection, Scientology seems tailor-made for actors. 'A culture is only as great as its dreams,' Hubbard once wrote, 'and its dreams are dreamed by artists.' And perhaps Hubbard's own involvement in the arts – he was a successful pulp novelist – made his theories of particular interest to other artists.

Even friends and commentators with a long-established affection and respect for Cruise were concerned by the newest development in his life, his involvement in the Church of Scientology, tagged 'The Cult of Greed' in a 1992 *Time* article. Cruise doesn't view it as a cult and credits his membership with helping him overcome his dyslexia (that drew an angry response from the Dyslexia Foundation of America who took offence to Cruise's assertion that dyslexia can be so 'miraculously' and easily cured. Cruise, on the other hand, had become convinced that he'd never been dyslexic in the first place) and enhancing his spiritual life. If anything, his devotion to Scientology has increased his drive and ambition, showing him how to channel his energy into success. Scientology, which has a worldwide following, teaches the concept of exorcising or healing the psychic scars caused by traumas in present or past lives and stresses the need to gain control of one's self and one's environment. This is achieved through a spiritual counselling process called 'auditing', sometimes with the aid of a device called an E-meter. By using it, members can cleanse themselves, free their creative spirit from past demons. This and other courses don't come cheap, and there's a host of videos, audio tapes and books. Hubbard's writings on Scientology were vast, beginning with the publication in the 1950s of *Dianetics: The Modern Science of Mental Health*, which has sold in incredible numbers. The use of such unorthodox electronic gadgetry merely serves to distance Scientology from other religions and adds credence to its wacky reputation and the accusations of brainwashing. The creed of acquiring self-control (members swear Scientology has enabled them to be in complete control of their own destiny) is what must have appealed to Cruise. He joined

some time during his marriage to Mimi Rogers, a Scientologist
since her teens, though insists he never enrolled via his then wife,
and that his involvement was of his own choosing. After turning
his back on the priesthood, perhaps Cruise has always been in
search of a Church where he could belong. Nicole Kidman is
another convert, agreeing to attend seminars soon after the
marriage because she knew the important role Scientology played
in Tom's life, though insisted she'd earlier dabbled with the cult in
Australia. She has remained as steadfastly tight-lipped on the
subject as her husband.

Cruise refused to go public about his faith until 1991, and when
challenged about Scientology he always goes on the defensive.
Certainly his continuing affiliation with the controversial
quasi-religion hasn't helped his public image. Exposés have been
written about the Church's increasing power, particularly in
Hollywood. The *Los Angeles Times* wrote about brainwashing
tactics, coercive and cult-like practices, that members were
deprived of their individuality, punished for aberrant behaviour
and worked like slaves. Most newfangled religions attract this kind
of paranoid journalism, but because Scientology attracts some of
the Hollywood elite its public image is therefore greater.
Scientologists lead ostensibly 'normal' lives; there's no head
shaving, no chanting along Sunset Boulevard or Oxford Street in
orange robes. Still, to the uninitiated, Scientology does come
across as rather weird. *Time* magazine in 1991 did a similar hatchet
job. Scientology's hierarchy are always quick to respond to
allegations it regards untrue or unfounded, launching for example
a pamphlet campaign fiercely disputing many of the claims made in
the *Time* article (they also successfully sued). They also took out a
full-page advertisement in *The Times* at a cost of more than
£20,000 in a bid to counteract the continuing spate of negative
publicity, which they claim hails from a handful of discontented
former members.

The Church's bad reputation, Cruise maintains, comes from
media ignorance and misunderstanding. He also adamantly denies
that he is surrounded by Scientology advisers who map his every
move, that they helped the couple choose their first adopted child
or that he frequently spends weekends at Gilman Hot Springs in
five-star luxury. He finds such rumours repulsive. 'To say that
someone advises me on my life or how I lead it – that's absurd.' He
does, however, count as one of his closest friends David

Miscavige, the head of the Church of Scientology. Miscavige was present at a post-wedding party CAA threw for Cruise and Kidman and also visited the location of *Far and Away*. So what? The press have painted Cruise's friendship with Miscavige as being somehow conspiratorial. 'Dave Miscavige is a good friend of mine,' Cruise told *Premiere* in response to the magazine's probing article on the religious cult in their September 1993 issue, 'and while we both wish we could see each other more often, due to my schedule and his we rarely ever see each other. This question is just off the wall. We are friends. And how is this relevant to anything? It's offensive that I should even have to answer this question.' Cruise's publicist, Pat Kingsley, castigated the magazine, insisting that writing an article about someone's religion was 'un-American'. Cruise also denies paying exorbitant fees and donations to the Church. To be fair, Tom Cruise has never personally made a big issue about his Scientology connections, it is others who make it so. He's based his whole life on utility: does something work or doesn't it? If it doesn't, like a relationship, he'll leave. Obviously Scientology works for him. Rob Reiner offered this: 'Look, I don't know anything about Scientology, but if Scientology means you're the way Tom Cruise is, then everyone should be a Scientologist! He cares and he works his butt off.'

14   The Cruise Image

'The first time someone called me a beefcake I almost threw
up. I don't want to be remembered for being just a set of
biceps and teeth.'

— Tom Cruise

Whatever that intangible 'it' is Tom Cruise has got it in spades.
Hollywood knows it, for producers fall over each other to acquire
his services at $15 million a time, and the public are only too
willing to buy; he pulls in huge audiences for almost everything he
does. In a business as superficial as the movies image is everything.
If you aren't beautiful you'd better be the next Al Pacino, because
nobody will want to know.

The Cruise trademark, and his fortune, is what tabloids boringly
refer to as that million-dollar smile, if anything a glaring
underestimate: each pearly white chopper is probably insured for
twice that. 'That guy has the most winning smile of anyone I have
seen except Eddie Murphy,' Disney chairman Jeffrey Katzenberg
once said. And according to casting director Ellen Chenoweth,
'He has that killer smile that Nicholson and Redford have.' One
sad journalist intrigued by this phenomenon even counted Cruise's
smile quota in *The Color of Money*: twenty-two. And that's not
all: what about those clear sea-green eyes of his that give women
hot flushes at fifty paces. 'His most attractive feature is his eyes,'
Valerie Golino, his *Rain Man* co-star once said. 'The way he looks
with them. They're very alive.' He's also prodigiously fit and
muscular, a body attained through a rugged training programme
and more than the usual quotient of self-discipline. The effect is
completed with a standard-issue Hollywood tan and tousled hair
crowning eternally boyish features – even as one of the undead,
Cruise looks scarcely out of prep school. With his apple-pie looks

(he's handsome in a film star-next-door kind of way), Tom Cruise sometimes comes across as the Osmond that never was; association with wacky modern religions (the Osmonds being Mormon) compounds the link. It's as if someone sat down with instructions to create from scratch the perfect movie star (Jeffrey Katzenberg once urged his animators to redesign the hero of *Aladdin* to look more like Cruise), but missed out by about five inches. Slight he may be, but he's scarcely in the same league as Alan Ladd, who had to stand on orange boxes to reach his leading ladies' lips. At 5 feet 9 inches, Cruise equals the height of Mel Gibson, Julia Roberts and Sylvester Stallone. Nicole Kidman is an inch taller. When they're seen out together in public she daren't wear high heels for fear of towering above him. For *Days of Thunder* Kidman was forced to wear flat shoes, though it's obvious that she's taller than him. It's a shame for Cruise that all actresses aren't the size of Woody Allen. Height is a perennial Cruise obsession. He's probably got this super sensitivity for good reason. *Legend*'s Ridley Scott wanted Mickey Rooney to play one of the elf characters. 'But at 5ft 2in next to 5ft 9in Tom Cruise, he didn't look that tiny.' Such remarks hardly do the ego much good. Cruise may have looked every bimbo's idea of a hunky naval pilot in *Top Gun*, but he's actually an inch short of the minimum height requirement for officers in the US Navy.

Cruise has been voted sexiest man on earth more times than Oliver Reed's had hangovers. He's so good-looking one wonders if he's ever had an ugly day in his life. A female author wrote in a German women's fashion magazine that Cruise could take a ninety-minute shower, and we would not get bored watching. 'On screen the camera adores him so much that there's a risk that he may come out looking even more gorgeous than his leading lady,' concedes *Cocktail* producer Bob Cort. Readers of *Playgirl* voted him sexiest man alive in 1990: 'That smile, those eyes – and he's muscular in all the right places,' quivered editor Nancy Martin, who has a standing offer to feature Cruise in a nude pictorial. 'We'd take off from whatever his last movie was,' Martin dreamed. 'He'd look pretty good in a race car, or maybe in the cockpit of a plane. He'd look good on top of a white sheet. He'd look good in anything. Or, better yet, out of anything.' *People* magazine couldn't help but agree:

His blockbuster portrayals of red-blooded all-American youths struggling for glory have made him the Hollywood hot-rod de jour. He has a boyish, but pulsating intensity that, no matter what the activity – shooting pool, piloting a jet, speed-pouring drinks – edges him further and further into the danger zone. Each brush with movie peril has chiselled another notch of experience into his clean-cut sensuality making him darker, sexier and more handsome. He's the boy next door as daredevil.

Cruise tends to be an advocate of the belief, propagated by good-looking people, that being handsome is a curse, that the whole sex symbol bit gets in the way of his being considered a serious actor. 'Tom is at a disadvantage,' agrees Barry Levinson. 'He's got a pretty face, so his abilities are underestimated. He's just too good-looking for some people to take seriously.' If an actor's popular and handsome they usually don't get great acceptance from critics (probably out of jealousy). Newman didn't get it for years, and Cary Grant remains one of America's most underrated actors. Being very good looking, very successful *and* young is naturally resented in Hollywood – he's obviously too pretty to be talented, too young to have taste. He grows irksome if journalists dwell too long on the point. The media, to his mind, fixates too much on the physicality of stars as opposed to their abilities. But surely he must get a kick out of being lusted after. 'People shouldn't be admired for their looks. Beauty is only skin deep.' But Cruise belongs to a Hollywood where everyone seeks the elixir of youth and where growing old is almost a capital offence, yet, revealingly, he once commented: 'Thank God that nobody stays beautiful forever.' One feels he almost yearns for middle age, when his heroes like Newman and Hoffman came into their prime, when he can finally get his teeth into some really decent and challenging roles. Perhaps he is growing tired of playing the callow youth who evolves into a responsible adult through the course of ninety minutes.

Self-evidently he's getting better offers now than he did, say, ten years ago, but the tag of America's golden boy is one Cruise hasn't quite been able to shake off – despite gallant attempts in top-drawer adult dramas like *Born on the Fourth of July* and *Interview with the Vampire*. Indeed, he was so sensitive about being exploited that after *Top Gun* he expressly forbade the release of beefcake posters that might brand him as a male bimbo. That was not the way he wanted to promote himself. To be typecast as a hunk, where's the future in that? 'I'm an actor. I don't take my shirt off to sell tickets.' Shrewdly, though, Cruise knows when to play serious and when to turn on the heart-throb act and use it to his advantage. He's hardly been averse to ripping off his shirt and flashing those pectorals on screen: during his film debut in *Endless Love* he remains bare-chested throughout, and, most notoriously the volleyball scene in *Top Gun*, having no narrative function at all, serves merely as an erotic display for the male physique. Nor did Cruise wish to capitalize on his screen image by endorsing products; as the man who put Ray-Ban on the fashion map, he could have made a bomb as the company's teen figurehead. He also refused to promote Budweiser beer in a tie-in campaign for *The Color of Money*, even though Newman was keen on the idea.

It seems Cruise guards his image as closely as his privacy. He seems genuinely amazed, nay embarrassed, by the sex-symbol tag. 'When I look in a mirror all I see is someone who needs a shave.' He doesn't take it at all seriously, seeing it as a label he's been lumped with and one that doesn't amount to much. Of course it's helped, but it's something he prefers to play down. On the other hand, Cruise has methodically exploited this sex appeal in a succession of movies where he played young cocky, hormonally charged studs. In *Risky Business* he gets down to some serious adolescent self-abuse under the bedclothes before making wild love to Rebecca DeMornay's prostitute all over his parents' furniture and on public transport. 'Even with his pants on,' wrote *People*, 'Cruise always manages to pump the screen with heat. Riding the El with Rebecca DeMornay he generates enough electricity to keep the trains live all night.' Cruise is an 'electric' actor who can infuse a film with its primary ingredient – energy. He tries something similar to girlfriend Lea Thompson in the back seat of his car in *All the Right Moves*; untempted, she later succumbs to the inevitable teenage sex scene. In *Top Gun* Cruise and McGillis try it against a wall first before realizing it's only a PG-rated film and they'd better hop into bed. *Rain Man*'s one and only sex scene is the Cruiser's finest, making love with his Italian girlfriend in Dolby stereo as Dustin Hoffman looks on, mimicking the grunts and groans and achieving simultaneous orgasm.

Curiously as the increasingly prudish Cruise took on more serious roles so the sex scenes have receded. He barely touches his own wife in *Far and Away* ... I suppose they didn't want to give too many clues away. Audiences for this 'romantic' pioneer epic had to wait one-and-a-half hours for the first tremulous kiss and when it came there was a singular lack of sparks. Was this Ron Howard taking safe sex to extremes? This film is devoid of sex, save for Kidman's occasional ogle at the Cruiser's bottom. Only this director could fill the screen with whores and then forbid his hero and heroine to make love. The *Independent on Sunday* got it right: '*Far and Away* is a one kiss nonsense, with a schoolboy's fascinated terror about sex. The film is in awe of Cruise and Kidman's privacy.' Neither does Cruise indulge in a romantic clinch with Demi Moore in *A Few Good Men*, and even had to be shown what to do by the beach hooker in *The Firm*. 'Is our newly chaste megastar purposely neutering his onscreen image from cocksure lust-bucket to sexually-repressed Scientologist, or is he just getting sheepish in his old age?' pondered *Empire* magazine in 1993. Possibly it was the influence of married life or the belief that a star of his magnitude shouldn't have to indulge in gratuitous sex on the screen. His role as the vampire Lestat was merely the dark side of the sexually athletic Cruise of old.

Perhaps it's because he's always hated doing love scenes. Admittedly there's something very odd about climbing into bed with a near stranger surrounded by a lot of staring eyes and being photographed simulating sex. It's a bit perverted to be honest. And not the least bit romantic. Making love with Elizabeth Shue in a tropical jacuzzi might sound like paradise but after hours in the tub you start to freeze to death. 'It's not quite as romantic as it looks. It was more like "Jesus, let's get this shot and get out of here." Actually, in certain shots you'll see that my lips are purple and, literally, my whole body's shaking.' For the sex scenes in *Risky Business* director Paul Brickman cleared the set, save for the cameraman, in an effort to relax his actors – even the sound people were asked to leave. 'Those scenes were hard work,' Brickman admitted later. 'It was hard to get them started, but it was harder to get them to stop.' And how far do you go? The actors are obliged to make it exciting for audiences, but there's a line that can't be crossed. Presumably you've got to be as professional as possible about it, approach it as just another scene, shove your embarrassment in the drawer, respect the other person's feelings and get on with it. Mindful of his own acute unease about love scenes on *All the Right Moves* Cruise fought tenaciously with the producers to limit the amount of nudity required of his grateful co-star Lea Thompson. 'He was very supportive in not making it exploitative,' the actress said. 'He was really protective and really open ... Tom took all his clothes off as well.'

The perfect example of Cruise's shyness yet thorough professionalism concerning sex scenes is *Born on the Fourth of July*. The sequence in the Mexican brothel where the sexually crippled Ron Kovic spends the first night of his life with a woman was Cruise's most demanding of the entire shoot. 'He's a very shy boy,' said Stone, 'and he had to do several scenes with whores. It was tough for him.' Lying in bed, a naked woman astride him, Cruise felt the emotion and touchiness of the subject matter conspire against him. He just couldn't loosen up. Take after take was rejected, and Stone cut altogether one scene where a prostitute attempts to pleasure Cruise by giving his nipples a blow-dry. It was a tough few days but Stone persevered with his camera until Cruise, an actor known for the physicality of his performances but who here had to convey emotion solely through facial expression, finally let go and began weeping. The reaction was spontaneous and unscripted, but came welling up in thoughts of losing virility, never being able to enjoy what it feels like to make love to a woman, never being able to create a life. 'On that one take something happened inside him,' remembered Stone. 'Those tears came from some place in Tom.'

15 Fathers

'My father was not very successful at living life. He had a
very unhappy life'

— Tom Cruise

Cruise was in Los Angeles preparing to fly to London for *Legend*
when a call he'd been dreading came through. 'You know how
sometimes the phone rings and – ping! – you just know?' His father
was dead. The news, however much it was expected, devastated
him. And yet there were conflicting emotions over his passing.
Cancer had been ravaging his body for years, and in 1983 he'd
been rushed to hospital for major surgery. The cancer was cut out
but clumps of this vile disease still laid waste to other areas in his
stomach, spreading all the time. Everyone knew it was too late to
stop its stranglehold. Death seemed the only cure. It came in
January 1984.

Father and son had not spoken for years. After the divorce he
vanished from their lives, severing all contact; perhaps he was
ashamed of the chaos he'd inflicted upon others or maybe he
simply couldn't cope with normal family life. Throughout his teens
Tom seldom got to hear about his whereabouts, much less saw
him. By all accounts Thomas Cruise Mapother III's self-imposed
'lost years' were spent on the road, a pathetic hand-to-mouth
existence that saw him wandering across California and the
western states, never staying long in the same place, working odd
jobs – a virtual hobo who never let go of his dream of making a
fortune with one of his inventions. He remarried, only to divorce
later. By then the road had taken its toll. Illness forced him back to
Louisville and into the forgiving arms of his parents, but it was a
sad and bitter re-entry. He never truly adjusted to life back home
and played out his final years in a cheap rented apartment, which

197

he shared with another man's wife. The cancer from which he was eventually to die was already eating away at him, and though he remained gallantly dignified throughout his battle with the disease, by the end it had physically ravaged him.

Thomas Cruise Mapother III had followed his son's career (the walls of his hospital room were adorned with photographs of Tom, though he was never to see any of his movies) without seeking out publicity on his own account. 'I can't take any credit for his success. I'm the last person who'll ever criticize him. Maybe that's one favour I've done for him.' When Tom and his sisters visited, ending years of estrangement, the emotion was too much; all their father could do was weep, tears that were contagious. Did they suddenly realize then that the strain of the divorce had destroyed a little bit in each of them, that the casualties had been on both sides? Was the fact that their father hurt too enough to forgive him the mistakes of the past? He never thought Tom would come, or if he did, would it really be him? The pictures in the papers, those film publicity shots – that wasn't his son, the lad whom he'd last seen straining for breath because he was crying so hard. When Tom walked in to his father's humble room, both saw each other for who they really were. Thomas found it difficult afterwards to express how much his children's visit had meant to him. He died soon after. Had his soul found the absolution it sought?

That final meeting cleared up much of the confusion Cruise had about the father he never truly came to know, the man who even before the divorce was never much of a father or much of a husband to Mary Lee. He was never the kind of dad who played in the garden with his kids, and it was Tom's mother who took him to his first ball game, usually a father's responsibility. Though he remained an important figure in his life (mythical perhaps?), Tom's values and motivations all stem from his stepfather and he grew up resenting the lack of a father's encouragement, love and guiding influence through the burdensome hurdles of being a teenager. It bred insecurity, bitterness and a raging anger that one suspects he's only recently come to terms with. The violent discipline which father meted out to son alone is also etched deep in Cruise's memory. Though he's testified that his father was capable of love, Tom's subjection to regular beatings would today be classified as child abuse. The young Cruise was often exposed to violent games of catch. His father's idea of teaching his son how to catch a hard baseball was by whipping it at 65 miles per hour towards his nine-year-old's body. 'He'd start lightly with the ball, then just start hammering this baseball into my glove. Sometimes, if it hit my head, my nose would bleed and some tears would come up. He wasn't very comforting.' Steadfastly refusing for years to be drawn on the topic of his father, Cruise finally broke his silence about the violence he suffered at his hands for *Vanity Fair* in October 1994. 'If I came home from a fight and I had lost, then I had to go back out there and do it again. He was one of those guys: "You go out there and you don't lose. Period." And I certainly wasn't the biggest guy on campus.' Rather than an insistence that his son be macho, it was more to do with him not losing.

> It also had to do with his own way of loving me. He was the kind of guy who really got picked on a lot at school himself when he was growing up. He had also been small, though he ended up being six foot two. People had been quite brutal to him. Inside, I believe he was a really sensitive individual. He just didn't want me to have to go through the kind of pain that he had felt in his life. I think that all this was a solution to solving that problem. He was very, very ... ah ... tough on me. Very, very tough. In many ways. As a kid, I had a lot of hidden anger about that. I'd get hit, and I didn't understand it.

This making painful peace with his past derived from an understanding that his father was a complex and troubled individual whose lifetime of mistakes ate him alive and who finally felt remorse and shame for much that had happened. Even at the end, on his deathbed, the man refused to talk about the past, allowing his children to come to the hospital on the strict condition that no uncomfortable questions were raised. Tom never once pressed his father for answers to questions that must have been torturing him since adolescence. He learned later that his father had opened his soul to the nurses on the ward, telling them the mistakes he'd made over his children. Instead Tom held tenderly on to his father's hand, said he loved him, forgave him, and was going to miss him. 'But he said to me before he died, "Look, I'm gonna get better, and you and me are gonna go and have a steak and a beer and talk about the whole thing." Well ... ah ... that dinner never ... eventuated.' The memories are painful, even today; they'll never go away. Cruise must have felt like the leading player in an old fashioned Hollywood potboiler – father and son estranged for years, then reunited on his deathbed, as themes of forgiveness and deliverance are played out. Thomas Cruise Mapother III is buried in Louisville. His son is a rare visitor.

Having already agreed to star in *Legend* prior to his father's death, Cruise could easily have walked, and he refused an offer from agent Paula Wagner to get him out of his commitment to the project. Instead he saw the film as a kind of therapy, a way of refocusing his mind away from the emotional wreckage of the last few months. Keeping himself busy and productive would stave off any wallowing guilt trips and grief. After suffering the body-blow experience of a close bereavement, the first of his life, Cruise felt it important to claw back the innocence 'within my own soul' by playing Jack o' the Green. Somehow Jack's purity of spirit helped Cruise through the double whammy of his father's death and his encroaching stardom. 'I'm just glad I had acting then,' he told *Rolling Stone* in June 1986. 'I don't know what I would have done without my work. It gave me a place to deal with all those emotions.'

Interestingly, since his father's death in 1984 Cruise has consistently attached himself to older mentors or surrogate father-figures like Dustin Hoffman and Robert Duvall. The latter commented during the making of *Days of Thunder*, 'Tom's father wasn't around. I guess he grew up having to prove something on his own. I'm sure it's something of a catalyst. It drives you further into new areas. To prove some things.' Jack Nicholson, Gene Hackman, even Ron Kovic, but especially Paul Newman all found themselves in the role of paternal mentor. This is also reflected in the roles Cruise has chosen throughout his career, characters haunted by the ghosts of fathers – making him the most suitable Hollywood star to play Hamlet. Maverick in *Top Gun* is haunted by the memory of his father who perished in the skies over Vietnam: 'My father wasn't a fighter pilot and he didn't die a hero, but I think a lot of the gut-level, emotional stuff – the love of the father and the conflict in that – is in there. And the love of my mother, also.' (*Rolling Stone*, June 1986). In *All the Right Moves* Cruise's high school jock has an inadequate relationship with his father. Scorsese's moody drama of quasi-parental rivalry, *The Color of Money*, deals with the theme of surrogate father and rebellious son. As does *Days of Thunder*, with Duvall cast as his grouchy father figure. Tom felt one of the great tragedies in *Rain*

Man was that the father dies without reconciling the difficulties with his son. 'The dynamics of the relationship with my father were different but there are similarities. The relationship between a father and son is one of the most profound.' (*Time Out*, March 1989). In *A Few Good Men* his lawyer struggles to put his father's ghost to rest once and for all and become his own man by destroying the patriarchal Colonel Jessep (Jack Nicholson) in the witness stand. The subtext speaks of a younger man defying a father figure. 'I was never really in the shadow of my father, because I didn't see him for many years,' Cruise told *Empire* in February 1993 of his ability to relate to Daniel Kaffee's inner demons. 'But I think my father would have enjoyed seeing me and seeing the success I have attained. I think he would have enjoyed seeing that an awful lot. I never got a lot of acknowledgment from him.' In *The Firm* Cruise plays a hot-shot lawyer whose coalminer father died in a pit disaster and who is tempted into a law practice by the security of a close family atmosphere. By the time of his next film, *Interview with the Vampire*, the tables had turned and it was Cruise inhabiting the father figure/mentor role for Brad Pitt, whom he's created for company and as a hunting partner.

'I have cried tears of frustration. I'd love to have kids. I'd turn down an Oscar to see my little boy in a baseball game or my little girl in a song and dance recital'

— Tom Cruise

The emotional wreckage of his parents' divorce, his father's rejection and the failure of his first marriage accounts for Cruise's desperate drive to have a stable family life of his own. If you believe the tabloid press Kidman has had more phantom pregnancies since marrying Cruise than a London Zoo panda. Complete strangers felt justified in waltzing over to enquire whether or not she was pregnant yet. One woman even had the temerity to say loudly to a friend, 'Of course she's pregnant – look at that little belly!' It was degrading to have to put up with such ill-mannered people, but not unexpected. 'I can understand people wanting to see a little Tom Cruise running around.' Being in the spotlight of so much media attention could well drive you crazy but as a kid Nicole idolized movie stars, reading all she could about them; now on the receiving end herself she understands and has learned to live with it.

In the summer of 1991 speculation reached fever pitch, sparked off by inaccurate quotes about Tom 'bursting with pride' about imminent fatherhood. 'It's a miracle,' he allegedly exclaimed. 'She's pregnant and I did it. I can't wait to hold my first-born in my arms.' Newspapers even claimed that, fearing another childless marriage, Cruise insisted Nicole take a fertility test before tying the knot. It was all nonsense and Kidman scotched the rumours by going skydiving with her husband, an activity not exactly recommended for expectant mothers.

Like an annoying house guest the rumours didn't go away. Intrusive interviewers were told that though they'd love to have kids in the future now was not the time – they were just too busy, too caught up in their careers and each other to worry about the responsibilities of parenthood. The pressures were enormous. Tom felt them more having recently turned thirty, and he sought out top medical advice as to why Nicole wasn't pregnant yet, as he'd done previously with Mimi. It was the second time mother nature had thwarted him from becoming a father. People were starting to ask why.

In December 1992 a joint decision was made to privately adopt a baby in Palm Beach, Florida, and the relevant papers were filed. Under local law prospective parents were required to be residents, but that wasn't a problem as they owned a luxury condominium there and Cruise's parents had lived in the area for years. Despite every precaution to keep things quiet, to the extent of Cruise's PR woman Pat Kingsley rubbishing the very existence of the adoption papers, news of the arrangement leaked out. Before a D-Day-style media invasion could be launched a furious Cruise ordered the adoption be cancelled. It was a massive setback, but the secret search continued for another child. The mere fact that the couple were seeking adoption fuelled growing speculation about Cruise's own fertility. Unable to conceive a child with his first wife, it seemed the same problem had surfaced with Nicole; people were starting to whisper. Then a healthy baby girl was born to a married mother who already had two children and couldn't afford the burden of rearing a third. Cruise and Kidman are only too aware of the plight of these unwanted babies who are in need of a good home and loving parents, and both sincerely endorse adoption programmes. Kidman flew in from Los Angeles on hearing the news, and Cruise, who was in Memphis shooting *The Firm*, rushed down to join his wife for a few days to bond with their daughter, whom they named Isabella Jane Kidman Cruise. 'In 20 years of working with adoptions,' a nurse told the *National Enquirer* in February 1993, 'I have never seen anyone so overjoyed as Nicole was when she first held her new daughter.' The actress knew from the moment their eyes connected that this was the perfect baby for, well, the perfect couple. When asked if there had been a reason for adopting their first child Kidman told *Vanity Fair* in October 1994, 'No. It just happened that way. Isabella was meant for us. I think when things come into your life at a certain time you have to take them. It's destiny.'

Cruise and Kidman's high-profile lifestyle and heavy-duty workload must give rise to doubts about whether superstars can truly devote themselves to baby care. Their irregular work hours mean they often have little time for family life. Are those stars who adopt prepared to add another complication to their lives? Certainly parenthood took its predictable toll on the Cruises' marriage, both finding they had less time for each other. Cruise certainly seems committed to offering Isabella a loving, stable home and putting her before his career, instead of palming her off to nannies all the time. 'I want to be there for my family,' he said. 'My family is the most important thing in my life. Becoming a father makes you realise what it is all about.' But can an individual as ambitious as Cruise keep to such a commitment? And how do they hope to avoid the curse of the messed-up Hollywood kid? 'By sending her to a normal school,' says Kidman. 'By not treating her with kid gloves. By allowing her to be who she is. By always being there for her, like my parents were always there for me.' And Cruise insists: 'We're not going to raise them in LA, where all the kids get Ferraris when they're 16. There's just no way in hell that's ever going to happen with ours.' Both believe in lavishing love on their children, but being strict and having rules, guidelines and boundaries. 'As my father says, "with love but firm," ' continued Kidman. 'I think that's the key to it: being firm but knowing that it's always based on love.'

Cruise is by nature a traditionalist and intends raising Isabella in an environment that's as near normal as possible, despite the fact his life has changed beyond recognition since stardom. He's no raving recluse, as some might suppose; in fact he leads a quite regular existence that runs contrary to his reputation as one of entertainment's most intensely private people. They do not tend to venture forth into public much – Cruise is nervous of crowds – but are nonetheless an active family, in a low-key sense. They go shopping in malls, attend movies and plays, visit museums, stroll in the park. Because of their easy-going attitude they are pretty much left alone by the *paparazzi*, making them one of the most 'normal' high-profile families in Hollywood. Well, not always. On a family yachting holiday in the Mediterranean Tom had to inveigle the local police to disperse hordes of happy snappers.

Cruise is adamant that Isabella shouldn't miss out on activities other children enjoy, even sharing with her his work. Making *Interview with the Vampire* Isabella was often on the set. The first time Cruise was made up as the dandyesque bloodsucker Lestat he was concerned that she wouldn't recognize him or that his face would terrify her. It was decided that next time she would sit on her father's lap while he was in make-up, so as to grasp as much as she could what was going on. Cruise would show Isabella pictures of Lestat and ask, 'Who is that?' to which she'd reply, 'Daddy.' The Cruises often travel as a family unit, maintaining their nomadic habits, (Kidman is as much a wanderer as Cruise, 'I feel trapped if I have to stay in one place too long'), and offering their children as they grow up a varied and cosmopolitan upbringing. The whole family spent months together in London while Cruise was shooting *Mission: Impossible* and Kidman shot the English scenes for *Portrait of a Lady*. Isabella and Tom were frequent visitors to the *Batman Forever* set, but Nicole barred her daughter from the set of *To Die For*; it was a difficult enough role without the added distraction of visiting offspring. So Tom, who's more than happy in the caring role, looked after her. 'He's fantastic,' Kidman said to *Vanity Fair* in July 1995. 'He sits with the mothers in the playgroup; he goes to the playground. He'll be the only guy there.' Both try to alternate their work, plan it so at least one of them can be home to devote time to the kids. Cruise took nearly a year off after filming *Interview with the Vampire* to be with his family – he seems not to be shirking the responsibilities of fatherhood, despite his workload.

Is it fair dropping kids into the home of a celebrity given the risks involved? Cruise is only too aware of the pressures fame places on children and has done his utmost to shield Isabella from photographers and public scrutiny. No Cruise family portraits in *Hello* magazine like other sad celebrities, and for that both are to be applauded. As Kidman put it, 'I don't want my children splashed across the cover of magazines, I don't want them put into the spotlight like that.' But the intense media interest on the couple (which intensified, as if that were possible, the moment they adopted baby Isabella) could be damaging, and not just in a general psychological sense: she could face kidnap threats or be bullied by other kids for having such famous parents.

'Being a father is what I always dreamed of – only a hundred times better. I couldn't be happier. She has changed my life.' In some interviews Cruise talked in that irritating way new fathers have, at once boastful and resentful about this screaming bundle that's divebombed your life: 'I remember when I used to go out and party all night and sleep in till noon. Now 9.30am seems decadent.' In other interviews, however, every word, every syllable resonates with the incredible joy he derives from being a father. 'Seeing Nicole with Isabella, I see a whole other side to her,' Cruise told *Vanity Fair* in October 1994. 'Sometimes I just stand there and listen to them play. Sometimes Nic will forget to turn the baby-speaker off, and I'll just sit there and listen to them. Those are the little moments in life when you stop and think. I want to make sure I'll remember this forever. I'm a daddy,' the journalist heard Cruise whisper, more to himself than to his guest, 'I'm a daddy.' Cruise had waited a long time to say that. 'I think he desperately needed family,' observed Dustin Hoffman once. 'Whether it was my family or the makeshift family of the crew. Now, when he's playing with his kids, I can see it in his eyes. He loves it and needs it.'

Reports soon filtered out of plans to adopt a second baby, fuelled by the couple's open admission that they still hoped to have children of their own. These rumours turned out not to be false, only premature. Early in 1995 Isabella got a baby brother and Tom Cruise the son he'd always wanted. The fact that the Cruises had adopted a second child, christened Connor Antony Kidman Cruise, an African-American boy, prompted yet more gossip. But no one was letting on. 'I would like to give birth to two children,' was Kidman's response. 'I would like to experience that. But if I don't, it's not going to destroy me.' The couple proudly posed with their children when they flew into Sydney in January 1996 to attend the wedding of Nicole's sister Antonia. Tom gladly took charge of the stag night and offered his private jet to ferry guests up to Queensland for weekend frolics, frittering away a reported $45,000 at the casino tables. It was the first time that Connor had been photographed with his father, mother and sister.

Having a family of his own has made Cruise more appreciative
of his parents and what they accomplished and led to a
re-evaluation of how his own father treated him as a child. 'I think
sometimes what it would have been like for him to see me with my
son and daughter.' When Cruise looks at his kids he can never
understand how a father could desert his own flesh and blood and
it makes him all the more determined to prevent Isabella and
Connor from ever experiencing the trauma of parents who
divorce. It's politically correct always to blame parents for kids'
problems. Cruise believes you've got to take responsibility for
yourself. His parents did the best they could. He acknowledges
that his own father worked damn hard but was of the old school
that believed a woman's place was in the home, one arm
handcuffed to the stove, the other to the pram. Cruise, by
contrast, wanted to become involved in every aspect of raising his
children – and that meant nappies, the curse of the nineties man.
His first confrontation with them scared him half to death. 'I didn't
know what the hell I was doing.' And one mustn't forget the
ungodly horrors of getting up at all hours of the night to soothe a
crying baby who'll do anything but go back to sleep. Once, Cruise
attended a meeting to plan the intricate climax to *Mission:
Impossible* with Connor in tow. The group included director Brian
De Palma, the art director and the actors. The meeting was called
to order when Cruise suddenly asked for absolute silence. Connor
had dozed off. 'We couldn't talk too loud because Connor was
sleeping,' Jon Voight remembers. Essentially he sees the role of a
parent in terms of a teacher. Every time Isabella or Connor falls he
wants to be there for them before it happens. 'But that's not
helping them. What you have to do is teach them how to solve
their own problems. I'll try to be there for them, but not solve
their problems.'

16   Cruise Law

The script conferences are getting more heated, voices are raised, fists pound desks. *A Few Good Men*, Aaron Sorkin's old-fashioned courtroom drama, a nineties *Caine Mutiny*, ran on Broadway for 449 performances, garnering standing ovations every night. Now he's being told it's not good enough to be a movie. Sorkin was warned about Hollywood.

Physically there's no mistaking the one doing most of the yelling. Big, bearish, and looking as if he missed a vocation as a nightclub bouncer, Rob Reiner is one of the most respected and commercially sure-footed megaphone men working in Hollywood today. His output – *This is Spinal Tap*, *Stand By Me*, *The Princess Bride*, *When Harry Met Sally*, *Misery* – reveals a talent for diversity. It's difficult arguing against someone who's never directed a flop. Every day on the set of *A Few Good Men* he wore white trousers and a white shirt. Reiner didn't want to think about anything else, so he always wore white.

Given the movie's lack of car chases, explosive mayhem, special effects and wanton sex, Reiner's challenge was to find drama in the dialogue; he wanted a rationale behind every utterance, every inflection. 'Why does Cruise's character say this, instead of just walking out the door?' Reiner demands, staring at Sorkin above the table, which he thumps for emphasis. The 29-year-old playwright thinks that if he just closes his eyes for a moment before opening them again it will all have been a horrible dream. This is a terrified, thoroughly cheesed-off shell of a man who hasn't the energy left to come up with an answer that will satisfy Reiner. 'It'll work. Okay? Trust me,' he finally bleats. 'We'll fix it later.' Reiner does an impression of a pressure cooker that's just flipped its lid. 'It will not work! No, NO! NOOO!! I gotta know now! Because if you can't tell me here, I can't tell Tom Cruise on the set.'

Sorkin couldn't care less what Reiner tells Cruise on the set. With each passing day more of his precious text is trounced, violated, until it begins to resemble something other than what played on Broadway to such stirring acclaim. 'I've never worked with anybody before,' Sorkin confided to *Premiere* in January 1993. 'I felt like somebody was living in my house and rearranging the furniture. Reiner starts on page one, where you've written "Fade in," and before he gets to the next sentence he stops and says, "Okay, tell me why we're fading in." I'm not exaggerating.'

Slowly Sorkin's pain began to alleviate: the script was improving right in front of his disbelieving eyes. In fact, it ended up being so much better that Sorkin rewrote his original play. *A Few Good Men* became a play based on the screenplay, which had been based, in turn, on the stage play.

Cruise was the first of the high-voltage cast on board. Kidman had seen the stage play, in which Tom Hulce starred as hot-shot Navy lawyer Lieutenant Daniel Kaffee, and told her husband it was a must-see. 'There's a great role for you.' But he was too busy. A week later and he got a call from Reiner. 'Hey, Tom, I'm directing this movie, whaddya think?' Cruise had always wanted to work with Reiner – 'He's never made a bad movie' – so bought a ticket for the show. That night he phoned back: 'Yeah, let's make it.'

In the winter of 1991 Cruise went over the script with Reiner prior to shooting to discuss his role, which was tailor-made for him and perhaps a homage to the Mapothers of old. Tom's uncle William Mapother was a local judge and his grandfather Thomas Cruise Mapother II a respected lawyer. Back in uniform as another shallow maverick, with a chip the size of New Jersey, Cruise is haunted by the corpse of his celebrated attorney father, frightened to strike out on his own for fear of comparison. As an easy way out, Kaffee arranges plea bargains for every vagrant that he represents. Their guilt or innocence is irrelevant; he is interested simply in sliding up the greasy pole of success. Then he is goaded into defending two marines accused of killing a platoon weakling whilst doling out a code red – an illegal punishment – at a US military base in Cuba. The film questions how far marine discipline turns out men who put morality second to orders – it's about cold war values in changing times. But these potentially interesting themes are buried beneath a compost of courtroom cliches. *A Few Good Men* is high-style pulp, and you can almost feel the movie groaning under its own self-importance. The subtext is oedipal: only when Cruise can stand up to his nemesis Jessep (the bad father figure) – a jingoist in charge of the marines who connives in covert murders and cheap cover-ups – and smash him in court will he be able to count himself a man. There's a great moment in court where Jessep sneeringly refers to Cruise as 'son'.

Kaffee's co-counsel and voice of conscience, Jo Galloway, was a plum role in an industry starved of decent parts for actresses, though it is still a mere satellite to the Cruiser's male heroics. Reiner wanted to avoid the cheap ploy of throwing these two characters into bed together. The no-romance scenario, the only unexpected 'twist' in a thoroughly formula-bound work, caused consternation when the film was viewed at TriStar. One studio executive made these notes about the script: 'Why is Jo a woman? She doesn't take her top off and there's no love scene.' A sad commentary. 'We talked about Michelle Pfeiffer,' said casting director Jane Jenkins, 'but decided that if you put two of the most beautiful people in the world together, the audience would be disappointed if there wasn't a love story.' After Jodie Foster turned down the part (she rejected it because the male lead, not the female, was the focal point of the film), Demi Moore was chosen in spite of being eight months pregnant at the time of the audition. This was just one month after the Moore/Willis bulge was famously premiered on the cover of *Vanity Fair*.

Demi Moore's alleged prima donna behaviour has for years been the subject of professional gossip, earning her the unfortunate nickname 'Gimmie Moore'. *A Few Good Men* was irrefutably Tom Cruise's film, yet she insisted on playing dressing-room politics. Cruise has it written into his contract that his dressing-room trailer be positioned closest to the sound stage. Apparently, the bigger the star the less far you should have to walk. Not to be outdone Moore demanded and got a double trailer, arguing she needed extra space to accommodate her children, who visited the set daily. Then she embarked on negotiations with Cruise to have her trailer moved into his spot. Jack Nicholson, an old hand at dealing with temperamental co-stars, shrugged his shoulders and laughed at such petty little games.

It was a cast to die for, an agent's dream list, and in Hollywood Reiner's film earned the nickname 'A Few Big Names'. But it didn't come cheap: Cruise bagged $12.5 million, Moore about $3

million and Nicholson around $5 million (not bad for ten days'
work). *A Few Good Men* would have been a cheap movie to make
had you dispensed with the actors. And can you imagine how
many personal assistants were huffing and puffing around the set.
When filming began Sorkin imagined 'it would be a huge car crash
of egos'. Remarkably production passed off smoothly, with plenty
of opportunities for everyone to grandstand – great ensemble
playing, actor power at full throttle. But it's Nicholson who towers
over everyone, playing to the gallery. It says much for Cruise that
he doesn't come off too much like second best in their combustible
showdown, in which Jessep goes ballistic in court. Cruise brings
conviction to his wastrel-turned-hero, and he's a good enough
actor to bring off the legal jousting. Starting out cynical and cocky
Kaffee's character evolves during the second reel. Alarmed at the
thought of going to trial, with Galloway feeding him dark talk of
facing up to daddy's ghost, he finally squares up to his
responsibilities as a lawyer. The problem is that Cruise is so readily
pigeon-holed as the crusading good guy audiences never doubt
he'll pull his socks up by the end.

Going to work each morning to act opposite Jack Nicholson
Cruise often had to pinch himself, though that didn't stop him
from doing the odd wicked impersonation of the veteran, unlike
Christian Slater who has made an entire career out of doing it. In a
classic case of hero-worship, eighteen-year-old Cruise and pals
Sean Penn and Emilio Estevez used to drive past the great man's
house late at night. If the lights were on they'd think, Wow, he's
home – let's go knock on the door. But they always chickened out.
Nah, nah, he'll never let us in. Cruise told Hoffman this years later
and he said, 'Wrong. You should have knocked.' And Cruise
knew it. 'Damn it,' he raved. 'I should have.' One day on the set
Cruise finally confessed all to Nicholson who roared with laughter.
They had got the wrong house. Who knows, maybe fans drive past
Cruise's home waiting for his lights to go on. When Nicholson
walked into the first rehearsal the young cast, which also included
Kiefer Sutherland and Kevin Bacon, were so reverential that the
veteran star told Reiner afterwards, 'Rob, it was so strange, I felt
like the fucking Lincoln Memorial.' Nicholson confessed to
actually blushing.

Cruise's near-legendary generosity manifests itself in many
forms. One of the consequences of growing up poor is that if
you're lucky enough to come into money you never forget your

poverty, your roots, and are more likely to help those still in distress. Cruise, for example, often makes charitable donations or unpublicized visits to children in hospital (in South Carolina, filming *Days of Thunder* Cruise found time to raise the spirits of a ten-year-old girl in desperate need of a heart transplant). While in Memphis filming *The Firm* Cruise donated $15,000 to a local children's hospital, and a lipstick imprint of the Cruise kiss once fetched $1,000 for an AIDS fund raiser. In March 1996 it was reported that Cruise paid the hefty medical bill of a destitute hit-and-run victim he'd found lying unconscious in the road near his Hollywood home. The actor called an ambulance and followed on behind, settling the bill once at the hospital. Such generosity also extends to the workplace; Cruise has been known to pick up the tab for 'wrap' parties, held to celebrate the end of filming, usually the duty of the studio, or to present crews with personal mementoes. On *A Few Good Men* he flew the entire cast in his private jet, a snip at $15 million, to Las Vegas for dinner and hired a private salon at the Mirage Hotel for an evening of betting (both Cruise and Kidman love to gamble). Crowds gathered when Cruise, Moore and husband Bruce Willis decided they wanted to play the slot machines in the main casino. 'I really enjoyed hanging out with Tom Cruise,' fellow guest Kevin Pollack said afterwards. 'It gave me a chance to see how the other one percent live.' Pollack, who played Tom's work buddy in the movie, was on the receiving end of another Cruise gift, an expensive pen identical to one he'd earlier admired Cruise using. When Cruise saw Pollack wasn't writing with the pen he had bought him – 'I'm scared to use it, Tom, because, I dunno, I might lose it or something' – one of the star's assistants dispatched another one to Pollack's trailer.

After the summer, the Christmas season is Hollywood's most lucrative box-office period and the last-chance saloon for studios to get their hottest product in line for Oscar contention. One of the most eagerly awaited movies of the year, *A Few Good Men* rolled out on 11 December on 1,800 screens with a massive media blitz. It needed all the help it could muster against some mighty big guns hovering on the holiday horizon – Kevin Costner's *The Bodyguard*, Coppola's *Dracula* and Disney's *Aladdin*. It comfortably held its own thanks to Cruise-charged firepower and four Oscar nominations, including Best Picture; commentators were pleasantly surprised that a movie not reliant on special effects or action could do such big business. What seemed to be re-emerging was the kind of well-crafted movie, fuelled by the power of a popular star, that Hollywood traditionally has done best, but had lately eschewed in favour of more obvious pyrotechnics. Cruise also picked up a Golden Globe nomination for his bravura performance. But yet again it was his elder co-star who garnered the most plaudits and press attention. Nicholson's extended cameo was Oscar-nominated, while Cruise, who barnstorms through the film like a mad dervish, was overlooked again by an Academy ever contemptuous of too much success. Moreover, like the film, the young pretender courted decidedly mixed reviews: '*A Few Good Men* is a handy American product like Teflon or I Can't Believe It's Not Butter – it's nontoxic and durable, and I would be pleased to have it under my sink, next to the soft scrub and acrylic floor wax. *Men* is a product of old fashioned American know-how, like napalm and Cheez Whiz.' Thus jibed *Premiere*. Indeed Cruise's performance was one of his least critically admired. The *Independent on Sunday* was the most venomous: 'Cruise tries to project thwarted brilliance, but his strutting and fretting never convince for a moment. It's all one note: he does nervous the way he does angry the way he does cocky. His performance is mush. His fuming-drunk act after a set-back in court is the most embarrassing thing he's done since his stupid cue-twirling jive in *The Color of Money*'.

The word bestseller could almost have been coined for *The Firm*: John Grisham's Americanized version of the Faust legend was scooped up by Paramount for $600,000 on the strength of a one-sentence pitch and before even a word had been written. It then went on to sell seven million copies, becoming the blockbuster novel of 1991 and that summer's beach page-turner. Today lawyer-turned-author Grisham ranks alongside Michael Crichton (*Jurassic Park, Disclosure*), Tom Clancy (the Jack Ryan series) and Stephen King as the most Hollywood-friendly novelist, in spite of writing books that make average cinema. I'd defy anyone to stay awake, let alone enjoy, *The Pelican Brief* or *The Client* or, for that matter, *The Firm*.

Brand names help to sell movies to the public. Was it author John Grisham or Julia Roberts who got bums on seats for *The Pelican Brief*; Tom Clancy or Harrison Ford who got box office tills ringing for *Patriot Games*? You don't have to guess that hard. Tom Cruise singlehandedly turned *The Firm* into an international money-spinner. I doubt any other actor could have kick-started such a deadly dull movie towards mega-grosses. Superior it may have been to Alan J. Pakula's formulaic *The Pelican Brief*, but like its literary companion, read on a long-haul flight and binned at the arrival airport, Sydney Pollack's star-studded adaptation of Grisham's effective but trashy legal thriller is as disposable as a Big Mac, only less good for you.

Kevin Reynolds was originally slated to direct the picture, but his reported asking price of $3 million was turned down flat. Pollack, his replacement, himself classified *The Firm* as nothing profound, just a good dose of entertainment. Nothing wrong with that, but at two-and-a-half hours the line between entertainment and harrowing torture begins to blur. We watch Cruise meander through the film looking as mystified as the rest of us by what the screenwriters are asking him to do, secure in the knowledge that we won't become over-excited. Pollack has created a tension-free zone, a thriller that hinges on its hero photocopying incriminating papers without anyone noticing, hardly edge-of-the-seat stuff. Pollack blames himself for the insufferable length and given more post-production time would have drastically shortened it. 'I thought that the length would be its downfall,' he admitted, 'but people seem willing to sit.' Critics weren't. '*The Firm* is a very long haul and you could take half an hour out for a drink and a sandwich and not miss all that much,' condemned the *Guardian*. However, compared to the usual summer thriller fare of body-count pap, *The Firm* is quite a literate piece; it's not dumb, just boring. The book was a toughie to convert to celluloid, Pollack claiming it to be the most demanding adaptation he'd ever attempted. Severe changes to the text were inevitable, and the three writers (including *Days of Thunder* veteran Robert Towne) beat themselves senseless for months on end. Production was held up as they disgorged rewrite after rewrite, unsure whether to remain as faithful as they could to Grisham or try something more ambitious. Whilst the book's Mitch winds up in the government's witness protection programme, a permanent fugitive from the mob, Pollack redeems his hero. Instead of staying in purgatory Cruise/Mitch learns his moral lesson with barely a scratch, which suggests a star flexing his box-office muscles at the plot's expense.

Cruise loved the book, which he read during lulls in making *Far and Away*. 'I thought, this is a terrific yarn, this could be a great character for me.' At thirty-one Cruise is just plausible as grin-flashing law-school graduate Mitch McDeere, lured to

Memphis by a law firm promising big bucks and a Mercedes, only to tumble, after what seems like an eternity, that his new employers are on nodding terms with the Mafia. The dilemma facing Mitch, to go with the flow and get busted by the FBI or rock the boat and risk cement footwear, is what drew Cruise to the part. Mitch is an idealist, dedicated, hard-working, ambitious – quite a catch for any company. McDeere's inherent goodness, in conflict with an earnest drive and dark greed, was an interesting combination to play. From a poor background, Mitch has petty-bourgeois ambitions, which makes him a vulnerable target for the firm; he's the boy-next-door offered the American dream only for it to turn into a nightmare. He has sold his soul without even knowing it. Much like *Rain Man*, *The Firm* is a condemnation of the spiritually empty values of yuppiedom – young guns going after rewards of salary and status but at the price of their own morality. Mitch considers this price too high and takes on a corrupt system single-handedly (the mob and the FBI). Naturally, because he's Tom Cruise, he wins, finally nailing the lawyers for serious fraud.

The moral Hollywood of the nineties is preoccupied with correcting the perceived sins and indulgences of the eighties, and the reputation of lawyers has been one of the casualties of that decade's boom-and-bust philosophy. Not surprisingly lawyers, who rate just above serial killers in the popularity stakes, accused *The Firm* of being a negative portrayal of the legal profession – that it was 'attorney-bashing'. Cruise is passable in the role, and his legion of fans will be satisfied by their idol's angst-ridden heroics. *The Firm* makes no bones about its star attraction: Cruise gets close-ups galore and is scarcely off-screen ('like Hollywood's star vehicles of old, the main point here is not the plot, but the hallowed one's very presence' – *The Times*). But because here he cannot fall back on the flashy courtroom histrionics of *A Few Good Men*, his weary, bruised innocence isn't quite enough to save the movie. No guessing who was first choice for the role. 'He was a natural for this part,' said executive producer Michael Hausman. 'It's a very high-profile actor movie.' Grisham, who regularly visited the set with his family, also deemed Cruise perfect casting. For the star there was the opportunity to work with another master film-maker in Sydney Pollack, who after filming had nothing but praise. 'I think he is the most voraciously curious actor I have ever worked with,' the director told *The Times* in September 1993.

He's dying to learn. He sits there with his ears and eyes open, waiting for you to tell him. He has much more range than many people realise. He throws himself into his roles with no vanity at all. At the end of *The Firm*, I wanted him to look as if he had really been through something. John Seale, the director of photography, whispered to me, 'Are you sure you want him to look this awful?' He had no vanity about looking pale and red-eyed. I expect great things from him.

Julia Roberts declined to play the Cruiser's wife and newcomer Jeanne Tripplehorn inherited the part. Pollack was at one time toying with the idea of giving Gene Hackman's character – a womanizing, ball-busting attorney at the all-male firm – a sex change to attract Meryl Streep. Even with the mouth-watering possibility of Cruise and Streep on the same screen Grisham was apparently less than thrilled at the prospect of several key scenes needing a drastic revamp. The idea was dropped.

The film's one redeeming feature is the sterling support cast, many of whom steal the Cruiser's thunder. Notable among them are Holly Hunter, Ed Harris (less an FBI agent than Hannibal Lecter's loonier kid brother) and Gene Hackman as a burned-out lawyer, dimly aware of his original ideals, who becomes a mentor of sorts to Mitch. Hackman's name was conspicuously absent from the credits and the film's posters. Hackman is used to seeing his name in lofty places, but Cruise has it etched into his contracts that his name alone stands above the title and that his face dominates a film's publicity material. Such is the man's power that he can effectively oust one of America's most respected actors from his film's poster. Informed there was no way he'd get equal billing (Paramount argued that would make audiences confuse the thriller with a buddy movie), a dismayed Hackman, then hot stuff having recently won a supporting-actor Oscar for *Unforgiven*, elected for complete anonymity. 'I am not going to be a supporting actor to Tom Cruise,' ranted Hackman. 'Where are his Oscars?' Kevin Costner was quite happy the following year to share top honours with Hackman for *Wyatt Earp*, so why wasn't Cruise?

The film looked a sure-fire summer hit. After all Cruise hadn't misfired yet doing what his public like him for best: acting the arrogant upstart who battles against seemingly insurmountable odds and wins. Yet Hollywood had been so preoccupied by the astonishing success of *Jurassic Park* that no one had paid much attention to *The Firm*, which in its opening weekend knocked the Spielberg picture off its box-office perch. In the process it raced past the significant $100 million mark in a mere twenty-three days – reminding everyone that in Cruise here was an old-fashioned movie star who didn't need dinosaurs or explosions to sell tickets. *The Firm*, if little else, confirmed Cruise as possibly the leading male actor of our time. A grateful Paramount rewarded him with a spanking new Mercedes convertible. But Cruise was less than ecstatic when he received a hefty bill for the 'free' gift after the tax authorities heard of the studio's generosity. Nor was he happy about *The Firm*'s lukewarm critical reception. 'It is a rotten movie, far too long, poorly constructed, frequently preposterous, in parts downright incomprehensible' – *Daily Mail*; 'This is crap. Another wearisome thriller-cum-chase movie, which has all the formulaic appearance of being concocted by a computer' – *Morning Star*, not mincing their words.

17 Top Fang

Before: 'Cruise is no more my vampire Lestat than Edward
G. Robinson is Rhett Butler.'

After: 'The charm, the humour and invincible innocence
which I cherish in Lestat are all alive in Tom Cruise's
courageous performance.'

— Anne Rice

Not in living memory has the casting of a movie caused such public
acrimony. Hollywood's collective mouths dropped when it was
revealed that Anne Rice's bitchy, androgynous and diabolical
bloodsucker was to be none other than the squeaky-clean,
all-American Tom Cruise. Rice went ballistic; some dark cloud
had deliberately sought her out and was now ruining her parade.
She interpreted the choice of Cruise as a personal affront, and
regarded those responsible as idiots. As for Cruise, who could
never be her blue-eyed, golden-haired vampire, she subjected him
to a stream of vitriol rare even for Hollywood; no opportunity was
missed to badmouth him in public. 'I'm puzzled as to why Cruise
would want to take on the role,' she said to the *Los Angeles Times*
in August 1993. 'He's a cute kid, on top of the world and on his
way to becoming a great actor (note the condescending manner),
but I'm not sure he knows what he's getting into. He should do
himself a favour and withdraw.' After that things got really ugly.
The legions of Rice readers, who follow her work with an almost
religious fervour, were just as implacably opposed to Cruise
inhabiting the cloak of their beloved Lestat. They protested *en
masse*, with demonstrations, petitions and hate mail; 'No Tom
Cruise! No Tom Cruise! No Tom Cruise!' placards read at Rice
book signings – though only in the United States. Director Neil

Jordan was confronted in a New Orleans bar by a fan protesting about Cruise – she'd tattooed her choice of actor on her stomach! Did the pulp Gothic scribblings of Rice really warrant such fanaticism? Certainly the industry was stunned by the vehemence of Rice's campaign to discredit the actor and the movie.

The film's backer, David Geffen, whose influence on Cruise stretches back to the hit *Risky Business*, was so enraged by Rice's conduct that he communicated with the author only through their respective lawyers. Over the years Cruise has befriended a high number of Hollywood power brokers, and two of the biggest leapt to the star's defence with public proclamations of support. 'I was astounded by the flak we've gotten,' Geffen told *Vanity Fair* in October 1994. 'Especially since Cruise is certainly one of the two or three greatest actors of his generation. The only thing that bothered me about people's reaction to Tom was that I know how sensitive Tom is and I knew that it would hurt his feelings.' Next up for damage limitation was Jeffrey Katzenberg, chairman of the Walt Disney Studios, who has known Cruise for ten years.

> Tom keeps putting himself at risk as an artist. He's done it again with *Vampire*. For all of us – as moviegoers – there's nothing more fun than watching someone like that walk on a high wire. I've even experienced that with him when it's going over falls at the Grand Canyon (the rafting expedition in question took place in August 1989 and was organized by Katzenberg. Cruise was joined by numerous executives, directors (including John Badham), Don Simpson and a flock of agents. One participant told *Premiere* in December 1989 the fun he had watching everyone court Cruise. 'It was hysterical watching these producers and agents chasing him around. Then you had an agent from his own agency making sure no one laid a hand on him. The poor guy could not go up in the woods and have a peaceful sit on the potty without somebody pursuing him.') and saying, 'OK! Let's carry our boat back up there and do it again!' He does it for sport. He does it for craft. He does it for art. He does it for life.

Two such high-profile champions amounted to a very public raspberry to Rice. By this stage the author had become convinced that the project was cursed – just ask River Phoenix, who died of a drugs overdose weeks before filming. Christian Slater replaced him as the journalist who hears a vampire's confession. The derogatory rhetoric failed to dent the confidence of the film-makers, merely made them more resolved to prove Rice wrong. The brouhaha just fired up Cruise all the more, made him work harder (if such a thing is possible). But how much damage did she inflict, apart from bruising the Cruise ego, that is? Rice had pierced Cruise's two most sensitive areas by claiming he was too short and his voice too high to play Lestat – 'just too mom and apple pie'. If anything, the controversy boosted interest in the film, making it even more of an 'event'. It became the most anticipated movie of the year.

When Geffen sent Rice a videotape of the film, her expectations were upended. The repentant author made an astonishing public apology, placing notices in the Hollywood trade press fulsomely applauding Jordan for preserving the 'heart and soul' of her book. 'The high point was to see Cruise in the blond hair speaking with the voice of my Lestat. He makes you forget the boyish image of his past films. He is that mysterious and immortal character.' Talk about swallowing pride. After viewing the tape Rice called Cruise. It was the first time they had ever spoken. 'She was very nice,' he told *Interview* in November 1994. 'She just went on about the movie and how she was very happy with the handling of her characters, and specifically Lestat, and told me how much her son loved the movie. It was a very classy thing to do, because she didn't have to do that.' Vindicated, Cruise still couldn't hide the hurt and public humiliation he'd suffered at her hands, yet remained politely diplomatic about the whole affair, a gentleman as always. He knew how personal the work was to her. Like Mary Shelley, Rice wrote while grieving the death of her first child at the age of five from leukaemia. Her daughter's spirit is resurrected in the vampette Claudia, the raging woman trapped in a child's body, a sort of Shirley Temple from hell. I guess actors need thicker skins than most (armour plating in the case of Ms Rice), though if a Jack Nicholson had been in Cruise's shoes, Rice might well have been joining the beloved undead of her books.

The journey from page to screen had been a long and tortuous path; the novel originally appeared in 1976. Scripts floated around Hollywood like so much confetti, ideas too ridiculous to contemplate. For all those whingers upset by Cruise's casting what would they have made of a television mini-series or, worse, a Broadway musical? Paramount were first to realize its potential, optioning the work for $150,000, but really didn't know what to do with it once they had it. A script was written with John Travolta in mind but hopes of turning that into a movie faded almost as quickly as his career (until *Pulp Fiction*, of course). Richard Gere was pursued for the role and might have got it had his asking price been lower.

The project languished for years in development limbo until 1989, when David Geffen, Hollywood's first openly gay mogul and one of Cruise's most powerful Hollywood allies, acquired the rights, inheriting enough useless scripts to wallpaper his office tenfold. He decided to go straight to the source – Rice. She had already had a few stabs at adapting her novel for the screen, including one version with a female Lestat earmarked for Cher. Rice was outspoken in who should direct her baby – David Cronenberg, Ridley Scott (practically every director worth his salt in the fantasy milieu was approached – Steven Spielberg, David Lynch, John Boorman, Brian De Palma, Roman Polanski – but nobody would touch it) or Neil Jordan would do nicely. She adored Jordan's *Company of Wolves*, and the surprise success of *The Crying Game* had made this reserved and soft-spoken Irishman hotter than a vindaloo in a microwave. Jordan signed on to his first Hollywood blockbuster – with a gigantic budget of $60 million and star names.

With Rice's blessing Geffen offered Lestat to crowd favourite Daniel Day-Lewis, who declined on account of being fed up with recycling himself in costume drama. Rice had always envisaged Rutger Hauer in the role, but by 1993 she was thinking along the lines of John Malkovich and the suitably cadaverous Jeremy Irons, actors she deemed as being in a different league to Cruise. Too old, thought Jordon; Lestat was in the bloom of youth when he contracted immortality, not middle aged. Other names tossed about were William Baldwin, Ralph Fiennes, Mel Gibson – just about anyone with an Equity card and his own teeth. The idea of casting Cruise against type came out of discussions between Jordan and producer Stephen Woolley; Geffen loved the idea and approached Cruise personally. It was a huge departure for such a school prefect of a star. But, then, isn't there something infinitely more sinister about Mr Nice Guy, the person you trust the most, turning out to be your worst nightmare?

Cruise had grown up on a late-night diet of horror movies and claims always to have been fascinated with vampires. The lure of the role, his riskiest yet and a further example of Cruise's obsessive desire to stretch himself, was impossible to resist – stuff anyone who didn't like it. Certainly he was nervous about taking it on, but those who carped about his unsuitability didn't seem to understand that moviemaking should be all about taking risks. Actors in the DeNiro/Hoffman mould are regaled for playing diverse roles, so why not Cruise? He is perpetually criticized for being too wholesome, but the moment he tries to subvert the good-guy stereotype he's attacked for that, too, as if stretching oneself artistically were a capital offence. This film was deeply important, because he hoped it would raise cinema-goers' expectations of what he was capable of as an actor and at the same time prove his doubters wrong, as he'd done with *Born on the Fourth of July*.

Cruise set about altering his appearance over the course of five months, shedding 18 pounds to achieve a skeletal figure and dyeing his hair blond. Initially he baulked at taking on Lestat's signature golden locks, afraid he'd look ridiculous. 'Finally we did the whole make-up test on him,' Michele Burke, the make-up supervisor told *Premiere* in February 1995. 'He says to me, "If Nicole buys it, that's going to be it." The minute she saw him, I could hear this shriek in the corridor.' Cruise eventually bleached his eyebrows and the hair on his temples, arms and chest an ash blond and wore special contact lenses to intensify his eyes. Lestat's skin is the texture of blue-veined cheese. Cruise spent three and a half hours every day in the make-up chair and was the quintessential pro, anxious that everything looked as near to perfection as possible, that his hair did not look like a wig, make-up not look like make-up. His dedication impressed Jordan, who had only superlatives to describe his close encounter with the Cruiser. 'It's just that the guy is kind of amazing,' he said in *Empire* in February 1995. 'I had no idea of the kind of energy he brings to a movie, he kind of carries it on his shoulders. It wouldn't have been one tenth of the movie with any of those other actors.' What struck Jordan particularly was how passionate Cruise was about playing someone as evil as Lestat. 'He had this incredibly direct instinct all the time for that character. He'd say, "Hitler didn't think he was a monster. Stalin didn't think he was a monster. Lestat doesn't think he's a monster." ' Indeed he's behaving as any right-minded vampire would; just as we kill animals to eat meat so Lestat feeds off humans to survive. It's probably the first horror movie that shows next to no interest in the victim and is told purely from the predator's perspective. The real challenge facing Cruise was eliciting an audience's sympathy for the happily malevolent Lestat, this narcissistic monster who loves being a vampire and kills with such sadistic relish, yet is tortured by the dilemma of eternal life and his own loneliness.

To psych himself up Cruise toured the museums of Paris, visited Versailles and worked on his diction, reading aloud from classic literature so as to familiarize himself with the language of the time. He took piano lessons from a teacher recommended to him by Holly Hunter and studied video footage of lions killing zebras to try to appropriate their predatory nature – scenes Cruise found violent yet strangely sensual. Never had he worked so hard on a character. 'I busted ass.'

Principal photography began in October 1993 in New Orleans, then moved on subsequently to Paris, San Francisco and London's Pinewood Studios, which was turned into a virtual Fort Knox. Security personnel stood guard after the British tabloids had gone to extraordinary lengths to snatch a picture of Cruise in vampire garb. When defences were breached by a US television show a canvas tunnel was constructed that allowed Cruise invisible passage on to the set. It was deemed vital to keep his frightening appearance a secret till premiere night, and extras and crew members had to sign nondisclosure forms (a showbiz version of the Official Secrets Act).

Jordan was amazed at the media feeding-frenzy and the cyclone of rumours that swirled about the set. According to these Cruise had taken over the show, was prone to temper tantrums when he didn't get his own way and flew into jealous rages because Brad Pitt came over as better-looking on screen. There is much more evidence to show that Cruise is probably the least vain actor in Hollywood, presenting himself as a burnt-out husk on wheels in *Born* and a putrid corpse in *Vampire*. That doesn't sound like someone obsessed with looking more gorgeous than anyone else. It was just more tabloid nonsense. A rift did exist between the current reigning Hollywood sex symbol Cruise and the challenger Brad Pitt. It was no secret that the two actors didn't hang out together either on or off the set. While there may never have been the level of animosity hinted at in the press, nor was there any love lost either. Tensions must have risen when Rice said Pitt would have made a wonderful Lestat and the producer should have reversed the roles. By the time of the premiere party the frostiness hadn't thawed, but both grudgingly agreed to have their picture taken together. But why should they have to get on? After all, their outlooks and temperaments are so different. Cruise is the child of the eighties, the yuppie movie star, brusque and businesslike; Pitt, by contrast, is helter-skelter, moody and soulful, a child of the nineties. Cruise's spartan regime of morning jogs and gym sessions would be anathema to the more laid-back and hip Pitt. 'Tom and I walk in different directions,' Pitt diplomatically admitted to *Premiere* in February 1995.

> He's North Pole. I'm South. I always thought there was this underlying competition that got in the way of any real conversation. It wasn't nasty by any means, not at all. But it was just there and it bugged me a bit. But I'll tell you, he catches a lot of shit because he's on top, but he is a good actor and he advances in the film. He did it. I mean, you have to respect that.

And their working methods are poles apart, too. Cruise self-assuredly plunged into the role of Lestat; the less-experienced Pitt lost himself in Louis's dilemma of having fallen under the spell of Lestat only to discover too late he has no stomach for blood. The actor haunted Pinewood like a raincloud of depression, fretting constantly over the worthiness of his performance. Unsurprisingly, though he loves the movie, he hated doing it.

Making movies is never easy, especially when everyone is against you even playing the role, egging you on to failure. These pressures were felt by Kidman. One night lying in bed she asked her husband why he wanted to put himself through such criticism. But it was that very fear which drove him to do it. One of his racing-car tutors always said that he didn't know whether he was the smartest guy around or the dumbest. 'I've always had this thing that when I was afraid I never backed off. I always went forward.' For the first few weeks Cruise felt tremendous pressure just walking on to the set. He had to find the Lestat dormant within himself. Stirring up that kind of emotion twelve to fifteen hours a day can take its toll, and Cruise found it difficult to relax. 'Before the cameras would start rolling, Tom would be getting into it,' recalled Christian Slater, 'and he'd say things to me like, "I'm going to rip your throat out, you filthy...." He was helpful that way.' Sometimes shooting took place at night, which meant that just as Isabella was awakening, at six or seven in the morning, Cruise was scrabbling into bed. It was up to Nicole to keep the house quiet so that Tom could get a decent stretch of sleep. Cruise rented a seven-bedroom mansion in Chester Terrace, close to Regent's Park, and most mornings went out jogging with his personal fitness trainer, with little Isabella in a three-wheel baby buggy by his side, both men taking it in turns pushing her. Despite all the strains and demands, the picture was a riot to make. The cast killed spare time by taking polaroids of each other pulling faces and sticking them up on a noticeboard christened 'the ugly wall'. During the notorious rat scene where Cruise bites the head off a rodent, draining the smoking liquid into Pitt's glass, the star had trouble stifling his laughter. The movie is one of Cruise's fondest professional experiences and he was especially proud of what had been accomplished. When it came time to leave Pinewood and pack up to go home Cruise felt more of a tinge of pain than usual upon saying goodbye to a character.

The film opened big, even for a Cruise movie, taking $38.7 million in the first weekend. It was the fourth biggest debut ever, and eventually topped the magic $100 million mark in America – staggering for a horror movie, though not for one starring Tom Cruise. In the end casting Cruise was a wise move, commercially; when your protagonist is a repellent bloodsucking ghoul you have to lure audiences in somehow and there's no star who can guarantee to open a movie quite like Tom Cruise. Granted, ticket sales tailed off dramatically after the first few weeks, but Cruise's job was done, while at the same time he'd been seen to extend his range. Cruise attended the LA world premiere with Kidman, who, in her vampish make-up, looked like a cross between Olivia Newton-John and Morticia Addams.

The gamble had paid off, silencing those carpers who'd labelled the film 'Cruise's coffin', another *Heaven's Gate*. If the high hopes for Jordan's film were not ultimately warranted, Cruise gained belated plaudits for his versatility and courage in tackling such a challenging role. 'Cruise is a revelation. Hollywood's strutting college kid is transformed. Demonism with a blinding smile, Cruise is the Ivy League's answer to Bela Lugosi' – *Financial Times*; 'Largely an exercise in sado-masochism. This really is offensive rough stuff. A parade of perversions. Cruise adopts an effete affrontery that's initially effective, but only because it's such a contrast to the red-blooded roles he usually plays. *Interview* doesn't bite; it sucks' – *Evening Standard*; 'Cruise is flabbergastingly right for this role. The vampire Lestat brings out in Cruise a fiery, mature sexual magnetism he has not previously displayed on the screen' – *New York Times*; 'Here's a chance to witness mega-watt star-power effortlessly wiping everyone else off the screen. Next to Cruise, poor old Pitt looks like so much dead wood' – *Sunday Telegraph*; 'A masterpiece, a brilliantly bold mixture of horror, pathos and camp comedy. Cruise is a revelation' – *Gay Times*.

The fear he'd alienate his fans, particularly his female ones, proved groundless; if anything he gained more admirers than dissenters. There were always going to be those who said this was one role he couldn't pull off. After all he'd not played anything remotely erotic onscreen for years (except for some adolescent fumbling in *The Firm*) and, more importantly, had never played a villain. Lestat supposedly personifies evil, yet Cruise had rarely played even a mildly dislikeable character. Throughout his career, however, he's hinted at the darkness behind that prairie-wide smile. Something unsettling and dangerous lurks within, as if the pain of his childhood is seeping through the pores of his all-conquering screen persona. 'He's got this cold fury,' Jordan observed. 'If we could get that into the role, it could be quite chilling.' And Rob Lowe on the set of *The Outsiders* spotted it, too. 'Cruise is this middle-class, kind of square, "Yes Sir", "Yes, Ma'am" God-fearing American kid. But something in the eyes says he'll snap your goddamned neck if you look at him the wrong way.' And here, with remarkable guts and audacious style, he gives full vent to his malevolent side. Instead of transforming himself completely Cruise took one of the trademark, likeable aspects of his screen persona – his casual, cocky arrogance – and hyped it up into something hateful. As Cyndi Stivers, the deputy editor of *Premiere*, noted, 'No one ever said that Cruise couldn't play cocky. He'd done it in *Top Gun, The Firm*, all his movies. This may be new territory for him, but his personality shows through. They could have called this *Top Fang*.'

In a performance better than you'd expected, though not as good as you'd hoped, Cruise cleverly conveys the pain of an endless existence without sacrificing the humour and menace that is essential to the part. There's much fun to be had watching him

sweep up a rat and bite its neck or plucking up a plague-riddled
corpse and cutting a rug. Ironically after Rice's viciousness Cruise
fares better than her screenplay, which lacks narrative thrust and
meanders when he's playing truant from the camera. Elegantly
mounted, Jordan has created one of the most visually sumptuous
films so far this decade, but what might have been a dark, brooding
tale of sexual decadence and torment comes over rather too often as
an over-stuffed historical TV mini-series. The film refuses to come
to terms with its controversial homosexual subtext – the victims are
mostly women – and, remarkably, there is no sex on show despite
the erotic nature of the piece. Killing becomes a substitute for
sexuality, the drinking of blood the ultimate orgasm. 'I think it has a
sexiness about it,' offered Cruise. 'It's vampire-erotic to me.'
Instead the film lurches between the homoerotic and the sado-
masochistic – Lestat and Louis indulge in implied paedophilia and
incest with their vampire 'daughter'. It is nothing like as gory, or
scary, as people made out; reports from the US of preview
audiences fainting in the aisles and running screaming from theatres
merely sound like crafty marketing. But there were genuine worries
that the film was too bloody for mainstream audiences, and
ultra-violent scenes ended up on the cutting room floor. A guest on
the Oprah Winfrey show, Cruise was made to feel very uncomfortable when Oprah admitted she'd walked out of a press screening
after just twenty minutes because of the violence and 'climate of
evil'. She joined hands and whispered prayers with several other
women who'd left the auditorium to form a circle in the foyer.
Cruise, ever the controller, responded by encouraging the audience
to roar their approval for the film. 'If you don't like being terrified or
if you're squeamish, don't go see the film,' he told his host.

In a smartly re-shot ending, Louis encounters Lestat in the
present day living as a pathetic recluse. Next thing we know the
Cruiser is sinking his teeth into Slater. Is this a blatant pretext for a
sequel? With each successive volume in what has become known as
'The Vampire Chronicles' both Rice and Lestat's popularity has
soared, and if the right script comes along Jordan and Cruise have
already 'tentatively' confirmed they'd be willing to return. The next
instalment could deal with Lestat's early life in France and his
confrontation with Antonio Banderas's European bloodsucker (the
film's most malevolent presence) in a time before his decadent
Theatre of Vampires. Surely if Cruise has any sense, this is one
sequel he can't afford to resist.

It wasn't a sequel that came next, rather a high concept remake of a classic sixties television show about a secret unit of government spies – *Mission: Impossible* – that Cruise had adored as a youngster. It was an idea that had been knocking about Paramount for ten years. On Cruise's arrival at the studio he was delighted to hear they owned the property, believing it to be the perfect vehicle to kick-start his production company, of which big things are expected in Hollywood. It's already developing a whole roster of projects, including *Pre* (Robert Towne's screenplay about an athlete, which Cruise hopes to produce) and *Criminal Conversation*, based on Evan Hunter's novel. Again Cruise is rumoured to be producing the film as a vehicle for Kidman.

In keeping with the hush-hush nature of the original series *Mission: Impossible* was filmed in top secrecy in Prague and London. It was director Brian De Palma's idea to base the movie in London, and having just shot *Vampire* at Pinewood the prospect of working with the same crew again appealed to Cruise. I managed to secure an audition to double for Cruise's hands in a scene where he's required to use a computer, and met the actor on the set at Pinewood. I found him to be courteous, sincere and not at all standoffish; he came across as someone who wanted to be one of the lads. And drop-dead gorgeous, I regret to report, looking too healthy by far. The man is strangely more handsome and radiant in real life; the screen seems to iron out his features.

The début offering from Cruise and Wagner Productions *Mission: Impossible* is Cruise's 007 homage, with its secret agents, leaping from exploding helicopters and the like. The stakes were always high, and with a script that wasn't finished and a high number of complicated hi-tech sequences to shoot, the pressure was enormous on Cruise the star and fledgling producer. This was to be a trial of fire. At the outset he established the tone by deferring his entire salary (opting instead for a percentage of the profits) and demanding his movie not be allowed to fly over budget or over schedule. Inevitably rumours circulated in Hollywood that Cruise and De Palma weren't getting along, that they were continually butting heads over spiralling costs. Cruise simply laughed them off, 'how can you make a movie and not have arguments'; he had no compunction about playing the heavy with the director when needs must. 'Tom's performance as an actor was brilliant,' confirmed Sherry Lansing, chairman of Paramount, who fully expects Cruise to go the way of Gibson and Eastwood, eventually becoming a major director. 'But his function as a producer was extraordinary.'

And what of the film itself? Reviews were mixed, some disappointed that screenwriters of the calibre of Steve Zaillian (*Schindler's List*), David Koepp (*Jurassic Park*) and Robert Towne could produce such an uninspiring and overly dense plotline. Instead it's left to three truly heart-grabbing action sequences to save the day – Cruise's spectacular exit from a restaurant, dodging a 30-foot wave when a giant aquarium behind the diners detonates. The tons of water cascading around the stunt guy just didn't look right. 'Tom,' explained De Palma. 'We have to do it with you or it's not convincing.' Cruise ponders awhile. 'Brian, I'm only an actor.' But his director is insistent. 'And he did it.' De Palma acknowledged afterwards. 'But I swear he could've drowned.' Another nail-biting episode where Cruise breaks into a top-security CIA computer room, and the climactic helicopter-train chase through the channel tunnel is truly awesome.

Because this was a Tom Cruise movie the box office tills didn't stop ringing all summer. The final tally worldwide was over $400 million, turning *Mission: Impossible* into one of the most popular films ever made and hurtling Cruise to the top of the action man stakes. Watch out Arnie and Sly seemed to be the message. Cruise was soon being sought to star in Columbia Pictures' CIA thriller *The Good Shepherd*, which Wayne Wang will direct for Francis Ford Coppola's American Zoetrope outfit.

In London the Cruise family took up residence in an eleven-bedroom mansion in Holland Park, complete with gym and indoor swimming pool. Although cocooned from London society by a six-foot security fence and electronic gates, Cruise prefers as much as possible to avoid the more extreme security measures of employing bodyguards. Both he and Kidman try to retain a modicum of normality in their lives, happily carting off the kids, who each have an American nanny, to a local nursery and playgroup, chancing the lung-clogging smog of Bayswater Road for a jog across Hyde Park (a temporary Londoner, Cruise was smitten hard by the craze for rollerblading and could often be seen whizzing through the streets around his rented mansion or taking his kids for a spin through local parks in a special joggers double buggy. Once he delighted onlookers in Hyde Park by joining pal Dustin Hoffman for a game of roller hockey) or going out to nightclubs and good old-fashioned boozers rather than hiding

away in VIP lounges. The couple found that staying in London
they were often able to escape the traditional entourage of security
staff and assistants to enjoy quiet evenings alone. 'With Tom and
Nic you never feel like you're hanging out with movie stars,'
Naomi Watts, Australian actress and close friend of Kidman's,
revealed to *Vogue* in October 1995. 'Until you find yourself being
chased down the street by 400 paparazzi. That's the only time you
see them click out of being free spirits and think, "OK, now I've
got to keep my guard up." '

18   *Cruise Might-Have-Beens*

He's hotter than July in a greenhouse, he's young, good-looking and he's at the top of everyone's wish list, but there's only one of him to go around. In nineties Hollywood Tom Cruise runs a high-stakes lottery. The players are producers whose projects call for a leading male hunk under thirty-five and Cruise is both the master of ceremonies and the grand prize. He's as bankable at the box office as Redford and Newman were in their heyday; what other actor could have turned a pilchard of a film like *Cocktail* into a $70 million hit simply by smiling.

Here are some premiere-league projects that over the years have been entered in the Tom Cruise Sweepstakes, only to stall in the pit lane.

That Was Then, This Is Now

The Cruise was due to co-star with close pal Emilio Estevez in this story of teenage angst based on the S.E. Hinton novel. Cruise even had a hand in trying to write the screenplay. He ultimately backed out and made *Legend* instead. Oh dear.

Bright Lights, Big City

This yuppie morality tale finally made it to screens in 1988 with Michael J. Fox as a young Midwesterner seduced by unscrupulous Kiefer Sutherland into a life of drugs in New York City. Cruise was first approached to star in the days before *Top Gun*. He'd read Jay McInerney's bestseller, which he called 'an interior piece. Very daring,' and hung out with the writer in New York, hitting the club scene. The two got on well and talked at length about the project. 'I'd like to do the movie,' Cruise said in May 1986, 'if I like the script.' He didn't and pulled out.

An Innocent Millionaire

Tom Cruise and James Ivory (the distinguished director of *A Room with a View* and *Howard's End*) seem the most unlikely of consorts, yet in 1987 Hollywood was alive with rumours that they were considering making a movie together, tentatively entitled *An Innocent Millionaire*. Ivory approached Cruise to head the cast of this adventure story about sunken treasure, to be filmed on location in the Caribbean. Alas, this intriguing enterprise never surfaced.

The King of the Mountain

The producers of this comedy set in the South of France had hoped to team veteran Michael Caine with one of the then new crop of young American actors known as the Brat Pack; Cruise was chosen. Alas, no money could be found to set it up. The film was made years later with Steve Martin in the role originally earmarked for Cruise and under a new title, *Dirty Rotten Scoundrels*.

Always

Cruise was first choice to play the third side of the love triangle in Steven Spielberg's flawed remake of 1943's *A Guy Named Joe*. He was unavailable and Tom Berenger lookalike Brad Johnson replaced him.

Edward Scissorhands

A fairy tale, with shades of Frankenstein, about a man-made boy whose creator dies before attaching human hands to his body. Cruise had three in-depth meetings with *Batman* director and all-round genius Tim Burton – the third lasting over three hours – but ultimately declined the role. Johnny Depp was cast.

The Doors

Cruise had 'discussions' with Oliver Stone, following their successful collaboration on *Born on the Fourth of July*, about playing dead pop star and lizard king Jim Morrison in the director's biopic of the legendary wild man of rock. Instead Tom's *Top Gun* co-star Val Kilmer got the role.

Backdraft

Action yarn, with stunning special effects, about the sibling rivalry between two fire-fighters. Director Ron Howard desperately wanted Cruise to play the younger brother opposite Kurt Russell, but he turned it down and the role passed to William Baldwin. Baldwin was less than complimentary about Cruise in an interview for *Sky* magazine in August 1993. 'He has surrounded himself with the most fucking talented people in the business. But he's not the actor that Pacino or Hoffman is, because anyone who walks around at 25 years old and says "I'm a great actor" is an asshole. The great thing about acting is the more you live life the more you can apply it to the characters you portray. You look at the stardom of Cruise, Julia Roberts and Willis – they need to work with great actors for a movie to be great.' Bitchy!

Rush

The story of two undercover narcotics cops who became addicts, based on Kim Wozencraft's autobiographical novel. Cruise was involved in the project from the beginning and filming was due to commence in the summer of 1990, under the direction of Robert Towne. Then Towne dropped out; Cruise subsequently followed suit, not wanting to glorify the act of drug-taking.

Prelude to a Kiss

When this romantic comedy took the New York stage by storm
Cruise was reportedly meeting with producers about playing on
Broadway the role originated off-Broadway by Alec Baldwin.
Sadly prior commitments ruled that out. So *Taps* co-star Timothy
Hutton took over. Director Norman Rene hoped Cruise might star
in the film version. 'If Cruise were interested in the role, we'd
definitely consider him' – he wasn't. Released in the summer of
1992 with Alec Baldwin and Meg Ryan in the leads it failed
miserably with critics and public alike.

Till There Was You

A tale of romance and intrigue about a man out to avenge his
brother's murder. Cruise's name was mentioned right away, but
the role inexplicably went to Mark Harmon. He was cheaper, $10
million cheaper. 'Frankly, Cruise isn't even good casting for it,'
the movie's spokesman Mark Urman said. 'He's too young.
Although I think they'd cast him for *Yentl* if they thought they
could get him.'

China Maze

If executive producer Bill Moya had got his way Cruise would have
played a man recruited by the CIA to perform a covert operation
in 1952 Manchuria. 'At one time, we were talking to his
management crew,' Moya told reporters around 1990. 'I don't
know at this point. Everything depends on his availability.' Cruise
was available, but not for *China Maze*.

What Makes Sammy Run?

Warner Brothers planned a film version of Budd Schulberg's 1941
novel about famed showbiz agent Sammy Glick. By all accounts
Cruise loved the book. 'We just had a couple of meetings,'
producer Gene Kirkwood said. 'He read the script, and he had a
meeting with Sidney Lumet, and then he went off to do the

racing-car movie. We'd love him to do it. But then I'd love my hunchbacked uncle to be able to straighten up.'

The Princess of Mars

Hollywood was bating its breath for this Tom Cruise/Julia Roberts team-up, until director John McTiernan dropped out, reportedly worried about possible clashes with the two leads. The whole thing promptly fell apart.

The Curious Case of Benjamin Button

The curious case of the movie that never was. This F. Scott Fitzgerald short story was rumoured to star Cruise under Steven Spielberg's direction. I doubt there's a studio in the world with money enough to team together those two.

Out West

This comedy western would have paired Cruise with his only serious box-office rival of the time – Eddie Murphy, with veteran Walter Hill at the helm. Fireworks were promised, but someone threw a bucket of cold water over it.

Indecent Proposal

Mr and Mrs Tom Cruise looked all set to re-team for Adrian Lyne's controversial sex drama about a young couple who agree to have Kidman bed a powerful industrialist (then played by Warren Beatty) for $1 million. Cruise backed out over moral qualms with the script's steamy subject matter. Johnny Depp or Tim Robbins were tipped to take over. In the end *A Few Good Men* co-star Demi Moore and Woody Harrelson replaced Cruise and Kidman.

Moby Dick

Acclaimed director Roland Joffe attempted, unsuccessfully, to hook Cruise as Ishmael and either Sean Connery or Clint Eastwood as Captain Ahab in a proposed $40 million version of Herman Melville's classic seafaring tale.

Some Like It Hot

Rumours circulated that a remake of Billy Wilder's classic (and, let's face it, unremakable) *Some Like It Hot* was in 'the talking stages'. Madonna (who else) was mooted for the Monroe role with Michael Keaton and Cruise playing Jack Lemmon and Tony Curtis. To the benefit of all humanity it never materialized.

Sommersby

When Hollywood remade *The Return of Martin Guerre* in 1992 with Richard Gere and Jodie Foster, Gerard Depardieu's role was first offered to Tom Cruise. 'I was intrigued by the idea,' he said. 'But then I went back and screened the original and when I saw Gerard, I said no way am I going to do this picture. There is no way I can match what he conveyed on the screen. He was awesome.' The Frenchman, on hearing Cruise's comments, replied in kind. 'I feel myself completely feminine in this craft. I don't believe in the Stallone image of the invincible hero. The biggest success goes to actors like Cruise and Hoffman, who prefer to show their faults and weaknesses, rather than project an image of invulnerability.'

The Heiress

Plans were afoot to cast Cruise in a remake of William Wyler's 1949 film of the Henry James novel, ironically as the fortune-hunter who woos a lonely spinster, a role originally played by the classic movie star Cruise most evokes – Montgomery Clift. But after watching the film he wisely backed off, aware he'd never be able to match the original performances.

Sliver

Paramount's feeble screen adaptation of Ira Levin's bestselling sex thriller about the voyeuristic inhabitants of a skyscraper. Merchant and Ivory it ain't. Cruise wisely wanted nothing to do with this turkey. Had he accepted though, and pocketed an estimated $20 million, he'd have been teamed with Hollywood siren Sharon Stone. It's interesting to note here how Cruise has rarely been cast opposite a female superstar (much like Clint Eastwood). Is this a career strategy? Would a star actress dim his glow? Perhaps mega-stars such as Cruise don't really need a major co-star; their name alone is enough to reel in the punters. And yet he's worked with some of the biggest male stars around. While rarely cast opposite major female stars, the Cruise women are nevertheless smart professionals, older and more experienced. Additionally, these screen romances strangely emphasize Cruise's comparative inferiority: Kelly McGillis in *Top Gun* is not only older but his teacher; Nicole Kidman in *Days of Thunder* is the doctor, Cruise the patient; Rebecca DeMornay's whore in *Risky Business* points up the Cruiser's sexual inexperience; Kidman, again, in *Far and Away* belongs to a higher social class and takes Cruise along with her to the new world as *her* servant. They all fall in love with him at the end, of course.

Thunderbirds: The Movie

Hollywood planned a big-screen version of Gerry Anderson's cult 60s television show. Cruise was reportedly interested in playing TR 1 pilot Scott Tracy, without the aid of strings. File in the not-to-be-taken-too-seriously department. Whatever next, Woody Allen as a geriatric Joe 90, Keanu Reaves as Captain Scarlet, Arnold Schwarzenegger as Torchy the battery boy?

Pulp Fiction

The role of the charismatic heroin-soaked hitman, which rejuvenated John Travolta's career, and got him an Oscar nomination to boot, was originally offered to Tom Cruise. And he turned it down, a decision the Cruiser may well live to regret.

Legends of the Fall

Tom Cruise and Sean Connery were tentatively approached to star in this tale of two brothers and their stern Scottish father (guess who?) whose lives are played out against the panoramic grandeur of turn-of-the-century Wyoming. In the end *Vampire* co-star Brad Pitt and Anthony Hopkins were cast.

The Saint

In 1993 Cruise was rumoured to be stepping into the shoes of Roger Moore in the big-screen version of one of Britain's greatest-ever television exports. No thanks.

City Hall

Early in 1994 Tom was approached by *Taps* director Harold Becker to star in *City Hall*, a political thriller penned by Bo Goldman, an Oscar-winner for *Scent of a Woman*. The Cruiser's salary for this one was tipped to top $20 million. Becker eventually opted for his *Sea of Love* star Al Pacino.

The Chamber

It was only natural to link Cruise, having just starred in *The Firm* with a screen adaptation of John Grisham's other legal dull-buster. The writer was paid $3.5 million for the film rights before he'd even plugged in his word processor.

Cutthroat Island

Both Cruise and Keanu Reeves had been approached to star in this actioner directed by Renny (*Die Hard 2*) Harlin, but turned the chance down. Michael Douglas signed on, only to quit two weeks before shooting began.

Zorro

Zorro hits the screens again via the Spielberg route. Sean Connery and Andy Garcia both play the gay blade, with Connery as an ageing Zorro training Garcia to take over where he left off. Plans for Cruise to play the young swashbuckler were bismarcked when he decided to make *Mission: Impossible* instead. Someone sunk the film too.

Wild Wild West

Producers hoped in vain to lasso Cruise into starring in a big-screen version of Robert Conrad's dire sixties television series.

Sunset Boulevard

In February 1995 London papers revealed Cruise was lined up for his first musical role in the film version of Andrew Lloyd Webber's hit show and was set to bag $20 million to play opposite Glenn Close, who was being tipped to repeat her critically acclaimed stage performance of Norma Desmond. The *Evening Standard* reported a 'Hollywood insider' as saying 'He has quite a high-pitched voice, but very good range. With coaching and his determination he should carry it off.'

Phil Spector Biopic

In May 1995 news broke that Cruise was keen to produce and star in a biopic of eccentric music mogul Phil Spector, who wrote a string of hits in the sixties and created the distinctive Wall of Sound for groups such as the Ronettes. A millionaire at twenty-one, Spector turned his back on the music industry for a reclusive lifestyle that would have made Howard Hughes green with envy. Though Spector has spurned movie offers in the past, he was willing to collaborate with Cruise on the project.

Top Gun 2

Although almost certainly guaranteed worldwide box-office attention, a *Top Gun 2* starring Cruise is about as likely as a *Police Academy* sequel being funny. When asked about this project (at nearly every press conference), Cruise has been known to give a you've-got-to-be-kidding look. If he'd wanted, Cruise could have made *Top Guns ad infinitum* and made even more money than he ultimately did, but it would have finished him as an actor. 'Top Gun* was an entertaining roller-coaster ride. And that's why I couldn't remake that kind of movie – I've done that ride already.'

Footnote:
Films Tom Cruise made but should have turned down: *Losin' It, Cocktail, Days of Thunder, Far and Away.*

19   *Thoughts on Cruise*

'I was lucky because I married a man who's incredibly sane and who conducts himself in a very pleasant manner, never allowing the celebrity thing to go to his head.'

— Nicole Kidman

'If Tom's feet were any more down-to-earth, you could plant them.'

— Don Simpson

'It's not fair, is it? Some of us are just lesser mortals.'

— Roger Donaldson on the Cruise smile

'When Tom comes on the set, the set works differently. It changes the rotation of the planets a bit.'

— Brad Pitt

'There's no sense of a crest in Tom. His talent is young, his body is young, his spirit is young. He's a christmas tree – he's lit from head to toe.'

— Dustin Hoffman

'I'm addicted to Tom. He's my drug.'

— Nicole Kidman

'I think Tom's wholly obsessed with being an original. He's going to take it out to the edge as far as his persona and soul will allow.'

— Oliver Stone

'Tom is a spokesman for his generation.'

— Paul Brickman

'Cruise is the boy next door, most likely to succeed.'

— Richard Corliss, *Time* magazine

'They were everywhere. The young ladies from fourteen to forty die for him. I used to hang around Cruise. I'd hang around and get all the castoffs.'

— Tony Scott on the advantages of working with Cruise

'He's the kind of guy who won't take yes for an answer. He wants you to really mean it.'

— Ron Howard

'Tom is an actor of extraordinary technique and huge experience.'

— Neil Jordan

'You'll see Tom and Nicole in all their hormonal glory. She and Cruise are something together.'

— Don Simpson

'Even Tom's flops make $80 million!'

— Rob Reiner

'When you're working with him you worry a bit. You think you've got to get everything right first time.'

— Nicole Kidman

'There is something different about Tom now. He's unbelievably sexy, but there's something a little rougher around the edges. I wanted to photograph him at this moment of change.'

— Annie Leibovitz on the post-Lestat Cruise

'All Cruise's pictures make big profits, not because they're good (sometimes they aren't) but simply because he is in them.'

— Barry Norman

'I really admire the approach Cruise has taken to his career, where he's treated it as a quest for excellence.'

— Ron Howard

'Cruise commits himself to being the best he can possibly be. He's got, like, blinkers on.'

— Jerry Bruckheimer

'He's a good fella. A good egg.'

— Brad Pitt on a fellow vampire

'Tom reminded me of those guys you see in boot-camp films, doing push-ups, and the sergeant is saying, "One more! One more!" And Tom is not only the guy doing the push-ups, he's also the guy saying, "One more!" '

— Dustin Hoffman

'Well, the good thing is that I get to go to bed every night with Tom Cruise.'

— Nicole Kidman on the advantages of being Mrs Tom Cruise

'He's like a champion. He's like an athlete in the way he attacks work. He's incredibly focused.'

— Sean Penn

'I loved working with Tom. I think he's a terrific actor. I had always admired his work very much, but when you actually get to work with someone, that's the real test.'

—Vanessa Redgrave

'He's a man who always believes his reach can extend beyond his grasp. And so far he's been right.'

—Robert Towne

Filmography

ENDLESS LOVE (1981)
Polygram Pictures

DIRECTOR: Franco Zeffirelli
PRODUCER: Dyson Lovell
SCREENPLAY: Judith Rascoe, based on the novel by Scott Spencer.
PHOTOGRAPHY: David Watkin
MUSIC SCORE: Jonathan Tunick; featuring songs by Diana Ross, Lionel Richie, Blondie, Kiss
RUNNING TIME: 115 mins
CERTIFICATE: AA

CAST: Brooke Shields, Martin Hewitt, Shirley Knight, Don Murray, Richard Kiley, James Spader, Tom Cruise

TAPS (1981)
20th Century-Fox

DIRECTOR: Harold Becker
PRODUCERS: Stanley R. Jaffe and Howard B. Jaffe
SCREENPLAY: Darryl Poniscan and Robert Mark Kamen
PHOTOGRAPHY: Owen Roizman
MUSIC SCORE: Maurice Jarre
RUNNING TIME: 122 mins
CERTIFICATE: A

CAST: George C. Scott, Timothy Hutton, Ronny Cox, Sean Penn, Tom Cruise, Brendan Ward

THE OUTSIDERS (1983)
Warner Bros.

DIRECTOR: Francis Ford Coppola
PRODUCERS: Fred Roos and Gray Frederickson
SCREENPLAY: Kathleen Knutsen Rowell, based on the novel
by S.E. Hinton.
PHOTOGRAPHY: Stephen H. Burum
MUSIC SCORE: Carmine Coppola; featuring songs by Stevie
Wonder
RUNNING TIME: 91 mins
CERTIFICATE: PG

CAST: C. Thomas Howell, Matt Dillon, Ralph Macchio, Patrick
Swayze, Rob Lowe, Diane Lane, Emilio Estevez, Tom Cruise,
Leif Garrett, Tom Waits, Sofia Coppola

LOSIN' IT (1983)
Embassy Pictures

DIRECTOR: Curtis Hanson
PRODUCERS: Bryan Gindoff and Hannah Hempstead
SCREENPLAY: B.W.L. Norton
PHOTOGRAPHY: Gil Taylor
MUSIC SCORE: Ken Wannberg
RUNNING TIME: 100 mins
CERTIFICATE: 18

CAST: Tom Cruise, Jackie Earle Haley, John Stockwell, Shelley
Long, John P. Navin Jnr, Henry Darrow

RISKY BUSINESS (1983)
Warner Brothers

DIRECTOR: Paul Brickman
PRODUCERS: Jon Avnet and Steve Tisch
SCREENPLAY: Paul Brickman
PHOTOGRAPHY: Reynaldo Villalobos and Bruce Surtees
MUSIC SCORE: Tangerine Dream

RUNNING TIME: 97 mins
CERTIFICATE: 18

CAST: Tom Cruise, Rebecca DeMornay, Curtis Armstrong, Bronson Pinchot, Raphael Sbarge, Richard Masur, Kevin Anderson

ALL THE RIGHT MOVES (1983)
20th Century-Fox

DIRECTOR: Michael Chapman
PRODUCER: Stephen Deutsch
SCREENPLAY: Michael Kane
PHOTOGRAPHY: Jan DeBont
MUSIC SCORE: David Campbell
RUNNING TIME: 90 mins
CERTIFICATE: PG

CAST: Tom Cruise, Craig T. Nelson, Lea Thompson, Charles Cioffi, Paul Carafotes, Christopher Penn

LEGEND (1985)
20th Century-Fox

DIRECTOR: Ridley Scott
PRODUCER: Arnon Milchan
SCREENPLAY: William Hjortsberg
PHOTOGRAPHY: Alex Thomson
MUSIC SCORE: Jerry Goldsmith (Tangerine Dream in US)
RUNNING TIME: 94 mins
CERTIFICATE: PG

CAST: Tom Cruise, Mia Sara, Tim Curry, David Bennent, Alice Playten, Billy Barty

TOP GUN (1986)
Paramount

DIRECTOR: Tony Scott
PRODUCERS: Don Simpson and Jerry Bruckheimer
SCREENPLAY: Jim Cash and Jack Epps
PHOTOGRAPHY: Jeffrey Kimball
MUSIC SCORE: Harold Faltermeyer; featuring songs by Kenny
Loggins, Berlin, Giorgio Moroder
RUNNING TIME: 110 mins
CERTIFICATE: 15

CAST: Tom Cruise, Kelly McGillis, Val Kilmer, Anthony
Edwards, Tom Skerritt, Michael Ironside, John Stockwell, Meg
Ryan, Tim Robbins

THE COLOR OF MONEY (1986)
Touchstone

DIRECTOR: Martin Scorsese
PRODUCERS: Irving Axelrad and Barbara De Fina
SCREENPLAY: Richard Price, based on the novel by Walter
Tevis
PHOTOGRAPHY: Michael Ballhaus
MUSIC SCORE: Robbie Robertson
RUNNING TIME: 119 mins
CERTIFICATE: 15

CAST: Paul Newman, Tom Cruise, Mary Elizabeth Mastrantonio,
Helen Shaver, John Turturro, Forest Whitaker, Iggy Pop

COCKTAIL (1988)
Touchstone

DIRECTOR: Roger Donaldson
PRODUCERS: Ted Field and Robert W. Cort
SCREENPLAY: Heywood Gould, based on his novel
PHOTOGRAPHY: Dean Semler
MUSIC SCORE: J. Peter Robinson; featuring songs by Robert

Palmer, The Beach Boys
RUNNING TIME: 100 mins
CERTIFICATE: 15

CAST: Tom Cruise, Bryan Brown, Elisabeth Shue, Lisa Banes, Kelly Lynch, Paul Benedict

RAIN MAN (1988)
United Artists

DIRECTOR: Barry Levinson
PRODUCER: Mark Johnson
SCREENPLAY: Ronald Bass and Barry Morrow
PHOTOGRAPHY: John Seale
MUSIC SCORE: Hans Zimmer
RUNNING TIME: 140 mins
CERTIFICATE: 15

CAST: Dustin Hoffman, Tom Cruise, Valeria Golino, Jerry Molden, Jack Murdock, Michael D. Roberts

BORN ON THE FOURTH OF JULY (1989)
Universal

DIRECTOR: Oliver Stone
PRODUCERS: A. Kitman Ho and Oliver Stone
SCREENPLAY: Oliver Stone and Ron Kovic
PHOTOGRAPHY: Robert Richardson
MUSIC SCORE: John Williams
RUNNING TIME: 144 mins
CERTIFICATE: 18

CAST: Tom Cruise, Willem Dafoe, Raymond J. Barry, Caroline Kava, Kyra Sedgwick, Bryan Larkin, Stephen Baldwin, Tom Berenger

DAYS OF THUNDER (1990)
Paramount

DIRECTOR: Tony Scott
PRODUCERS: Don Simpson and Jerry Bruckheimer
SCREENPLAY: Robert Towne
PHOTOGRAPHY: Ward Russell
MUSIC SCORE: Hans Zimmer
RUNNING TIME: 107 mins
CERTIFICATE: 12

CAST: Tom Cruise, Robert Duvall, Nicole Kidman, Randy Quaid, Cary Elwes, Michael Rooker, Fred Dalton Thompson

FAR AND AWAY (1992)
Universal

DIRECTOR: Ron Howard
PRODUCERS: Brian Grazer and Ron Howard
SCREENPLAY: Bob Dolman
PHOTOGRAPHY: Mikael Salomon
MUSIC SCORE: John Williams; featuring songs by Enya
RUNNING TIME: 140 mins
CERTIFICATE: 12

CAST: Tom Cruise, Nicole Kidman, Thomas Gibson, Robert Prosky, Cyril Cusack, Colm Meaney

A FEW GOOD MEN (1992)
Columbia

DIRECTOR: Rob Reiner
PRODUCERS: David Brown and Rob Reiner
SCREENPLAY: Aaron Sorkin, based on his play
PHOTOGRAPHY: Robert Richardson
MUSIC SCORE: Marc Shaiman
RUNNING TIME: 138 mins
CERTIFICATE: 15

CAST: Tom Cruise, Jack Nicholson, Demi Moore, Kevin Bacon, Keifer Sutherland, Kevin Pollack

THE FIRM (1993)
Paramount

DIRECTOR: Sydney Pollack
PRODUCERS: Scott Rudin and John Davis
SCREENPLAY: David Rabe, Robert Towne and David Rayfiel, based on the book by John Grisham
PHOTOGRAPHY: John Seale
MUSIC SCORE: Dave Grusin
RUNNING TIME: 155 mins
CERTIFICATE: 15

CAST: Tom Cruise, Jeanne Tripplehorn, Gene Hackman, Hal Holbrook, Terry Kinney, Wilford Brimley, Ed Harris, Holly Hunter, David Strathairn, Gary Busey, Steven Hill

INTERVIEW WITH THE VAMPIRE (1994)
Geffen Pictures

DIRECTOR: Neil Jordan
PRODUCERS: David Geffen and Stephen Woolley
SCREENPLAY: Anne Rice, based on her novel
PHOTOGRAPHY: Philippe Rousselot
MUSIC SCORE: Elliot Goldenthal: Featuring songs by Guns N' Roses
RUNNING TIME: 122 mins
CERTIFICATE: 18

CAST: Tom Cruise, Brad Pitt, Kirsten Dunst, Christian Slater, Antonio Banderas, Stephen Rea

MISSION: IMPOSSIBLE (1996)
Paramount

DIRECTOR: Brian De Palma

PRODUCERS: Tom Cruise and Paula Wagner
SCREENPLAY: David Koepp and Robert Towne
PHOTOGRAPHY: Stephen H. Burum
MUSIC SCORE: Danny Elfman
RUNNING TIME: 110 mins
CERTIFICATE: PG
CAST: Tom Cruise, Jon Voight, Emmanuelle Beart, Henry Czerny, Jean Reno, Ving Rhames, Kristin Scott-Thomas, Vanessa Redgrave, Emilio Estevez

JERRY MAGUIRE (1997)
TriStar Pictures

DIRECTOR: Cameron Crowe
CAST: Tom Cruise

EYES WIDE SHUT (1997)
Warner Brothers

DIRECTOR: Stanley Kubrick
CAST: Tom Cruise, Nicole Kidman

Index